ALL
ABOARD

STACKS

Amtrak's California Zephyr prepares for the climb up Donner Pass in California's Sierra Nevada mountain range at the Truckee River Canyon. PHOTO BY ALEX RAMOS

ALL ABOARD

THE COMPLETE NORTH AMERICAN
TRAIN TRAVEL GUIDE

Fourth Edition

JIM LOOMIS

CHICAGO REVIEW PRESS

The Library of Congress has cataloged the third edition as follows:
Loomis, Jim.
  All aboard : the complete North American train travel guide / Jim Loomis. —
3rd ed.
    p. cm.
  Includes index.
  ISBN 978-1-56976-309-4 (pbk.)
  1. United States—Guidebooks. 2. Canada—Guidebooks. 3. Railroad
travel—United States—Guidebooks. 4. Railroad travel—Canada—
Guidebooks. 5. Copper Canyon (Mexico)—Guidebooks. 6. Railroad travel—
Mexico—Copper Canyon—Guidebooks. I. Title.
  E158.L59 2011
  917.304—dc22
                                                          2010036923

Cover and interior design: Jonathan Hahn
Cover image: The California Zephyr runs daily in each direction between Chicago and Emeryville, across the bay from San Francisco. Arguably Amtrak's most scenic ride, the Zephyr is shown here more than halfway through its eastbound journey, threading its way along rocky ridges as it descends into the Denver area. Photo courtesy of Mike Danneman.
Map design: Chris Erichsen

Copyright © 1995, 1998, 2011, 2015 by Jim Loomis
All rights reserved
Fourth edition
Published by Chicago Review Press, Incorporated
814 North Franklin Street
Chicago, Illinois 60610
ISBN 978-1-56976-176-2
Printed in the United States of America
5 4 3 2 1

"You get a real feeling of this country and the people in it when you're on a train." —HARRY TRUMAN

"These railroads . . . are positively the greatest blessing that the ages have wrought out for us. They give us wings; they annihilate the toil and dust of pilgrimage; they spiritualize travel!"
                          —NATHANIEL HAWTHORNE,
                            The House of Seven Gables

"I have seldom heard a train go by and not wished I was on it."
                          —PAUL THEROUX, *The Great Railway Bazaar*

CONTENTS

ACKNOWLEDGMENTS

This book contains a lot of information. All of it has to be accurate and current. And that means I had to do a lot of checking with people who have a large store of specific knowledge or immediate access to whatever it was I needed to know. It's just not possible to adequately thank all those people, but the very least I can do is acknowledge them as a group. I do so gladly and with gratitude. You know who you are.

Then there are the good-hearted folks who answered my questions and sent me information and double-checked what I wrote for accuracy—and went through that drill multiple times. These include:

Harris Cohen, one of the very best of a new generation of leaders at Amtrak. If we're lucky, he'll be running things one of these days.

Ryan Robutka, genial go-to guy for VIA Rail's long-distance trains, who had the answers almost before I finished asking the questions.

Sue Stilwell of S&S Tours—font of all the best information on the Copper Canyon experience.

Ross Capon, President Emeritus of the National Association of Railroad Passengers and all-around passenger rail expert.

Dave Randall, NARP board member, for his encyclopedic knowledge of passenger train equipment.

Adam Auxier of Altiplano Rail, who actually makes a living by riding around North America in classic railcars.

Charlie Treuhold, who keeps finding little details that need fixing and makes this a better book every time he does.

And my profound gratitude to both the professional and non-professional photographers who have allowed me to use their outstanding photos in this book. Please note their names as you turn the pages.

To all of these, and to the one or two I have invariably—but inadvertently—missed, my heartfelt thanks.

Mahalo and aloha.

—JIM LOOMIS
Ha'iku, Maui

REDISCOVERING THE TRAIN

When I was a youngster back in the late 1940s and early 1950s, my family would take an annual train trip from our home in Connecticut to either St. Louis or Florida, where grandparents would be waiting.

Those train rides were great adventures. I remember standing on the platform of the Hartford railroad station, waiting for the train to arrive. I would impatiently crane my neck for the first glimpse, being careful to keep behind the yellow warning line. According to my father (a master of hyperbole), anyone standing too close to the train as it rolled into the station ran the risk of being "sucked under the wheels."

The anticipation was almost unbearable. But finally, a rasping monotone would blare out over the PA system: "Your attention, please. Now arriving on track two . . ."

The platform came alive with that announcement; baggage carts rattled past, last-minute passengers ran up the stairs from the waiting room, and mothers anxiously corralled their kids. After the general confusion subsided, 30 or 40 people would be craning their necks. Still we saw nothing, just the tracks curving away beyond our line of sight.

Then, suddenly, a black steam locomotive materialized, bearing down on us, even appearing to accelerate as it loomed larger
and larger. It always seemed so much bigger than I remembered—
and noisier, although the locomotive's bell, clang-clanging slightly
out of rhythm, was somehow clearly heard above the din as the
train rumbled past.

A train ride is still a great adventure for me. I'm always anx-
ious to board, always reluctant to get off. There is obvious irony,
of course, in the fact that someone who loves rail travel has spent
more than 50 years living in Hawaii, a place more than 2,000
miles from the nearest long-distance train. Strangely, it was for
this very reason that my love of train travel was revived after so
many years.

Back in the early '90s, a family reunion was being organized
in Florida. While discussing plans to attend the event, I realized that neither my wife nor my daughter had ever really seen
America. Both had been born and raised here in the Islands, and
most of what they knew of "the mainland" was what they had
seen from 30,000 feet. Neither had any real idea of how *vast* our
country was.

Though I was not even sure it was possible, I suggested flying
straight to Florida for the reunion but from there taking a train
back to the West Coast. Then we would fly home to Honolulu.
My wife, Paula, thought I was crazy and said so. Our daughter
was six at the time, and Paula had visions of trying to occupy an
active youngster in cramped quarters for hours on end. Eventually I worked out an itinerary that included overnight stops in
Williamsburg, Virginia; Washington, DC; Chicago; the Colorado
Rockies; the California Sierras; and, finally, San Francisco. My
wife still wasn't completely convinced, but she agreed to give
Amtrak a try.

We had a wonderful trip. Williamsburg was charming; Washington was inspiring (and, thankfully, cool for June); the Rockies

and the Sierras were spectacular. Just as important, our train experience was all I had hoped it would be.

Since then, the train has become the preferred means of long-distance travel for our family. My daughter, in particular, has become a train enthusiast. She's a grown woman with a family of her own now; but when she was about ten years old, we combined two of our passions into a wonderful three-week excursion. We logged several thousand miles on Amtrak as we followed the Boston Red Sox on one of their road trips, hitting Oakland, Seattle, Chicago, and finally "home" to Boston. Neither of us will ever forget it. We had a priceless opportunity for a special father-daughter time together, we saw magnificent scenery, we saw the Red Sox win six of seven games—and we did it all by train.

The idea for this book grew from those experiences. It was written for the person who is naturally inquisitive, who notices and finds delight in little things, and who knows that people in a hurry miss a lot. It is my hope that this book will significantly add to the experience of every train ride for such a person, and I take a great deal of pleasure in that thought.

1

WHY TAKE A TRAIN?

Sophie Tucker once said, "I've been rich and I've been poor. Believe me, rich is better." Well, in my many travels I've been comfortable and I've been uncomfortable. Believe me, comfortable is better. A lot better. And that's why I take the train.

There are a lot of societal and environmental reasons for being pro-rail, and we'll talk about those in another chapter. But for long-distance travel, the train is the only civilized option left for us. You think not? Just consider the other choices.

See America Through a Windshield?

Forget it. Droning great distances across the country by car or—I shudder at the very thought—by bus is, for the most part, a waste of time. If you're the driver, it's tiring. If you're a passenger, it's boring. Either way, it's confining and uncomfortable.

In Charles Kuralt's delightful book, *On the Road with Charles Kuralt*, he said, "Thanks to the Interstate Highway System, it is now possible to travel across the country coast-to-coast without seeing anything." Kuralt's exaggeration can be forgiven, but you won't come close to seeing much of the real America until you leave the interstate. When we build superhighways in this country, we level everything, carving swaths hundreds of yards wide across the land from horizon to horizon. When we're through, there's nothing much left to see. The only conceivable reason for traveling long distances by car is to save money; that, I'll argue, is only possible when costs are divided among a number of passengers.

Flying Really Is for the Birds

Perhaps it's because of deregulation. Maybe it's just the shifting economic conditions that have caused the airlines to cram more people into fewer flights. And all the increased security is certainly a hassle. Whatever the reason, flying is no longer a pleasurable experience for the ordinary traveler.

Unless you have the money or enough frequent-flier miles to fly first-class, you're forced to spend hours crammed into a narrow seat with virtually no legroom. Once, on a flight to Los Angeles, I sat next to a rather large woman. She was only moderately overweight, but the seats were so narrow I was forced to eat my meal left-handed. Add jet lag into the mix, and a cross-country trip is exhausting. A longer flight—Honolulu to Paris, for instance—often involves back-to-back red-eye flights, an ordeal from which it takes two or three days to recover. Everyone has horror stories about the routine discomforts and inconveniences of flying; yet we have come to tolerate these conditions as an acceptable trade-off for getting somewhere quickly.

Flying isn't all bad, of course. It's quite true that occasionally—*if* you are flying during daylight hours, *if* you can arrange a window seat, and *if* there is no cloud cover—you can see some pretty spectacular things from a jetliner. Once on a flight out of Fort Myers, Florida, I had a ringside seat for a space shuttle launch. No doubt about it: that really was something to see from 25,000 feet.

But how exciting is it when the captain says, "That city off to the left of us is Wichita, Kansas"? Assuming you have a window seat on the left side, Wichita looks a lot like Topeka . . . or Boise, Duluth, or Portland (Oregon or Maine, take your pick). The fact is, you really can't see much of America from a plane.

Finally, the technology of modern aviation is incomprehensible to most people. Instead of entering through that long Jetway, have you ever boarded a Boeing 747 from ground level? It's an unnerving experience. You stand there on the tarmac, looking up at that monstrous machine. You just *know* it will not—cannot possibly—fly! Only blind faith gets you aboard. I know just one thing for certain about a plane trip: the sooner we land, the better I like it.

A Simple Attitude Adjustment

Long-distance train travel isn't the best choice for everyone on every occasion. If you have to get somewhere fast, an airplane is admittedly the only practical answer. And some people just can't

Passengers traveling overnight on Amtrak's northbound Coast Starlight wake up to this stunning view of Mount Shasta near Dunsmuir, California. PHOTO COURTESY OF AMTRAK

gear down sufficiently to enjoy the train, whether they're really in a hurry or not.

For most people, though, all it takes to enjoy a long-distance train trip is a simple attitude adjustment before starting out. Just remember that the train is part of your whole vacation experience; the plane is nothing more than the fastest way to get there.

On the Coast Starlight, en route from Los Angeles to Seattle, you roll almost silently through the Cascade Mountains of Oregon on a single track cut through the wilderness. (You'll notice that long-distance trains are traditionally given names as well as numbers.) Heading east out of Seattle on the Empire Builder, you fall asleep in the Cascades and wake up the next morning in the Rockies as the train skirts Glacier National Park. The eastbound Lake Shore Limited takes you along the banks of Lake Erie on your left and the original Erie Canal on your right; and the Adirondack follows the Hudson River into New York City. If you want to gaze on some of the prettiest country views anywhere, ride the Cardinal across the Blue Ridge Mountains from Virginia into Kentucky.

Just out of El Paso on the Sunset Limited, you pass a teenage boy sitting bareback on his horse and wonder if he's as curious about you as you are about him. From the California Zephyr, just west of Burlington, Iowa, you see a man and a woman sitting with their arms around each other on a tractor in a field of corn that stretches to the horizon. On the City of New Orleans, you pass a man putting tar paper on the roof of a shed and, as he straightens and stares, you can tell that his back hurts. As you roll slowly through Palatka, Florida, on the Silver Meteor, you see an elderly woman tending a small vegetable garden in her backyard. Her tomatoes are ripe. Twenty-four hours on a train will yield not only a thousand mental snapshots of America and its people but also the time to savor them.

More than anything, your train ride should be relaxing. That doesn't come automatically to everyone, so you may have to work a bit at making that mental adjustment. Some people just can't manage it. My sister once talked her husband into taking the train from Denver to San Francisco. He enjoyed the spectacular scenery as they wound their way through the Rockies west of Denver; but somewhere in Nevada the next morning, as they were rolling along beside a highway, he suddenly sat straight up in his seat. "Good God! Those cars are moving faster than we are! They'll get there before we do!" Not true, of course, and he never could explain why that should matter anyway, but he was agitated and impatient for the rest of the trip.

Why travel by train? Because compared to the alternatives, it's comfortable, relaxing, and *civilized*. Most of all, it will broaden and elevate your appreciation and understanding of our country and its people. That's the United States of America out there, passing by right outside your living room window.

2

HOW IT ALL BEGAN

Railroads have been around for a long time. As far back as the 16th century, they were used to haul coal out of mines in England and Wales. Really, those were hardly what we would call railroads—just horses and mules pulling wagons along crude tracks—but they had the same fundamental advantage that modern railroads offer. By reducing friction, more weight could be moved with less energy. The people who ran those coal mines understood the concept in even simpler terms: the easier it was for a horse to pull one of their carts, the more coal they could put into it.

The potential of steam power had been understood for a long time; in fact, steam engines had been used for years to pump water out of those same coal mines. The big breakthrough came about 1803 when Richard Trevithick, an English mining engineer, figured out how to mount a steam engine on a movable platform. Within a few years, the very first steam locomotives were being used to haul coal from mines to seaports, where it was shipped all over the world. In 1825, the first passenger rail service began, and word of this new means of transportation started spreading beyond England's shores. It found fertile ground in America.

A Mobile Society Is Created

America's first railroad was the Baltimore & Ohio (B&O), which
started service in 1830 and immediately captured the imagina-
tion of the country. That's hardly surprising. Up to that time, no
American had ever traveled faster than a horse could run. Almost
overnight, ordinary people were traveling for greater distances at
higher speeds than had ever been possible. Other railroads followed on the heels of the B&O.

For the average American in the early 19th century, it all took
some getting used to. Individual families and entire communities had always been pretty much self-sufficient. The railroads
changed all that in a matter of a few years, first by linking towns,
then states, and finally the entire continent. Suddenly Americans
had mobility; almost anyone could go almost anywhere. It's an
interesting paradox that while railroads were bringing Americans
together as one people, they also made it possible for the country
itself to expand.

By the mid-19th century, people were heading west by the
thousands, chasing after the gold that was discovered in California in 1848 or just looking for some land of their own. But however efficiently the railroads may have linked the North, South,
and East, they could only take people halfway into the great
American West—just as far as Omaha, Nebraska.

The Biggest Construction Project Ever

There had been talk about extending the railroad to the West
Coast for some time, but the men who proposed it were largely
written off as fools. It was indeed a huge, daunting project, arguably one of the largest and most ambitious engineering projects
ever attempted. Furthermore, not everyone thought California
was the promised land, even if the transcontinental railroad did

prove feasible. Probably the best-known naysayer of the time was Daniel Webster, who described the West as a "region of savages and wild beasts, of deserts of shifting sands and whirlwinds of dust, of cactus and prairie dogs."

Nevertheless, President Abraham Lincoln decided to move ahead with the transcontinental railroad and signed the Pacific Railway Act in 1862. Although foresight and vision were no doubt involved, the main reason for the decision was a very real concern that California, which had become our 31st state in 1850, would use the Civil War as an excuse to leave the Union and become a separate nation. Then, too, with the Gold Rush in full swing, there was always the threat of attack by a foreign power. Without a transcontinental railroad, the United States could never get troops or supplies to California in time to deal with that potential problem.

When the work finally started, it was certainly in earnest—in spite of the fact that the Civil War had begun. The Union Pacific Railroad headed west from Omaha, Nebraska, while the Central Pacific (CP) Railroad began in Sacramento, California, and went east. The CP had problems from the outset. Most of the able-bodied workers were busily mining gold, and those who were recruited proved to be largely unreliable. Finally, as a desperate last resort, the railroad hired Chinese laborers. As it turned out, they were much better workers. During the six or more years of construction, the Central Pacific used a total of 10,000 workers, of which 90 percent were Chinese.

It was tough, dangerous work over terribly difficult terrain. In some areas, laborers were suspended from cliffs by ropes in order to hack the roadbed out of the mountainside. While digging the Summit Tunnel in the Sierras, work crews had to blast through 1,600 feet of granite so hard that in spots they were able to progress just one foot a day. A new explosive, nitroglycerin, speeded the work, but in its early form it was extremely unstable, which meant it was always dangerous and frequently fatal. Nevertheless, work on the tunnel went on from both ends and, when the crews finally met, the two holes were only a few inches off. Still, after five years of prodigious effort, the Central Pacific crews had laid only 100 miles of track.

Meanwhile, the Union Pacific didn't have the awful terrain to deal with and was making much faster progress heading west across the Great Plains. There were still problems aplenty, however, such as finding wood from which to fashion cross ties, since there were no trees on the Nebraska prairie. To fill this obvious need, the railroad contracted with men called tie hacks to cut ties from trees in the western mountains and haul them eastward to meet the railroad.

The Union Pacific paid its railroad workers $1 per day, and all of them lived in railcars that followed them as track was laid. Many were immigrants of Irish and German descent, and many had served in the Civil War. As the railroad moved farther west, it entered Sioux territory. The Indians had largely ignored the occasional wagon train, but this development was clearly a serious threat to their way of life. Attacks became more frequent and progress slowed as the ex-soldiers were diverted into armed units assigned to protect the remaining work crews. Through it all, fueled by relatively high wages and visions of huge profits, the work went on at a feverish pace. In fact, one Union Pacific crew laid just a little more than 10 miles of track in one day—an astonishing feat considering the backbreaking nature of the work and the lack of any kind of power equipment.

The transcontinental linkup finally occurred on May 10, 1869, when the two railroads met at Promontory Summit, Utah. Several hundred people gathered at the site for the event, which included prayers and lots of speeches by many dignitaries. Several ceremonial "last spikes" were used in the official dedication, including a gold one, but the actual last spike was an ordinary iron one. It was driven into place by one of the railroad workers whose name, as far as I can tell, has long since been lost to history.

One other item of interest to those of us who are trivia buffs: America's transcontinental railroad and another monumental feat of engineering, the Suez Canal, were both completed in 1869, a coincidence that gave Jules Verne the idea for *Around the World in 80 Days*.

The Stream Becomes a Flood

It's hard for us to imagine the impact on the country when the transcontinental railroad was finally opened. It had taken a full six months to reach California or Oregon by wagon train from one of the several jump-off points in the Midwest, and one out of every ten pioneers died during the crossing. Then, almost literally overnight, you could travel in relative safety and comfort all the way from New York City to Sacramento in just under a week. And people started to do so by the thousands.

If the western movement of people was a stream, then the mail they sent and received soon became a flood. Before the transcontinental link, mail was either carried by stagecoach or around South America by sailing ship, which took several months. Suddenly trains had the capacity to carry large quantities of mail at low cost and at unheard of speed: from the Atlantic to the Pacific in less than a week. Letters and packages were sorted en route in mail cars. Speed was everything. Bags of mail were thrown from trains or snatched from trackside poles as trains sped through small towns all across America. There was glamour attached to speedy mail service, and the railroads gave it top priority. Trains brought news for the masses, too—more of it and faster than ever before. Newspapers printed in major cities were being delivered by train to subscribers in small town America within hours.

America Starts Moving by Rail

By 1865, when the Civil War ended, there were some 30,000 miles of track in the country. During the next 25 years, steel rails spread out all over America until, by 1890, there were well over 200,000 miles of track running from sea to shining sea.

The federal government encouraged the spread of the railroads by giving them land—not just rights-of-way on which to lay their tracks but land adjacent to the tracks too, which totaled millions upon millions of acres. The railroads sold this land at very low prices, actually giving it away in some cases. Men called colonization agents were hired by the railroads to recruit families from the industrial East Coast. Many railroads actually operated what were called immigrant trains—which carried entire families, including their personal belongings and even their livestock—from the eastern United States into the newly opened areas. Thousands of people took advantage of this new opportunity, and as word spread across the Atlantic, European immigrants joined the flood of new settlers.

The railroads were eager, almost desperate, to encourage this resettlement, because if they were to succeed, people—*lots* of people—had to settle wherever tracks had been laid. It worked too, because the supplies these settlers needed to start and sustain their new lives on the American frontier were brought to them by the railroads. As they became established farmers and ranchers, they sent their wheat, corn, and cattle to eastern markets by rail as well.

In less than a quarter of a century, the railroads were prospering, and so were the cities and towns they served. Chicago became a thriving center of business and trade, not coincidentally because the eleven different railroads serving the city made it the busiest railroad center in the world. Factories full of new employees sprang up to process the cattle, grain, lumber, and other raw materials being delivered to Chicago by rail from the

West. And, naturally, the goods produced by these factories were then shipped by rail to consumers in every area of the country, including back to those people living in the now-prosperous western towns.

It was certainly a time for people with new ideas. There can be no doubt that Richard Sears and Alvah Roebuck had a good one when they started their catalog business in 1887, but it was the railroads and their efficient handling of letters and packages that made it all possible. In fact, it's hardly a coincidence that Richard Sears, the partner who first realized the potential of the mail-order business, began his working career as a railroad agent in Minnesota. The Sears Tower (renamed the Willis Tower in 2009) that dominates the Chicago skyline today is as much a monument to the American railroad as it is to those two far-sighted entrepreneurs.

Bigger, Better, Faster Trains

As the country grew, so did the railroads. There were more trains going to more places and getting there faster—and safer too. Air brakes had been developed by George Westinghouse and were in general use on most trains by the 1880s. About that same time, a simple but significant improvement in the design of passenger cars occurred when an elastic diaphragm was added to each end of every car. These diaphragms connected when the cars were coupled together, and just like that, the passageway between rail-cars became enclosed. Until this improvement took place, the business of crossing from one lurching car to another was not for the young, old, or faint of heart. Furthermore, once it became easy and safe for passengers to pass between moving railway cars, the modern version of the dining car suddenly became feasible.

The first regular onboard food service had begun in 1842, with credit again going to the Baltimore & Ohio. The food was

prepared elsewhere, brought aboard the trains, and served cold
to passengers. Then, in 1867, George Pullman introduced a very
early version of what we would come to recognize as a dining car.
Actually, he called it a "hotel car," and with good reason: since
passengers didn't move back and forth between railcars in those
earlier years, this one car contained cooking facilities, a dining
area, and sleeping accommodations for as many as 40 passengers.

George Pullman may have had a good idea with his hotel
car, but he really hit it big when his Pullman Palace Car Company in Chicago began turning out luxury sleeping cars that soon
came to be known simply as Pullmans. Not many people know
that the railroads hauling George Pullman's sleeping cars around
the country didn't actually own them. The Pullman Company
retained ownership of the cars and merely leased them to the
various railroads. Even the conductors and porters were Pullman
employees (it was what we would now call a turnkey operation,
several decades ahead of its time). In fact, for many years it was
said that on any given night more people were sleeping in Pullman
car berths than in the beds of the largest hotel chains in the world.

George Pullman went so far as to build a small town for his
workers adjacent to the Chicago plant where his railcars were
built. At its peak, some 12,000 workers lived in the community created by their employer—working in his factory, living in
his houses, buying from his stores. Pullman was not so much a
visionary as he was a relentless businessman, for he made a profit
on almost everything his employees bought, including the rent
they paid for their homes.

It all started to come undone in 1893 when the country slid
into a depression. As business declined and profits fell, Pullman
reduced the wages he paid to his employees. He did not, however,
see a corresponding need to reduce the rents they were paying for
their housing. As the depression deepened, unrest among Pullman
Company employees grew, and in 1894 they walked off their jobs

in protest. Things turned ugly in short order; in an ensuing riot, 34 people were killed at the Pullman plant. The US Army was sent in and restored order by simply arresting the union leaders and tossing them into jail.

The Government Gets Involved

For a number of years, George Pullman had been regarded as an enlightened and respected businessman, but that image changed quickly after the strike and the ensuing violence. He soon found himself the object of severe criticism from many quarters. Pullman wasn't alone either. Sharing the spotlight of harsh public opinion with him were a number of other men, all of whom had made millions from railroads: Cornelius Vanderbilt, J. P. Morgan, James J. Hill, Jay Gould, and others.

These men were portrayed as greedy robber barons, and in truth many of them richly deserved the label. After all, these were the days before government controls, and many of the railroad tycoons took full advantage of that lack of regulation through shady stock deals and shameless gouging. In many areas of the West, for instance, farmers and ranchers were at the mercy of the railroads that carried their cattle or grain to eastern markets. The railroads regularly increased their rates and were soon making huge profits while their customers continued to struggle for survival. In 1887 the federal government finally reacted, and the Interstate Commerce Commission was created by Congress to regulate the railroads, specifically to set the rates that could be charged for hauling freight.

The Unions Step In

Railroading in those early days was notoriously dangerous work. The combination of improving technology and the lack of anything approaching modern safety standards took a terrible toll. Brakemen worked on top of moving railcars in all types of weather. Bad track, usually because it was laid in haste, often caused derailments. Locomotive boiler explosions were not uncommon and were always fatal to the head-end crew. It's estimated that in the 30 years leading up to World War I, railroad workers were killed on the job at the rate of some 2,500 a year, an average of 7 deaths every single day. Many thousands more were injured. Even everyday working conditions were often appalling. Temperatures in the locomotive cab could reach –30 degrees in winter and 150–160 degrees in summer. Not surprisingly, these were the years when railroad unions were formed and began to gain acceptance. Gradually the lives of railroad workers began to improve.

Storm Clouds on the Railroads' Horizon

The pendulum began swinging a bit faster when the country's railroads were nationalized during World War I and major concessions to the unions were agreed to by the government. Many of the new rules made sense at the time. For instance, an eight-hour day was established as a standard for railroad employees—but at the same time the government also agreed that a distance of 100 miles would constitute a full day's work for a train's operating crew. In those early days, that was realistic. Operating one of those early steam locomotives was exhausting work, and with stops along the route for watering and coaling, it could easily take a full eight hours to travel 100 miles. But by the 1920s—long after the railroads had been returned to private ownership—the technology of steam locomotives had become more efficient, and trains were being run at much higher speeds. The railroads were not able to change or get rid of the old union rules, and they often found themselves giving a train crew four days' pay for eight hours of work because their train covered 400 miles during that time.

But then trucks appeared. Actually, the value of hauling supplies by truck had become apparent in Europe during World War I when the US Army used fleets of vehicles to haul supplies and ammunition to the doughboys at the front. From that experience, it was easy to see that trucks had considerable potential for peacetime application. In 1919 a convoy of trucks set out to cross the country from Washington, DC, to San Francisco. The journey took three months, and the vehicles averaged less than six miles per hour, but they did it. Suddenly it was clear that the only thing trucks needed to become a new and important mode of transportation was a decent road.

To provide jobs for the unemployed after the stock market crash of 1929, the government started building those roads, the beginnings of our Interstate Highway System. As soon as new roads were finished, trucks began hauling freight over them. Instead of traveling city to city in a railroad boxcar, goods were traveling door to door in a truck. Then came buses—Greyhound, Trailways, and a host of small-time carriers—and the railroads started losing passenger business too. Right behind the buses came private automobiles. Thanks to Henry Ford and mass production, ordinary people could now pile into the family car and visit friends or relatives several hundred miles away. As if competition from trucks, buses, and cars wasn't bad enough for the railroads, a few visionaries were talking about airplane travel becoming feasible for large numbers of people within 20 years. To top it all off, in some parts of the country railroads were even competing against each other for both freight and passenger business.

The Way to a Passenger's Heart

Whatever their other faults, the railroad entrepreneurs were not quitters, and they finally began to fight for their share of the passenger business. They competed by claiming faster trains, more

comfortable routes, and more service amenities. But many railroads had come to realize that what passengers remembered most
about their train trips were the dining experiences. (Still true, by
the way.) That's what they talked about with their friends, and as
we all know, word of mouth is the most effective form of advertising. Soon, to the delight of rail passengers everywhere, competition
between railroads had extended all the way into the dining car.

During the 1930s, '40s, and '50s—the exception being an
interruption for World War II—it wasn't unusual to have more
than a dozen entrées, including fresh fish and wild game, on a dining car menu, plus a lavish selection of desserts. Many railroads
became known for specific dishes served in their dining cars. The
Great Northern's dining cars featured rainbow trout that were
caught, handed aboard moving trains, cooked, and served in the
space of just a few hours.

After World War II, the railroads did their best to regain passenger business by promoting rail travel to the West. In addition
to traditional forms of advertising, many of the crack trains were
given what Easterners would perceive to be Indian names: Chief,
Super Chief, Scout, Hiawatha, and others.

The Golden Age

Beginning around 1890 and continuing until the outbreak of
World War II, Americans with the means to travel coast-to-coast
and between major US cities were able to do so in real style. It
was a time that's come to be known as the golden age of train
travel, as dozens of railroads vied for passenger business with
crack trains that featured every manner of luxury and service.

The very, very rich—investment bankers, industrialists, the
railroad tycoons themselves, and others of that ilk—traveled in
their own private railcars. But until the railroads actually got into
the business of providing luxury rail travel, it was simply not

available, not even to the merely wealthy. Then, in the fall of 1911, the Atchison, Topeka and Santa Fe Railway—aka Santa Fe—began offering once-a-week service between Chicago and Los Angeles with a train appropriately called the de Luxe. And indeed it was. Passengers slept in real brass beds. There were maids, a manicurist for female passengers, and a barber for the men. The latest books and magazines could be found in an onboard library. Newspapers and the latest stock reports were put aboard at regular stops en route. In promoting the de Luxe, the railroad boasted that passengers would stay comfortable regardless of the outside temperature, thanks to a technological breakthrough the company described as an "air washing device" (a primitive form of air conditioning).

As the years passed and passenger demand grew, Santa Fe added more luxury trains to its popular Chicago–Los Angeles route. The Chief made its debut in 1926 and soon became the choice of movie stars traveling between coasts, a fact the railroad promoted relentlessly with publicity photos of the stars waving from the observation platform on the rear car. There was a barber, a hairdresser, a manicurist, and a hostess in the lounge car. In the Chief's dining car, the menu offered a dizzying variety of dishes, expertly prepared and served with a flourish. There was even a private dining room where Hollywood moguls could dine and make their blockbuster deals in private.

The Chief proved very popular, so to meet the additional demand and broaden its passenger base, Santa Fe added other new trains to the route. The Scout wasn't as fancy as the Chief, but it catered to middle-income families traveling on a budget and helped bring long-distance train travel to a whole new market. The El Capitan was an all-coach train, and the California Limited served only first-class passengers. Finally, in 1936, Santa Fe introduced the Super Chief, which soon became a standard in its own right. Gradually the traditional Pullman cars gave way to gleaming stainless-steel consists, with the now-classic bullet-shaped lounge car bringing up the rear. Even after auto and air travel forced rail passenger service into serious decline, Santa Fe steadfastly maintained its standards of quality and service to the very last.

Competition for passengers among railroads themselves was probably fiercest on the routes between Chicago and New York City. There were a number of railroads serving those cities, but most of the competition was between the Pennsylvania Railroad's Broadway Limited and the pride of the New York Central System, the famous 20th Century Limited. Both trains ran at high speeds, both offered fine dining and many service amenities, and (for a time anyway) both left Chicago heading east at about the same time. Old-time Chicago train watchers tell of waiting at any one of several vantage points in the suburbs to see which train would be leading as they came thundering past, still running on parallel tracks at that point.

Other railroads were also contributing to the lore and legacy of the American luxury long-distance train. The Baltimore & Ohio operated a number of excellent trains but probably considered the Capitol Limited—which ran between Washington, DC, and Chicago—to be its flagship. One of the Great Northern's best was the Oriental Limited, so named by the railroad's founder, James J. Hill, because he thought that his northern route from Chicago to Puget Sound would open the way for a vast amount of trade between the United States and Asian markets.

The Wabash Railroad's Cannonball began providing daylight service between St. Louis and Detroit in 1946. Curiously, even though the famous song, "The Wabash Cannonball," had been around for decades, there's no record of any train with that name before the Wabash got around to using it.

During this so-called golden age, there were dozens of railroads operating hundreds of trains. Many developed their own identity and reputation—for speed, service, color scheme, a special dish in the dining car, or just their own peculiar *élan*. And, of course, in that wonderful railroad tradition, the trains were all given names. Some were clearly regional (Connecticut Yankee, Southern Belle), while others touted destinations (Dixie Express, Texas Eagle). Some trains were named for people, both real and fictional (Commodore Vanderbilt, Pocahontas, Rip Van Winkle). Some of the names were highly evocative (Black Diamond, Flying Cloud, North Wind); some tried to be clever (Silent Knight) or cute (Seven O'Klocker).

Many of us actually recall riding on some of those trains, and they were wonderful, perhaps even as luxurious as we remember. Still, it's important to keep things in perspective. The fact is that during all those "glory years" of rail travel, most Americans rode on trains that were quite ordinary. They were slow and probably neither clean nor comfortable. Then, as now, luxury was for the fortunate few.

First It Rained, Then It Poured

When trouble came for the railroads, it came from many directions at once, and it wasn't pretty. Trucks by the hundreds of thousands began hauling commodities of all kinds over a new system of interstate highways. Mom, Dad, and their 2.5 kids traveled wherever they wanted to go, coast-to-coast over that same highway system in a family car that ran on gasoline costing 25 cents a gallon. Airplanes became larger and faster, which meant they carried more people farther, faster, and cheaper than ever. With all those fast new jets flying everywhere, the US Post Office decreed that all first-class mail would henceforth travel by air. (Remember? We used to pay one rate for letters sent by surface mail and a higher rate for airmail.) Revenue from first-class mail carried on fast passenger trains had been an important source of revenue for the railroads.

Any one of those factors alone would have hurt; altogether they were fatal. Some railroads had seen it coming and tried to fight back, but one after another they all came to realize it was a losing battle. At that point, the problem became how to get *out* of the passenger business. It wasn't easy in those days before deregulation. The same Interstate Commerce Commission that had been created in the late 1800s was now a way of bureaucratic life for the railroads. The commission approved requests for routes and reviewed and approved the fares the railroads charged. Unfortunately, from the railroads' perspective, the Commission also had to approve whenever a railroad wanted to cut passenger service. Usually that approval would only be given if the railroad could demonstrate that there was little, if any, demand for the service.

And so the game began. Railroads allowed both their equipment and their service to deteriorate in the hope that train travel would become such an unpleasant experience that passengers would turn elsewhere for their transportation. Certainly a lot did, but for many unlucky souls, the train was the only way to get where they had to go. (That's still the case today in many rural communities, by the way, where an Amtrak train is literally the only public transportation in or out of town.)

Gradually it settled into a standoff between the federal government and the railroads: the government refused to let the railroads stop providing passenger service and the railroads refused to provide more than the most basic service. The traditional dining car soon gave way to dirty lounge cars, where vending machines dispensed stale packaged food. Sleeping cars on overnight trains were replaced with coaches, forcing passengers to sit up all night—even those willing and able to pay for first-class accommodations. It was a frustrating, maddening situation that went on for years. And everyone knew that sooner or later, it could only end one way.

3

AMTRAK TO THE RESCUE

The great trains are gone, and it's a pity. But with the advantage of 20/20 hindsight, most people agree it probably wasn't realistic to think that a nationwide system of privately operated passenger trains could have survived. It certainly hasn't worked out that way anywhere else in the world.

After a decade or more of struggle, by 1970 it had become clear that the private railroads were simply not going to provide the country with anything even remotely resembling a nationwide rail passenger system. Even government oversight and regulation of the railroad industry wasn't going to save the passenger train. The railroads' claim that their financial health would be threatened if they were forced to continue providing passenger service was quite true in most cases. In fact, the Interstate Commerce Commission had all but officially acknowledged the plight of the railroads during the '60s by granting various railroads permission to eliminate what amounted to almost 60 percent of the nation's passenger trains. Even that relief wasn't enough help for some, however, and private railroads continued to go broke at an alarming rate.

Time for Some Hard Decisions

The politicians had been watching these convulsions in the railroad industry with consternation, and most members of Congress had come to realize that sooner or later they would have to confront a very fundamental question: Did America really need some kind of national passenger rail system? There were loud and vocal arguments on both sides, but the answer finally came up "yes," helped along at least in part because there was already a mandate to that effect on the books in the High Speed Ground Transportation Act, which was passed by Congress in 1965. It created and funded a federal office to look into the feasibility of, among other ideas, high-speed rail. Some of the funds had gone into the study of far-out futuristic schemes, but a lot of the money was put to practical use, such as helping the Penn Central railroad begin high-speed passenger service between Washington, DC, and New York.

Things came to a head during the summer of 1969, and after a great deal of argument and discussion, a variety of bills were introduced by several different members of both the House and the Senate. There was the usual dithering, and the several versions became mired in the legislative process. Then, in June of 1970, the Penn Central collapsed into bankruptcy. The resulting shock waves galvanized Congress into action. What emerged was something called the Rail Passenger Service Act, which finally allowed the private railroads to give up their passenger service. But it also created a half-private, half-public company—eventually known as Amtrak—that would take over the job of providing the country with a nationwide passenger rail system. Although a bit short on specifics, the bill was nevertheless a commitment of support for passenger trains by the federal government. It was also pretty much a bipartisan effort. (Cynics have noted—and continue to note—that support of passenger rail service has a lot less to do with political philosophy or transportation policy than it does with whether or not there are trains serving the district of any given member of Congress.)

The funding method devised to launch Amtrak was pretty complicated. Essentially it allowed private railroads to make cash payments, which would provide start-up funding for Amtrak while giving the railroads permission to get out of the passenger business. On a case-by-case basis, Amtrak could also elect to accept payment in the form of passenger equipment or operating crews. By the time it all shook out, 20 railroads had given Amtrak nearly 1,200 pieces of equipment and a total of slightly more than $197 million in cash. Congress added $40 million to the pot and another $100 million in loan guarantees, giving Amtrak some $340 million to begin operations.

The final hurdle was a presidential signature. Richard Nixon had been keeping a low profile on the subject, but in retrospect that part of the process was probably never in doubt. Nixon was already looking ahead to his reelection campaign in 1972 and worrying about how the unpopular war in Vietnam would affect his chances. As a matter of practical politics, he couldn't afford having the death of the passenger train laid at his doorstep too. He signed the bill on October 30, 1970.

Any sighs of relief from pro-rail people were premature, however. Many who were there at the time now believe that it was always the intent of the Nixon administration—if not the president himself—to give lip-service support to the creation of the new rail system and then quietly kill it behind the scenes. These suspicions were subsequently borne out by a succession of power plays and roadblocks aimed at undermining Amtrak, usually orchestrated by Nixon aide John Ehrlichman (later of Watergate fame).

A Shortage of Know-How

The formal name for this new public/private corporation was the National Railroad Passenger Corporation—as a matter of fact, that's still its name. Given the American propensity for nick-names, it's not surprising that the company almost immediately became known simply as Railpax, "pax" being common short-hand in the travel industry for "passengers." Within months—supposedly because a few critics of rail travel had begun referring to the new company as "Railpox"—the name was changed to Amtrak, an acronym for "*Am*erican *tr*avel by tr*ak*."

An arrow-shaped logo was adopted, and wags almost instantly dubbed it "the pointless arrow" (proving, I suppose, that someone will always find something to pick on). Amtrak adopted a new, more contemporary logo years later, but you will still see the old logo on some stations and platforms around the country.

As President Nixon began naming directors to the new company's board, it was soon noted that there was not one railroad person among them. Then, continuing this puzzling precedent, the board's choice to be Amtrak's first president was Roger Lewis, who was available for the job by virtue of having been recently fired from his position as head of General Dynamics. Lewis assumed his new job just one week before Amtrak's scheduled start date. Don Phillips, a Washington-based journalist whose credentials include stints as a transportation writer at United Press International, the *Washington Post*, and *Trains* magazine, came to like the man personally; however he publicly speculated on Lewis's real assignment. "I am persuaded," he wrote, "that [Lewis] took the job with orders from the White House—direct or indirect—to oversee an orderly shutdown [of Amtrak]."

Some were startled by Lewis's priorities as he began what was undeniably a daunting job. One early Amtrak employee, Kevin McKinney, recalled in a *Trains* magazine story that in Lewis's very first staff memo he complained about the appearance of the reception area outside Amtrak's executive offices, directing that thereafter the number of magazines permitted on the coffee table would be limited to no more than four.

In putting together his team, Lewis surrounded himself with other executives equally unfamiliar with the railroad business. W. Graham Claytor Jr., the head of Southern Railway at the time and himself a future Amtrak president, grumbled that "Amtrak doesn't have a railroader above the level of trainmaster" and dourly predicted that the new Amtrak brain trust (people Claytor considered to be near-hopeless amateurs) would "screw it up beyond . . . redemption."

It took a while—organizing a coast-to-coast system of passenger trains would be a monumental task under even the best of circumstances—but on May 1, 1971, the first train to operate under the Amtrak banner rolled out of Washington's Union Station and headed north for New York City.

Off to a Rocky Start

An old Madison Avenue axiom says, "Nothing can kill a business faster than great advertising." Translation: If you create demand for a product or service, it had damn well better meet customer expectations. If it doesn't, the negative word-of-mouth can destroy you. Amtrak stumbled into that trap in its early days with the catchy advertising slogan, "We're making the trains worth traveling again." Unfortunately, they weren't.

From day one, Amtrak people found themselves with a maintenance and operations nightmare on their hands. Being saddled with a variety of equipment collected from more than a dozen railroads caused some nasty surprises. Employees often discovered, for example, that the electrical systems in one or two passenger cars of a train's consist were incompatible with the rest

of the train. Rolling stock, most of which had been old to begin
with, was deteriorating rapidly, and there was little money available for repairs, let alone any kind of orderly maintenance program. Worst of all, in Amtrak's first few years, locomotive failures occurred at the rate of ten per day. Per *day*! There was no
money for new ones, of course, so Amtrak had to scrape together
whatever cash it could and go back to the used locomotive market, buying poor equipment to replace terrible equipment.

In many areas of the country, Amtrak had to haul all that
run-down equipment over poor track, which added to the woes
of beleaguered passengers. Railroads were in poor financial
shape after the disastrous '60s, and rather than spend money to
maintain their track, most simply let it deteriorate and reduced
the speed of their freight trains accordingly. Amtrak passenger
trains running over that same track had two options: run at the
highest safe speed possible and cause discomfort to your passengers from the bouncing and swaying, or reduce speeds and frus-
trate your passengers with slow trains and late arrivals. Some
choice!

Finally, many of the onboard crews, which Amtrak had
inherited from private railroads along with all that run-down
equipment, brought with them casual if not downright hostile
attitudes. After all, they had probably been working for a railroad that had been actively trying to discourage passenger business for years.

For the record, however, a few railroads continued to guard
their reputation for quality and service. One was Santa Fe, which
had begun operating the deservedly famous Super Chief between
Chicago and Los Angeles in 1948. Amtrak had taken over the
route, but Santa Fe's chairman, John Reed, was so distressed
at the level of service being provided that he indignantly with-
drew permission for Amtrak to use the Super Chief name. That
decision was never reversed. Today, although it has become one

of the company's better trains, Amtrak continues to call it the Southwest Chief.

Too Many Trains, Not Enough Dollars

Despite these very serious concerns, Amtrak's biggest problem continued to be a financial one. Within months, the company's deficit had begun to mount alarmingly. For one thing, start-up costs had been huge. For another, Amtrak's route system was highly political from the get-go, with influential members of Congress insisting on having trains in their districts whether or not there was any serious demand for the service. Early in its existence, Amtrak began service between Washington, DC, and Parkersburg, West Virginia, at the behest of Harley O. Staggers, a powerful and influential Democratic congressman from, of course, West Virginia. In its first several years of operation, the Amtrak system had actually increased from some 23,000 miles to more than 27,000 miles despite mounting deficits.

About the only thing holding steady during Amtrak's early turbulent years was the public's support for rail. That support was reflected in opinion polls, which, as we all know, are avidly read by the politicians. So while Congress remained committed to the passenger train, it nevertheless recognized that too much was being demanded of the company. A service cut would be necessary. After months of hand-wringing—no one in Congress wanted his or her train eliminated—the Amtrak system was reduced by about 14 percent, which, ironically, left the company at just about the size it was on its very first day.

After several years of operations to provide some kind of track record, Congress at last began to evaluate Amtrak in a more realistic light. Clearly, the notion that Amtrak could operate at a profit had not been realistic—not as long as every other manner of public transportation, from airplanes to sidewalks, was being subsidized by one or more levels of government. In 1978 Congress formally acknowledged Amtrak's need for government support by ordering the company to generate enough revenue on its own to cover at least half of its operating costs. Then, a few years later, Congress finally dealt with the problem its own members created. Specific monetary guidelines were set up for judging every train in Amtrak's system. Trains that fell below certain minimums for ridership and revenue would face elimination, even over the inevitable objections of individual members of Congress.

No Friend in Reagan

Somehow Amtrak managed to muddle through the 1970s, meeting and at least trying to deal with one obstacle after another. Then a very large obstacle came along in 1981 when Ronald Reagan took office as the country's 40th president. Reagan was opposed to *any* subsidy for Amtrak. With budget director David Stockman leading the charge, the first of many attempts to reduce or eliminate the flow of federal dollars to Amtrak occurred. Instead of proposing plans for the future, Amtrak found itself having to justify its very existence to an administration that was almost blindly anti-rail. (Ironically, for many years Ronald Reagan the movie actor had appeared in advertising campaigns extolling the virtues of the Union Pacific Railroad's passenger service.)

Another Change at the Top

It had taken almost four years, but influential pro-rail members of Congress had finally gotten the idea that Roger Lewis was not the right man to be running Amtrak. One clue came when, in spite of all its problems, Lewis would not support a request to Congress for additional funding by the company he headed.

Responding to congressional pressure, the Amtrak board replaced Lewis with Paul Reistrup. He was a railroader, all right, but he proved to be artless when it came to dealing with the politicians. After a three-and-a-half-year hitch, he was replaced by Alan Boyd. And, yes, once again Amtrak found itself with a non-railroad man as its president. But Boyd had been the country's very first secretary of transportation and was the consummate Washington insider. Despite Reagan's policy of benign neglect toward Amtrak, Boyd managed to bring about a kind of political stability among the various players during his four-year tenure.

The timing for Amtrak's top leadership somehow always seemed to be wrong: When circumstances cried out for someone with operational know-how, they got a politician. When they needed someone who could talk turkey with the power brokers on Capitol Hill, they got a hard-nosed railroader. Fortunately for Amtrak, Graham Claytor became the company's fourth president in the summer of 1982.

The Cavalry Arrives Just in Time

First and foremost, W. Graham Claytor Jr. was a railroad man. On every Amtrak trip he took, he was known to "walk the train" relentlessly, looking for the smallest out-of-place detail. But Claytor also proved to be a skilled politician. Already respected by his peers, he soon came to be viewed in the same way by members of Congress as well. Many of them felt a good deal more comfortable about continuing federal support for Amtrak with the no-nonsense former president of Southern Railway in charge. Unlike most of his predecessors, Claytor was able to speak from experience and with authority. Happily, under Claytor's leadership, Amtrak actually began to deliver.

Claytor began a shape-up program at Amtrak that would continue all through the 1980s. Training improved for employees;

because of elaborate procedures required by union contracts, those with unsatisfactory performance records were gradually weeded out. Claytor knew, as the railroad barons of a century before knew, that what passengers remember most is having a good meal in the dining car. Little by little (when you're habitually underfunded, there's no other way), plastic was replaced by china and stainless-steel utensils in Amtrak diners, and airline-type food gave way to meals prepared onboard.

Claytor was a hands-on leader who took a personal interest in every aspect of the Amtrak operation. Many an Amtrak passenger who had written a letter of complaint about some lapse in service was surprised to receive a personal letter from Claytor himself, who assured them the matter would be addressed.

One day at a time, Amtrak was working through many of its problems. Engineers and conductors, who had continued to be employees of the freight railroads over whose tracks Amtrak trains operated, became Amtrak employees. New contracts with labor unions resulted in more productivity from onboard crews. In addition to support for operating expenses, Congress provided funds for new equipment. Bi-level Superliners were ordered in 1975 to replace traditional railcars on Amtrak's western runs; an order for new locomotives followed in 1976. In the late 1980s, Amtrak placed an order for a new generation of passenger car, the Viewliner, which would enable the company to start getting rid of the old single-level sleepers still operating on eastern routes. In 1993, a new locomotive appeared; it was the first in several decades specifically designed for passenger train service. A new order for updated Superliners was placed.

In December 1993, Graham Claytor retired at the age of 81. Sadly, he died in May of the following year, less than six months after retiring. Graham Claytor left quite a legacy, however; it is almost universally agreed that, without him, Amtrak would probably not have survived.

The More Things Change . . .

Amtrak's new president, Thomas M. Downs, had his hands full from the start. Bare-bones funding during the eight-year Reagan administration had continued under the first George Bush and was taking its toll. Replacement and maintenance for locomotives and railcars were being deferred because of a lack of money. As a consequence, equipment failures—the same problem that had plagued Amtrak in its start-up years—were happening all over again. President Bill Clinton was vocally pro-rail, but his budget requests for Amtrak (which were generous compared to those of the Reagan and Bush years) were drastically reduced by a conservative Republican Congress.

During his first year at Amtrak's helm, Downs moved quickly to streamline the company's operations, transferring both responsibility and authority farther down toward the frontline employees. With that shift of responsibility and with reduced costs clearly part of the picture, some 600 middle-management people were laid off. Then, in December 1994, Downs had the dubious distinction of announcing the most drastic reduction in service in Amtrak history—a reduction of more than 20 percent.

The mid- to late '90s was not a great time to be carrying the Amtrak banner into the halls of Congress. In order to keep desperately needed federal dollars coming, earlier Amtrak executives had assured members of Congress that it was just a matter of time before Amtrak could wean itself off any federal subsidy. In fact, a document known as Amtrak's Road Map to Self-Sufficiency had been floating around for some time. Pro-rail people used it to get continued funding, even though most realized it was a pipe dream. Anti-rail people used it as an eventual justification for choking off those federal dollars on the grounds that Amtrak had been unable to meet promised goals. As one pro-Amtrak observer said at the time, "Congress put a gun to Amtrak's head and said, 'Lie to us!'"

That was the political climate facing George Warrington when he took over as Amtrak president in 1998. There is no doubt that during Warrington's tenure, cost cutting continued, and as a result Amtrak service deteriorated. Nevertheless, looking back it is quite remarkable that no routes were discontinued under his tenure. George Warrington's legacy can be described quite simply: Amtrak survived.

The climate in Washington certainly didn't improve with the election of George W. Bush in 2000. In fact, though it hardly seemed possible, things got worse. Bush's annual budget proposals continued to include painfully low funding for Amtrak—so low that, if not for intervention by Congress, still more severe service cuts would have been necessary.

In 2002, David Gunn was named Amtrak president. He quickly endeared himself to Amtrak supporters for the honest and straightforward—although sometimes blunt—manner in which he dealt with Congress and the Bush administration. Gunn vigorously defended federal support for Amtrak by pointing out that every form of public transportation in the United States requires subsidizing from one level of government or another, but that many of these subsidies are disguised as user fees, such as the dedicated fuel taxes that raise billions every year for the nation's highways. Furthermore, Gunn was not shy about criticizing the Bush administration's attempts to starve Amtrak with budget proposals that would have forced more and more cuts. Gunn predictably paid the price for his vigorous defense of Amtrak: he was fired by the Bush appointees on Amtrak's board of directors in 2005, a move that devastated and demoralized many of Amtrak's long-suffering management people.

Things seemed to be changing for the better in 2006 when the Democrats regained control of Congress and again in 2008 when Barack Obama was elected president. That same year, Amtrak got a new president: Alex Kummant came to Amtrak after having been an executive with the Union Pacific Railroad. Kummant ran Amtrak during a period of unprecedented increases in ridership, due in part to $4-a-gallon gasoline and chaos in the airline industry. Then in November 2008, amid rumors of conflict with the Amtrak board, Kummant suddenly and unexpectedly resigned.

Within weeks, the Amtrak board announced the interim appointment of Joseph Boardman as the railroad's newest president. Boardman was certainly familiar with Amtrak and its operations—he had been serving as administrator of the Federal Railroad Administration for the prior three years and, for three decades before that, in various roles within the surface transportation industry. As of this writing, Boardman's appointment has been extended through May 2015.

Also in 2008, Congress authorized funding for Amtrak that would do two important things: (1) provide adequate operating funds and (2) commit funding at that level for five years. It's hard to believe, but in its entire history, Amtrak had never known from one year to the next how much money it would have for operations. You and I would have a terrible time running our households like that; yet Amtrak was somehow expected to operate a national rail transportation system efficiently and intelligently under those circumstances.

Then came the American Recovery and Reinvestment Act of 2009 (ARRA)—the so-called stimulus bill. It included additional funds for Amtrak to repair railcars that had been sitting in storage. The ARRA also provided $8 billion in capital grants to be awarded for initial work on high-speed rail corridors and intercity routes. Several states jumped at the opportunity and used federal dollars to improve rail service within their borders. Illinois, for example, was awarded $1.5 billion to upgrade track between Chicago and St. Louis, thus increasing maximum train speeds from 79 to 110 mph and reducing running time by about an hour. A similar project is underway in Michigan to improve running times between Detroit and Chicago. Unfortunately, in moves that most impartial folks say were politically motivated, Republican governors in Wisconsin, Ohio, and Florida refused to accept several billion federal dollars each for true high-speed rail lines in their states. Nevertheless, for the first time in its history, Amtrak found itself with a federal administration at least nominally supportive of more and better passenger rail service.

Still—and it's hard to overstate this—day after day and month after month through all those frustrating years, Amtrak trains continued to carry Americans to and from thousands of cities and towns, from one end of the country to the other, setting new ridership records almost every year over the past two decades. And they did it at bargain prices. Even to this day, it is a fact that revenues from rail fares and other sources cover nearly 90 percent of the company's operating cost. That's really quite extraordinary. In the facetious words of one veteran employee, that makes Amtrak "the most profitable money-losing national passenger rail system in the world."

4

PLANNING YOUR OWN TRAIN TRIP

If you want to fly between two large US cities, there will probably be several airlines from which to choose. But if it's a long-distance train ride you're after, Amtrak is your only option. The Amtrak system covers most parts of the continental United States, and fully half of all Americans live within 25 miles of an Amtrak station, which means you can reach or get close to most major cities by train (see Amtrak's system map on page 42). Before you begin to work out the details of any rail trip, however, there are a few things you should know about present-day train travel.

Beware of Great Expectations

To avoid disappointment, it's important to have a clear understanding of what you can reasonably expect from your train trip—and, probably more important, what you shouldn't expect. One Amtrak train attendant I spoke to is still astonished about the couple on a cross-country honeymoon train trip who had somehow gotten the idea that there would be a fireplace in their compartment. Many of these misunderstandings, at least according to the onboard crews, are caused by people who have somehow gotten the idea that a train is like a cruise ship. There are indeed some similarities, but the two experiences are opposite in the most fundamental way: Cruise ships focus on a wide variety of onboard activities because most of the time there's nothing to see but ocean out there beyond the railing. Trains, on the other hand, offer constantly changing scenery outside the window and, for the most part, leave passengers to create their own activities and diversions.

A Few Things to Know Before You Start

First, and probably most important, do your planning as far in advance as possible. Your first priority should be deciding on specific dates for your train travel. Most long-distance trains, especially the sleeping-car accommodations, sell out very quickly. That's particularly true during the busy summer months. But no matter when you travel, it's a very good idea to make your train reservations at least 90 days in advance (ideally sooner than that).

Most trains operating east of the Mississippi River are comprised of single-level coaches and Viewliner sleeping cars, while long-distance trains running west of the Mississippi are equipped with Amtrak's bi-level Superliner cars. Superliners are also being used on the Capitol Limited, the City of New Orleans, and the Auto Train in the East. (For detailed information about the differences between these two types of railcar, see chapter 9, "Passenger Train Equipment.")

On all long-distance trains, regardless of equipment, Amtrak offers its passengers a choice between two distinct types of service: coach or sleeping car (usually just called "sleepers").

All-coach trains run in the Northeast and in parts of the Midwest and California. These are shorter-haul trains operating mostly during daylight hours. Most of them have one car designated as business class where you will get a somewhat more comfortable seat and complimentary beverages (more about this later). There is, of course, a surcharge for these extras.

Almost all of the coach trains operating in the East and Midwest also have a quiet car in which passengers are expected to refrain from using their cell phones or any electronic gear that makes noise, and conversation must be subdued. In fact, *any* conversation is likely to draw scowls from other passengers. There is no extra fare for a quiet car, and they are very popular.

The information and suggestions in the following pages will help you plan a rail trip that's best suited to your individual preferences and budget. While most of the examples discussed refer to longer and more detailed itineraries, shorter rail trips deserve no less attention. Whether you're considering a three-day excursion through New England to admire the fall colors or a three-week rail tour of the West, the planning process should be the same: as thorough, as unhurried, and as far in advance as possible. After all, any vacation requires an investment of your leisure time and money, neither of which should be wasted.

Consider a Package Tour

This chapter is about planning your own train trip—it's fun to do, and you can design it exactly the way you want. You should be aware, however, that Amtrak offers a nice variety of rail tours of varying lengths, which include train fare, hotels, and some sightseeing. These trips can usually be scheduled at your convenience, and the cost could be a bit lower than if you had booked the identical itinerary yourself. You are limited to the preplanned itineraries, however. For information and a detailed brochure, call Amtrak Vacations at 1-800-AMTRAK-2, or 1-800-268-7252. You can also go to their website at www.amtrakvacations.com. Vacations By Rail (www.vacationsbyrail.com) and Rail Travel Adventures (www.railtraveladventures.com) are two other companies specializing in escorted rail tours, including tours not involving Amtrak and many operating in other parts of the world.

Amtrak's Frequent Rider Program

Just about everyone is familiar with the frequent-flier programs initiated more than 25 years ago by the airlines. Amtrak has something similar that they call the Amtrak Guest Rewards program, and it works pretty much the same way. You earn points for traveling on Amtrak, and those points can be redeemed for future Amtrak travel or at hotels and rental-car companies. It doesn't cost anything; in fact, there are usually some free points awarded just for signing up. I certainly recommend it. There's nothing to lose, and you could end up with a free train trip. You can sign up by going to www.amtrakguestrewards.com.

A Word About Rail Fares

When traveling by train, all passengers pay a basic rail fare that covers the cost of a seat in coach class.

Starting in 2013, Amtrak broke down their rail fares into three categories: "Flexible" fares have no penalty if you decide not to travel and ask for a refund. You can save some money and still get a refund on "Value" fares, but there is a 10 percent penalty. The cheapest option is a "Saver" fare, but there is no refund for cancelation. However, no matter which of these options you choose, you can get a full refund in the form of an e-voucher, which is good for future Amtrak travel and is valid for a full year. In any case, if you must cancel, just be sure you do it *before your train leaves*. Many tickets aren't refundable at all, even for an e-voucher, once the train has left the station.

If you want an upgrade to one of the several different sleeping-car accommodations, you'll be paying the basic rail fare plus an additional fee for the sleeping car. The cost of the upgrade will vary depending upon the type of accommodation you select and how far you're traveling. Both the basic rail fares and the sleeping-car surcharges go up and down depending on the time of year you choose to travel. Fares tend to be lower between November and March, but you'll pay more at holiday times and during the busy summer months. And the cost also goes up when there are only a few rooms left on any given train—one more reason to book space as early as possible.

Once you have specific dates in mind, get a current fare quote by going to the Amtrak website (www.amtrak.com) or calling a reservations agent (1-800-USA-RAIL or 1-800-872-7245).

Rail Passes Are Another Option

The USA Rail Pass is Amtrak's equivalent to the popular Eurail Passes, which are sold for discounted train travel throughout Europe. Like the Eurail Pass, it's available for 15, 30, and 45 days of travel and for a varying number of segments. The USA Rail Pass is good for coach travel only, but you can upgrade into sleepers along the way if space is available. There are a number of conditions attached to this pass, so call Amtrak or go online to www.amtrak.com/railpass for those up-to-date details.

Amtrak also offers a California Rail Pass that's good for 7 days of travel within the state of California over a 21-day period. For current information about this pass, go to the Amtrak website, hold the mouse over the "Deals" tab to access the drop-down menu, and then click on "Rail Passes." An Amtrak reservations agent will also have that information.

Look for Other Discounts

At either end of the spectrum, age can also save you money. Children under 2 travel free; those between 2 and 15 pay half fare-when accompanied by an adult. Seniors 62 and over get a 15-percent discount on their rail fare, students get a 15-percent discount, and active-duty military can save 10 percent. Members of the National Association of Railroad Passengers (NARP) also

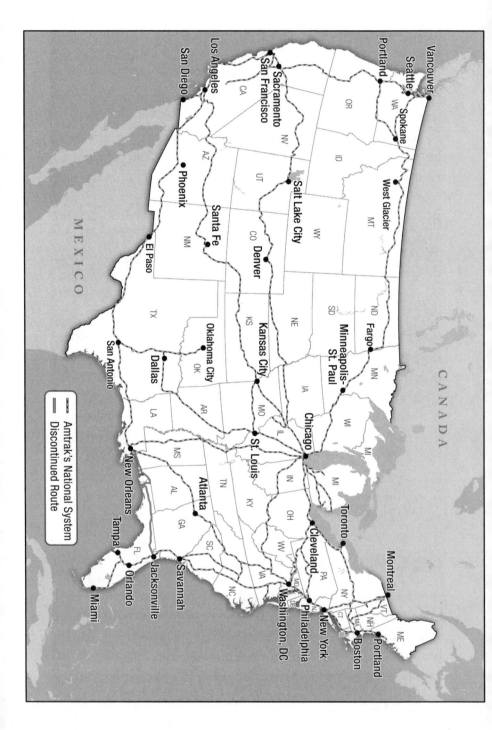

receive a 10-percent discount. But note that these discounts don't apply to sleeping-car accommodations, and there are other limitations and restrictions. As noted already, fares vary according to the season, so once you have tentative dates, check with Amtrak to see when those price changes occur. It may be that you can save some money just by changing the dates of your trip by a week or so. Check www.amtrak.com/hotdeals for special fares that pop up regularly. For last-minute one-way trips, go to that same page and, on the left side, click on "Weekly Specials."

Who Should Plan Your Trip?

There's no reason why you can't do all the preliminary planning yourself. For me, that's part of the fun. Besides, the more thought you personally put into your trip, the more successful and rewarding the whole experience is likely to be. Get as far into the details as you like, even selecting the specific trains you want to take.

When the time comes to make the actual reservations, you can work directly with an Amtrak reservations agent by calling 1-800-USA-RAIL. But don't just rattle off the trains you want— ask the agents if they have any suggestions. Their tips can make things go more smoothly all along the way. You'll find them very helpful.

You should also consider turning your preliminary itinerary over to a rail-savvy travel agent and letting him or her double-check all the details, make suggestions, and then handle the actual reservations and ticketing. A good agent can often work out a lower fare and will also know some tricks of the trade that could avoid some hassles. For instance, he or she will probably be able to wait-list you for a sleeping-car space on a sold-out train. Or make sure you're booked into a sleeping car that's right next to the diner so you won't have to walk through several cars on a moving train three times a day for your meals.

In the good old days, the services of a travel agent came at little or no cost to the traveler. Not anymore. Nowadays, you can expect to pay a fee to the travel agent that's based on the total cost of the booking. However, if your rail itinerary is at all complicated, a rail-savvy travel agent can be a big help and will probably be worth the money.

To learn how to find a train-smart travel agent—and, believe me, not all of them are—and for a list of a few travel agencies that specialize in train travel, see appendix B on page 383.

Customizing Your Train Trip

Can you do it yourself? Sure you can! Take a look at a map of Amtrak's coast-to-coast system and start with the two basic questions: Where do you want to go, and how long can you be gone?

Let's suppose you live in Washington, DC, and your two great passions in life are baseball and jazz. Great! How about taking Amtrak's Capitol Limited overnight to Chicago to see your Washington Nationals play the Chicago Cubs at Wrigley Field? The next evening, hop aboard the City of New Orleans and 24 hours later, after a fabulous dinner at Irene's (my personal favorite restaurant in the New Orleans French Quarter), you can be listening to real New Orleans jazz in Preservation Hall on Saint Peter Street. Since the Crescent passes through Atlanta on the return trip to Washington, you can stop there for a couple of days to visit your favorite Aunt Tillie. Sound good? OK, let's start the planning.

A Little Research Will Pay Off

Once you decide where you want to visit, find out something about those areas *before* deciding how long you'll stop there. Every state and most cities have offices established to promote tourism, and all offer a wealth of information on their websites.

Any good bookstore will have travel guides for most major cities and for every region of the country. Of course public libraries are excellent sources for free information. But please, take a little time for this before you start making specific plans. It will be time well spent, I promise you.

Amtrak Timetables

There are two ways to get an Amtrak timetable: (1) by going online to www.amtrak.com/schedules, or (2) by calling the nationwide toll-free number, 1-800-USA-RAIL. It may take a week or more to arrive. Just be sure to ask for the National Timetable (sometimes referred to as the System Timetable), which includes schedules for all coast-to-coast Amtrak trains. There is also a Northeast Timetable, which provides a detailed schedule of trains running between Washington and Boston. You may want to ask for both.

Amtrak has done a good job with their timetables. The format is simple and well presented, making them easy to read. The timetables contain much more than just train schedules. Depending on your specific itinerary, a lot of the information may be of little or no concern, but some could be very important.

Below each schedule, for instance, is a paragraph describing the different services available on that particular train. That's where you can find out if your train has a dining car serving full meals or if there's only a lounge car serving snacks. Most of Amtrak's long-distance trains run daily, but others don't. For instance, the Cardinal (Chicago–New York City) currently operates only three days a week. When you put a specific train into your itinerary, it's certainly important to know if it runs daily. The timetable will give you that and other important information.

Some cities not served by Amtrak may be reached by buses scheduled to connect with the trains. That information is also in the timetable, along with the locations of all Amtrak stations and whether checking baggage is allowed.

CALIFORNIA ZEPHYR

5			◄ Train Number ►			6
Daily			◄ Normal Days of Operation ►			Daily
Ⓡ 🍴✕ ☕🛏			◄ On Board Service ►			Ⓡ 🍴✕ ☕🛏
Read Down	Mile	▼		Symbol	▲	Read Up
🛏2 00P	0	Dp	Chicago, IL–Union Station (CT)	●&Ⓠℐ	Ar	🛏2 50P
R2 34P	28		Naperville, IL (METRA/BN Line)	●&Ⓠℐ		D1 43P
3 44P	104		Princeton, IL	○		D12 23P
4 38P	162		Galesburg, IL -S. Seminary St. 🗔	●&Ⓠℐ		D11 31A
5 25P	205		Burlington, IA	○&		10 36A
5 59P	233		Mount Pleasant, IA	●&		9 54A
6 53P	279		Ottumwa, IA	●&		9 09A
8 09P	359		Osceola, IA (Des Moines)	○&Ⓠℐ		7 40A
8 41P	392		Creston, IA	○&		7 04A
🛏10 55P	500	Ar	Omaha, NE	●&	Dp	🛏5 14A
🛏11 05P		Dp			Ar	🛏4 59A
🛏12 08A	555	Ar	Lincoln, NE	●&	Dp	🛏3 26A
🛏12 14A		Dp			Ar	🛏3 20A
🛏1 47A	652		Hastings, NE (Grand Island)	●&		🛏1 42A
2 34A	706		Holdrege, NE	○&		12 54A
3 43A	783		McCook, NE (CT)	○&		11 49P
5 05A	960		Fort Morgan, CO (Sterling) (MT)	○&		8 25P
🛏7 15A	1038	Ar	Denver, CO	●&Ⓠℐ	Dp	🛏7 10P
🛏8 05A		Dp	🚌 Colorado Springs, Pueblo, Vail, Glenwood Springs —see back		Ar	🛏6 38P
10 07A	1100		Fraser-Winter Park, CO	○&		3 50P
10 37A	1113		Granby, CO (Rocky Mt. Nat'l Park)	○&		3 12P
🛏1 53P	1223		Glenwood Springs, CO (Aspen)	●&		🛏12 10P
🛏4 10P	1311		Grand Junction, CO	●&		🛏10 23A
5 58P	1417		Green River, UT	○&		7 59A
7 20P	1488		Helper, UT (Price)	○&		6 37A
9 26P	1563		Provo, UT	○&		4 35A
🛏11 05P	1608	Ar	Salt Lake City, UT (MT)	●&	Dp	🛏3 30A
🛏11 30P		Dp	🚌 Ogden, Boise, Las Vegas —see back		Ar	🛏3 05A
3 03A	1871		Elko, NV (PT)	○&		9 31P
5 40A	2013		Winnemucca, NV	○&		7 08P
🛏8 36A	2202		Reno, NV	●&Ⓠℐ		🛏4 06P
9 37A	2237		Truckee, CA (Lake Tahoe)	○&		2 38P
11 48A	2301		Colfax, CA	○&		12 21P
12 57P	2336		Roseville, CA	○&Ⓠℐ		11 35A
🛏D2 13P	2353		Sacramento, CA	●&Ⓠℐ		🛏11 09A
🛏D2 44P	2367		Davis, CA	●&Ⓠℐ		🛏10 36A
🛏D3 26P	2411		Martinez, CA (San Joaquin Trains)	●&Ⓠℐ		🛏9 54A
D3 58P	2430		Richmond, CA	○&Ⓠℐ		9 22A
🛏4 10P	2438	Ar	Emeryville, CA (PT) 🚌 San Francisco—see back	●&Ⓠℐ	Dp	🛏9 10A

One more thing about timetables in general: Remember that minor changes in train schedules occur frequently. A train that departs at 10:00 AM today and is listed accordingly in the current timetable could leave 30 or 40 minutes *earlier* when you actually travel three months from now. So once you've worked out your itinerary and are ready to book your reservation, be sure to confirm all departure and arrival times for your specific dates, either by calling Amtrak directly or with your travel agent. Then check again a few days before you leave.

On the previous page is a sample of an Amtrak timetable. After studying it for a few minutes, you'll discover there is order and logic to the format. The schedule for the westbound California Zephyr, train 5, runs top to bottom in the left-hand column, while the schedule for the eastbound Zephyr, train 6, is listed bottom to top in the right-hand column. (Please note that this is just an example of a typical timetable's format. The Zephyr's current schedule will no doubt have a number of changes.)

Create Your Itinerary

So you've decided where you want to go and how long you can be away from home. Now you're ready to begin developing a detailed itinerary. Some travelers refuse to prepare itineraries in the mistaken belief that they will somehow become locked into a rigid schedule from which they can't deviate. Nonsense! An itinerary is nothing more than relevant information compiled in an orderly fashion. Not to have one with you as you travel is foolish; not to have one to leave behind with friends or family in case of an emergency is irresponsible.

Begin with a rough work sheet listing the days you'll be gone. At this stage, don't worry about specific dates. Remember that trip to Chicago and New Orleans and the visit with Aunt Tillie? Here's how it would look on a work sheet, planned to fit neatly into a 10-day vacation.

Day 1	Depart from Washington
Day 2	Arrive in Chicago; game at Wrigley Field
Day 3	Sightseeing in Chicago; depart Chicago
Day 4	Arrive in New Orleans
Day 5, 6	Sightseeing in New Orleans
Day 7	New Orleans to Atlanta
Day 8	Visit with Aunt Tillie
Day 9	Depart from Atlanta
Day 10	Arrive in Washington

Next, plug in real dates for your trip, beginning with those you can't change. In this example, you'll have to start with day 2 when the Cubs-Nationals game will be played. That's your one firm date, and the rest of your itinerary must revolve around it. Once that's done, use your timetable and add specific trains to the rough itinerary.

Date	Arrival or Departure	Time	Train
June 8	Depart from Washington	4:05 PM	Capitol Limited (train 29)
June 9	Arrive in Chicago	8:45 AM	
June 10	Depart from Chicago	8:05 PM	City of New Orleans (train 59)
June 11	Arrive in New Orleans	3:32 PM	
June 14	Depart from New Orleans/ Arrive in Atlanta	7:00 AM/ 7:35 PM	Crescent (train 20)
June 16	Depart from Atlanta	8:04 PM	Crescent (train 20)
June 17	Arrive in Washington	9:53 AM	

As you book sleeping-car space, reserve rental cars and hotel rooms, and decide on specific activities, your itinerary could go through many changes. One of my finished itineraries is reproduced at the end of this chapter (page 64) as an example.

A Word of Warning About Connections

If you're flying, a missed connection probably won't turn out to be a very big deal. Chances are there'll be another plane from either the same airline or another before too long. It's different with Amtrak. There are no other passenger railroads, and most of Amtrak's long-distance trains only run once a day. The Cardinal and the Sunset Limited operate just three days a week.

When you're traveling by train, a missed connection can be a real disaster. As you set about preparing your rail itinerary, be wary of any close connections. If there's a later train that would allow more time to make the connection, choose that one—even if it means spending a few extra hours somewhere. Or consider stopping at that point, spending the night, and continuing your journey the next day. Good travel agents and Amtrak reservations agents will be sensitive to this issue and will warn you if one of the connections in your itinerary is iffy.

If your inbound train is very late, Amtrak will do everything possible within reason to make sure you and other passengers affected make your connecting train. Sometimes that means holding the second train until yours arrives. As a practical matter, however, they can't delay the departure of a train for very long, since it will likely be connecting with another train somewhere else.

Every missed connection is handled on a case-by-case basis. If you do miss a connection with a train that runs once a day, any one of several things could occur. As a first choice, Amtrak will probably put you in a bus or van and take you cross-country to catch up with the second train. Or they may pay for your overnight stay in a hotel and put you on the same train the next day—assuming there's space, of course. Unfortunately, if you're traveling in a sleeper during one of the frequent busy periods, getting another sleeper is not likely. Even though you're holding a sleeping-car ticket, you could end up riding overnight in a coach seat. The eventual refund of the cost of your sleeping-car accommodations will be a small consolation. If the entire train is sold out the next day, you could be sent on your way by plane or bus—hardly the way you expected your carefully planned train trip to end up.

There are many factors that could affect how your missed-connection problem is solved, but you should keep in mind that the final decision is up to Amtrak. (For more on this subject, see chapter 8, "When Things Go Wrong.")

Should You Ride in Coach or in a Sleeping Car?

You'll have to make this choice before you book your train reservations, and there are a number of factors to consider. With a coach ticket, you'll ride in one of 50 or 60 seats in a standard passenger railcar and 70 or more in a Superliner coach. If you upgrade into a sleeping car, you'll be in small but private accommodations that include a bed to sleep in. There are other differences that we'll discuss in the next few pages, but the privacy and the bed are the main ones.

For short trips, even if it's an all-day ride, traveling by coach is a reasonable choice. For overnight journeys, the coach-versus-sleeping-car decision becomes much more difficult. Essentially, though, the decision comes down to cost versus comfort.

You Can Save Big Bucks in Coach Class

The biggest difference between coach and a sleeping car is cost. Coach is cheaper—a *lot* cheaper. Depending on the time of year, you can travel coast to coast for $250 or even less, as long as you ride in coach class. Of course, just like the airlines, the cost of your coach seat will vary according to the time of year, how far in advance you make the reservation, and how many seats are left on that particular train at the time.

There's a lot more about sleeping-car accommodations later in this chapter, but there are several things to note when considering the difference in cost between coach and sleepers.

First, if you're traveling with another person, remember that you both will pay a basic rail fare that entitles each of you to a reserved seat in coach class. However, if you decide to upgrade to a roomette in a sleeping car, there is only one extra charge for the room—meaning that, in effect, each of you will get that roomette for half price. And, second, the cost of all your meals is included in the charge for the roomette.

For a hypothetical example, let's assume you're traveling during the first three weeks of April between Los Angeles and Chicago on the Southwest Chief, train 4. Here's how the cost of riding in a sleeping-car roomette might compare with that same trip on the same train in coach. Remember, this is a two-night trip.

Los Angeles–Chicago, One Way, One Adult		
Class of Service	Coach	Roomette
Rail fare for one	$170	$170
Upgrade to sleeper	$0	$330
Total Cost	$170	$500

But note that the per-person cost drops when two people travel together. Both people pay the basic rail fare, but the charge for the sleeping-car accommodation—whether roomette or larger bedroom—applies to the *room* and not to each person. Here's what this same trip would cost if two people shared the sleeping-car accommodations.

Los Angeles–Chicago, One Way, Two Adults		
Class of Service	Coach	Roomette
Rail fare for two	$340	$340
Upgrade to sleeper	$0	$330
Total Cost	$340	$670

As I discuss in more detail a bit later, there's another important consideration when making the coach-versus-sleeper decision: dining-car meals are included in your sleeping-car fares. For this particular trip, that would mean a dozen meals at no additional cost for those two people.

Remember, fares are higher in June, July, and August, which is the peak travel period, or when any given train is close to being sold out. The bottom line? Coach travel wins hands down if cost is your most important consideration. But for privacy during the day, a real bed to sleep in at night, and free meals along the way, a roomette or bedroom is definitely the way to go.

Business Class: Another Coach Option

Amtrak offers an upgrade to business class on most of their all-coach trains; it comes with an additional charge above and beyond the basic rail fare. If you're traveling on one of the trains offering what Amtrak calls "regional service" in the Northeast, business class gets you into the first car behind the locomotive which may (or may not) be less crowded than the regular coach cars. You also get free nonalcoholic drinks in the cafe car. The basic coach fare between New York City and Washington, DC, varies, so whether or not it makes sense to upgrade into business class depends on which coach fare you choose. If you go for the cheapest nonrefundable fare, the upgrade could more than double your travel costs. You'll have to drink a lot of soft drinks to make the extra charge worthwhile.

The Unreserved "Reserved" Seat

You already know that securing a coach seat on any of Amtrak's long-distance trains requires a reservation. You also need to know that on most trains your reservation does not mean you have a specific seat assignment; it means simply that there will be one empty coach seat for you somewhere on that train. This is a small but important detail—especially if there are several people traveling as a group. See chapter 5 for some of the things you can do ahead of time and in the boarding process to get a good seat or to make sure that your family will be seated together.

Can You Sleep Sitting Up?

The seats in coach class are wide and comfortable—there is ample legroom even when they're fully reclined. Seats on the long-distance trains are equipped with special extenders for your feet and legs so you can really stretch out. All things considered, your coach seat on the train will be quite comparable to a first-class seat on an airplane. Make no mistake, however—it may be comfortable and roomy, but it's still a chair, and on an overnight trip you'll still have to sleep in it! If experience tells you that sleep just won't come under those conditions, consider opting for a sleeping car.

Are You a People Person?

Is privacy a big consideration for you? Coach seats are comfortable and the car itself is spacious, but if it's full, you'll be in fairly close proximity to as many as 70 other people. If you're traveling alone, you could be lucky and end up with an empty seat beside you, but you could also be sitting next to a stranger or find that there's a young parent with a couple of restless toddlers directly behind you. Some people see this as a great way to meet people and make new friends; others soon find themselves longing for the chance to be alone. Before letting cost alone dictate your decision, think about how much value you put on your privacy and your peace and quiet.

Comfort and Privacy in the Sleepers

Life in the sleeping cars is undeniably luxurious compared to coach class. While none of the accommodations can really be described as "spacious," they are private. Come nighttime, you've got your own room and a real bed to sleep in. Some of the sleeping-car accommodations are equipped with their own washbasins and toilets, but not all. In a Superliner roomette, the facilities are "down the hall." Sheets, blankets, pillows, and towels are all provided. For some travelers, the privacy and comfort found in the sleeping cars are essential luxuries for which they're happy to pay. I confess that I'm one of them.

Free Meals: A Sleeping-Car Bonus

While all passengers are of course welcomed in the diner, the cost of dining-car meals is included in the price of your ticket when you travel in a sleeping car. This can be a significant benefit for, as an example, a mom, dad, and two kids traveling in a family bedroom. That would be a total of 28 free meals on the California Zephyr between the Bay Area and Chicago. Coach passengers pay the regular menu prices for their meals; however they can always bring food aboard or purchase sandwiches and snacks in the lounge car.

Other Extras for Sleeping-Car Passengers

Coffee, juice, and bottled water are available at no charge during the day. There is an attendant for each sleeping car who will provide a number of other services either automatically or upon request. Some of these include wake-up calls, providing juice and coffee each morning, making up your berth each evening, and bringing food or beverages from the dining car to your room if you request that service.

Which Sleeping-Car Room Should You Choose?

Coach seats are all pretty much alike, but when it comes to sleeping-car accommodations, there will be several choices depending upon the specific train you've chosen.

Viewliners are used on most eastern trains and include roomettes accommodating one or two people and larger bedrooms that are also designed for two people. There is a washbasin and small toilet in the roomettes on older model Viewliners. Roomettes in newer cars have only the fold-down wash basin. Toilet facilities are at the end of the car. The larger bedrooms have a sink, a vanity, and an enclosed toilet, which also functions as a shower. There is also one shower stall at the far end of the Viewliner sleeper for passengers in the roomettes. Frankly, all the in-room showers are small and, in my view, it's a lot easier using the larger shower at the far end of the car. Doors between adjoining bedrooms can be opened to provide four-bed compartments for families. There is also a large bedroom at the end of the car that is wheelchair accessible and designed for two people.

Superliners operating west of the Mississippi River and on a few eastern routes offer roomettes for one or two people (no in-room lavatory), bedrooms for two adults and possibly a small child (in-room combination lavatory/shower), and family bedrooms that sleep two adults and two young children (no en suite facilities). Special compartments designed for elderly passengers or those in wheelchairs are also available.

Upgrading Once Onboard

Let's say you have bought a coach ticket and find yourself sitting next to a woman with squalling twins on her lap (my idea of a worst-case scenario). At that moment, a private roomette in one of the sleeping cars will sound awfully good. A conductor can sell you an upgrade even after you're onboard and the trip is underway, as long as there's available space. Failing that, you can always ask the conductor or train attendant if there's another seat, preferably in another car.

Finding and Booking the Right Hotel

Unless you have several Aunt Tillies scattered around the country, one or more nights in a hotel could well be part of your train trip. For some people, a hotel is just a place to sleep—almost any one will do. But others want each hotel they sleep in to be just one more interesting and enjoyable part of the entire experience. In other words, where you stay during a stopover is very much a matter of your own personal taste and budget.

You can always turn the matter over to a travel agent. Just give him or her some idea of the type of hotel you want and a price range. The agent will suggest a place to stay and take care of the booking.

If you want to make the arrangements yourself, the easiest approach is to go on the Internet. I usually go to Expedia.com or Hotels.com. Either of those websites will generate a list and a reasonably good description of hotels in the city where I'll be overnighting. At that point, you can either book through that website or go directly to the specific hotel's website. With a little surfing, you can also find websites listing bed-and-breakfast places. Any number of guidebooks in the travel section of your local bookstore can help you make your choice, be it deluxe accommodations or a listing of quaint bed-and-breakfast spots.

If you're not using a travel agent and will book the hotel yourself, the reservation will need to be "guaranteed" with your credit card. But be sure to check on the hotel's cancellation policy. Sometimes you may cancel with no penalty if you do so before

6:00 PM on the day you were to arrive. Some hotels will stick you for the full amount unless you cancel at least 24 hours ahead of your arrival. Often the lowest rate offered is nonrefundable, no matter when you cancel.

The Plane-Train Option

Here's another idea to consider, especially if your time is limited: Fly one way and take the train the other way. For instance, you could fly from Los Angeles to Chicago, take the Empire Builder from Chicago to Seattle, spend a couple of days in Seattle, and then take the Coast Starlight back to L.A. (My personal preference is to have the plane trip come first. I've done it the other way, and the plane trip home seems very anticlimactic. But, again, that's just me.)

What's All This Going to Cost?

After you've done it a few times, you'll be able to estimate the cost of your trip fairly accurately. Once you've decided when and where you're going, just call Amtrak (1-800-USA-RAIL) for a fare quote. Or you can go online (www.amtrak.com), plug in the appropriate dates, select the class of service, and have the computer figure it out for you. (Remember, however, that there are sometimes special fares being offered and you may be eligible for other discounts. Double-check with Amtrak reservations or your travel agent to be sure you get the lowest possible fare.)

Now start estimating the other costs of your trip. Don't try to anticipate every individual expense. Instead, think in terms of daily averages, either per person or for the whole party, whichever is appropriate. The following guidelines are the ones I use and should only provide you with a rough starting point. Adjust your own guidelines according to your personal tastes and preferences.

First, figure out how many nights you'll be in a hotel. For big-city hotels, I would allow no less than $200 per night—and a lot more than that in cities notorious for awful room rates (Washington, DC, or New York City, for example). Rates at hotels in smaller cities and rural areas will probably run half that amount.

For meals, allow $50 per day per person. That's $10 for breakfast, $15 for lunch, and $25 for dinner. Yes, it could be less, and obviously it could be much more, depending on where and what you eat. For kids, reduce your estimate appropriately—or you might have to raise it, I suppose, if you're traveling with a teenager. (Remember that a sleeping-car ticket includes the price of your dining-car meals. If you're riding in a sleeper, figure out how many meals you'll be having onboard the train and don't budget for those. Do remember the tips, though.)

If you'll be renting a car along the way, the rental car company's website will compute the cost when you enter the appropriate dates and times for pickup and drop-off. If possible, try to return the car at the same time of day you picked it up. Most rental car companies really whack you for those two or three additional hours. Should you have an accident in that rental car, your personal automobile insurance will probably cover you, but talk to your insurance agent before you leave to make sure of the details.

When it comes to sightseeing at the various stops in an itinerary, I would allow $20 to $40 per person per day. (Don't count the days you'll be on the train. All of that sightseeing is free!)

Going to be shopping and buying souvenirs? Don't guess at an average daily amount. Instead, decide what you can afford and budget that lump sum for the entire trip. If you're traveling with children, decide on an appropriate shopping allowance for each of them. Then give each child the money up front and—this is important—make sure they know that when it's gone, it's gone!

You'll also have small but frequent miscellaneous expenses, such as tips, snacks, fees for checked baggage, and others. Allow a total of $20–25 per day for such costs.

Be realistic and work with daily averages, and you'll be amazed at how accurate your estimate will be. A good estimate of your travel expenses, done now, is an important double check that your trip will be affordable. It will also be a valuable guide to keep you on budget during your vacation.

Book Your Space Early

Make your rail reservations as soon as your dates of departure and return are definite, when you've decided on your destination and other stopovers, and when you know whether you want to travel in coach or in a sleeping car. The other details—hotel rooms, rental cars, sightseeing tours, and the rest—can be filled in later. Early booking is especially important if you want sleeping-car accommodations. They're very popular, and space fills up several months in advance, particularly for travel in the summer months.

You can either have a travel agent handle the booking or deal directly with Amtrak by calling 1-800-USA-RAIL. If you do elect to call an Amtrak reservations agent, you'll find them very capable and most of the time extremely helpful. Do not call Amtrak if you're still uncertain about some of the significant details of your rail itinerary. The reservations agents are very busy and will not be able to give you the time needed to help you make up your mind. They may try, but that's when some small but important detail is sure to fall through the cracks. Besides, filling in those details is how a travel agent earns her fee.

Whether you use a travel agent or call Amtrak directly, there are a few things to cover before you hang up:

- Ask if she's sure you've been quoted the lowest possible fare.

- Ask if there are any minor changes you could make in your itinerary that might further reduce the cost.

- Ask if there are any connections in the itinerary that could be a problem.

- To avoid some of the less desirable accommodations, ask for specific room numbers if you're booking sleeping-car accommodations (see chapter 9, "Passenger Train Equipment").

- Be sure to ask for the cancellation date for your reservation. If you don't pay for your tickets by that date, your reservation will cancel automatically and your seats will go back into inventory for sale to someone else.

- Once you've paid for your ticket, the Amtrak reservations agent will e-mail both a confirmation and, if you wish, an e-Ticket to you. Your reservation number will be on both, and it's a good idea to note it on your separate itinerary. The e-Ticket is a great innovation because it allows Amtrak to store your record electronically. Even if you print out your e-Ticket and then lose it, your record can easily be brought up at any time along the way by a station agent or an on-board conductor.

Save Some Money in the Sleepers

As you will discover when checking the cost of sleeping-car accommodations, they can be expensive, especially during the busy times of year. But if you're traveling as a couple, here's a way to save some money: Instead of biting the bullet and booking one of the large bedrooms, consider taking two roomettes. (Try to get them across the corridor from each other.) Yes, you'll give up a lavatory in your room—but neither of you will have to climb up into one of those small upper berths, you'll have a view out of both sides of the train, and the cost of two roomettes could be less than the cost of one bedroom, sometimes a lot less.

Do You Need Extra Assistance?

If you or someone traveling with you should require any kind of special assistance or service—a wheelchair, for instance—call Amtrak at 1-800-USA-RAIL at least 72 hours before you leave (sooner than that if possible). And plan to arrive at the station early.

What About Special Diet Requirements?

Amtrak dining cars offer a standard vegetarian choice at every meal, but because of limited kitchen facilities in the dining car, it's likely to be the same option every day. That's something to consider if you're on a three-day cross-country journey.

Amtrak will accommodate special dietary needs, such as kosher or vegan, but you must notify Amtrak at least 72 hours before your scheduled departure so those special meals can be put aboard your train. However, the system is not perfect, and slip-ups do occur. Therefore, if your dietary restrictions are inflexible, I would strongly recommend bringing your own food onboard.

How to Get Last-Minute Sleeping-Car Space

If you have to make a train trip on short notice, you'll often find that no sleeping-car space is available. Don't despair. It might not be a very convenient hour, but try calling the Amtrak reservation number, 1-800-USA-RAIL, at about 3:30 AM Eastern Time. Every morning at 3:15, the Amtrak computer is purged of passengers who have failed to confirm reservations made earlier. At that hour, you'll probably be first in line if a vacancy has occurred for the train you want. If worse comes to worse, board the train with your coach ticket and ask the conductor right away if there's a vacancy in one of the sleepers. Chances aren't very good, but there are no-shows and last-minute cancellations more often than most of us would imagine.

If You Need a Refund

Stuff happens, plans change, and sometimes you just have to cancel a reservation.

If you bought your ticket through a travel agent, let them deal with getting you some kind of a refund. If you booked directly with Amtrak, talk to one of their reservations people before your scheduled travel date.

Once upon a time not so long ago, you could usually get all of your money back, even if it came in the form of a voucher for future Amtrak travel. It's not so simple anymore. Rules vary depending on whether your reservation is in a sleeping car or coach and on how far in advance you cancel. You may have to pay a 10 percent penalty, or you might get a full refund but in the form of an e-voucher for future Amtrak travel. Or you might even lose the entire cost of your ticket.

A few years ago, a seat or a room canceled at the last minute wasn't a big deal, but today, with much greater demand, that space could probably have been sold to another traveler. Cancellations, especially at the last minute, represent lost income for Amtrak. These days, I'm afraid the best advice I can give you is to be sure you understand what your options are *before* you purchase your tickets. The latest refund rules will be on the Amtrak website, and one of their very excellent reservations people can also explain it all to you.

What About Travel Insurance?

I've gone back and forth over this question for years and still haven't come up with a good answer. Travel agents all recommend that you buy this insurance, but they're hardly objective since they get a commission for selling it.

Travel insurance will compensate you if you have to cancel your trip, either before you start out or while you're traveling. It will also pay to send you home should you need "evacuation" because of a severe illness or a bad accident. Essentially, you have to ask yourself what the odds are that you'll have to cancel your trip at the last minute or interrupt it in progress. How old are you? How's your health? Are there any family or business circumstances that could cause you to abort your plans? Bottom line: Travel insurance is really a crap shoot, and only you can make the call. That said, the only time I would definitely recommend travel insurance is when you buy an expensive packaged tour and have paid for most or all of it up front.

A word of warning: Recently, a number of companies have offered "travel protection." Not all but many are fly-by-night scammers who avoid using the word "insurance" because that would legally require them to register and be licensed by the states in which they operate. Enough said?

If you do decide on travel insurance, go to www.insuremytrip .com. It's a website that will let you compare benefits and costs offered by different companies.

Putting Your Itinerary into Final Form

The last step in the planning process is to produce a final version of your itinerary. Remember that an itinerary is much more than just a day-by-day schedule. It should be your one written source of information, including everything you need to know about your trip: train arrival and departure times, the addresses and phone numbers of all hotels, confirmation numbers for all reservations (train, hotel, and rental car), other pertinent information, and any relevant notes.

The format can vary, but every itinerary should present its information in chronological order. Below is a section from one of my itineraries as it existed about a month before departure. I note relevant details, such as reservation and confirmation numbers, in the far-right column.

Date	Time	Activity	Notes
Sunday, October 14	2:45 PM	Depart from Maui	Hawaiian Airlines flight 30, seat 12A, confirmation number: OQZZVG
	11:05 PM	Arrive at Seattle; check in at Best Western Pioneer Square	Confirmation number: 274895, 77 Yesler Way, 1-206-340-1234
Monday, October 15	8:00 AM	Breakfast meeting with JTD at Sazerac Restaurant	
	11:25 AM	Depart from Seattle	Amtrak #513, reservation number: 218F37; pick up ticket, confirm double points
	2:55 PM	Arrive at Portland; check in at Benson Hotel	Confirmation number: BEN31796, 309 SW Broadway, 1-503-228-2000
	TBD	Dinner with SBD	He will call hotel
Tuesday, October 16	4:45 PM	Depart from Portland	Amtrak #28, Empire Builder Car 2830, Room 8, confirmation number: 218A2D

When finishing up your itinerary, avoid unnecessary verbiage, but be sure to include everything you will need to know once you've left home. I include other information I might need while I'm away, such as telephone numbers, e-mail addresses, and websites. Remember, this itinerary will be your bible while you're traveling—you'll refer to it many times each day.

By all means, store your itinerary in whatever electronic device you favor, but I suggest three additional hard copies—one for your shoulder bag (in case the airline sends your suitcase to Rio de Janeiro), one for your suitcase (in case your shoulder bag is lost or stolen), and one to leave at home with a trusted neighbor or relative.

That's it. You're just about ready to leave.

5

PACKING AND LAST-MINUTE DETAILS

Someone who no doubt learned the hard way once said, "There are only two kinds of travelers—those traveling light and those who wish they were."

Once upon a time, people got all dressed up to travel. I can remember my mother getting me into a white shirt, tie, and sports jacket for a 90-minute train ride from Hartford to Darien, Connecticut, to visit a cousin. And I was all of 11 or 12 years old!

Today it's different. People dress comfortably and casually on planes and trains and in all but the fanciest restaurants. And while some may take it to a tasteless extreme, casual traveling has one big benefit: you don't need to bring so much stuff with you when you travel. So think things through, organize, pack carefully, and you'll be able to head off on a two-week vacation with only one small-to-medium-sized suitcase and a shoulder bag. Yes, you can!

Pack Smart, Pack Carefully, Be Ruthless

There's a one-word secret to packing light: for women, it's *tops*; for men, it's *shirts*. Think about it: Tops and shirts are what you go through the most. They get wrinkled, they get dirty, and they get sweaty. For a two-week trip, I pack seven or eight shirts, mostly knits with a collar and made of synthetic fabrics so they won't wrinkle. I wear a nice pair of jeans and pack one decent pair of slacks. To that I add a sweater (lightweight or heavy, depending on the time of year), a very thin plastic poncho, a half dozen undershorts, six pairs of socks, and my toiletry kit.

Women should pack a half dozen or more tops, a pair of slacks or jeans, a decent skirt, and a minimum of whatever else you need according to your personal preferences. The key word is *minimum*. It's not as important for men, but women should make sure that every one of the tops can be worn with either the skirt or the slacks.

When it comes to toiletries, don't bring large sizes of *anything*, be it toothpaste, mouthwash, or tissues. Instead, buy the smallest available tubes or packages and replace them along the way if you need to. Some personal items you use at home every day can easily be left out altogether to save space and lighten your load—that bottle of aftershave lotion, for instance. Women should be sure to bring an adequate number of sanitary supplies; they are not sold aboard the train.

When considering possible clothing items to take along, opt for clothing made from synthetic fabrics, which will dry quickly and wrinkle less than natural fabrics.

I also pack a small, soft, down-filled travel pillow that compresses and rolls up neatly inside its pillowcase. I have a hard time sleeping on those uncomfortable foam pillows you get in some hotels. For me, this little pillow makes all the difference. I *never* travel without it!

If you're traveling in a sleeping-car roomette—either in a Superliner or in one of the new Viewliners—making a trip to a lavatory during the wee hours is a big hassle if it means struggling back into your day clothes. My solution is to sleep in a comfortable pair of gym shorts and a T-shirt. If I have to get up during the night, all I have to do is slip on a pair of flip-flops, which I pack for that very purpose.

A Catchall Carry-On Bag

In addition to your one suitcase, take a nice, roomy shoulder or tote bag. There will be some exceptions, but it's best to assume that while you're on the train it won't always be convenient to get to your suitcase. The shoulder bag, on the other hand, will stay with you in your room or at your seat. Knowing that, pack a short list of essentials in the small bag and everything else in the suitcase. You'll quickly develop your own list of tote bag items, but mine includes reading material, glasses, toiletry kit, gym shorts and a T-shirt to sleep in, a pair of rubber flip-flops, a small digital camera, a note pad, pens, and a clean shirt for the next day.

When it comes to packing, what's the bottom line? Less is better. As travel writer Rick Steves notes, how many people brag that on each new trip they take a little more baggage with them? It's an incontrovertible truth: the lighter you travel, the happier you'll be.

What About Electric Appliances?

If you can't do without your electric hair dryer or razor, you won't have to. There are standard 120-volt electrical outlets in all sleeping-car rooms, in coaches (although you may have to share), in lavatories, and in most of the lounge cars. If you're going to take a laptop with you, make sure your power cord includes a surge protector.

Packing for Kids

In addition to all of the usual and necessary items your kids will need during the time you'll be away, be sure to pack the usual assortment of books and games they'll need to occupy themselves while on the train. Adults may be able to enjoy the passing scenery for hours at a time, but not so with youngsters, who need plenty of distractions.

Here's some very good advice passed along to me by a veteran train attendant: If you're traveling with a small child, be sure to bring his or her favorite thing. When your toddler gets tired, bored, or cranky, that tattered blanket, teddy bear, or doll will help to make things all right.

Traveling in Coach? Bring a Blanket!

Amtrak coaches are air-conditioned, but sometimes the system is hard to regulate. Even during the summer it can get quite chilly at night in those large open cars. Amtrak does not provide complimentary pillows and blankets for coach passengers. However, lounge cars have "Comfort Kits" available for sale, which include a blanket, an inflatable neck pillow, eye shades, and ear plugs. The trouble is, they are often sold out. So if you're riding in coach, bring your own blanket and perhaps a small travel pillow, too. Heed this advice and you will thank me for it! A small thermal blanket or one for a twin-size bed that can be folded in half for extra warmth will be fine. Don't pack it; roll it up and tie it to your carry-on bag. As an alternative, take an extra sweatshirt—or two.

Boarding Your Sleeping Car

As a sleeping-car passenger, you've been assigned a specific room in a specific car. The room and car numbers will appear on your e-Ticket. Each car's number will be visible from the platform in a little window next to the car entrance. In any event, the first member of the train crew you see on the platform will be able to direct you to your car.

Your train attendant will be at the car entrance with a manifest listing all passengers assigned to that car, and he or she will be expecting you. The attendant will also carry your bags into your room if you need help doing so.

Finally—and this may seem obvious—make sure to board your train at the station stop showing on your ticket. A friend of mine once held tickets for sleeping-car accommodations between Miami and Washington, DC, on the Silver Star. At the last minute he had to change his plans and board the train in Orlando instead, some 250 miles north of Miami. He didn't change his tickets or bother to notify Amtrak, however, thinking that his bedroom would be waiting for him no matter where he boarded. Nope! Once the train left Miami, he was considered a no-show, and the conductor sold his bedroom to a coach passenger who had asked for an upgrade.

Coping with Baggage

While the rules are not always strictly followed, each passenger is allowed to bring two pieces of luggage onto the train, with a 50-pound limit for each. Additional items, such as tote bags or camera cases, are not included in these restrictions, but of course common sense tells you that these items should not weigh much anyway.

My first recommendation, of course, is that you should be traveling with just one carry-on-size suitcase and a shoulder bag to avoid this very problem. (A detailed description of how to deal with baggage in the various onboard accommodations is in the next chapter.) If you must travel with several pieces of large, heavy baggage, I'd recommend using Amtrak's checked-baggage service. Each passenger is allowed to check four bags, each no more than 50 pounds. The first two will be carried at no charge; the second two will cost $20 each. Be at the station at least 45 minutes prior to departure to arrange that. Each of the checked bags will be tagged and placed in the baggage car. Just remember that these pieces will not be available to you during your trip.

Remember, too, that checked-baggage service might not be offered at the station where you board or at your destination. This information is included in Amtrak's timetables, or you can always call Amtrak at 1-800-USA-RAIL to make sure.

If you have an unusual amount of baggage, or if you're not able to handle it yourself for any reason, call the above number at least 72 hours before your departure.

What About Bicycles?

If you have a bicycle and want to take it with you on your rail journey, check with Amtrak ahead of time. Then double check, because who gets to take what kind of a bike on which train and where it will be stored en route all seem to be subjects of endless debate. Furthermore, the rules keep changing.

First, let's talk about standard-size bikes, meaning maximum dimensions of 70" x 41" x 8½" and weighing no more than 50 pounds. A few of the short-haul trains have special bike racks in some of the cars and, as long as you can lift your bike into the rack by yourself, you can just walk onboard with it. But as of this writing, most Amtrak trains can only accommodate bicycles in the baggage car, and they must be in a bicycle container. You can provide your own container, or you can purchase one for $15 from most—*but not all*—staffed stations, so call that specific station ahead of time to be sure. There's a $10 charge for transporting your bike. Get to the station no less than 45 minutes ahead of the scheduled departure time. And remember: be sure there is checked baggage service *at your destination*, or you won't be able to retrieve your bike when you get there.

Will Your Train Be on Time?

If you're boarding at the train's point of origin, it will almost certainly leave on time. There could be a delay in its departure if your train is held for passengers making connections from an incoming train that's running late, but under no circumstances will your train leave ahead of the published departure time as it appears on the latest schedule.

If you're boarding somewhere along the train's route, there's always the possibility that the train will be late. That means you should find out exactly when it will arrive *before* you leave for the station. After all, if the station is a 90-minute drive from your home and the train is due at 5:45 in the morning, you'd probably like to know if it's going to be two hours late on that particular day.

Here's how to find out for sure when your train will arrive: First try calling the Amtrak office at the station where you'll board. If no one is there (you may need to leave home before Amtrak personnel arrive at the station), go online to Amtrak's home page (www.amtrak.com) and use the "Train Status" option on the left-hand side, or call Amtrak's toll-free number (1-800-USA-RAIL). If the automated system tells you the train is running on time, head for the station as originally planned. However, if they say the train is running significantly late, beware! Since Amtrak builds padding into their schedules, your train could make up a lot of that lost time. The fail-safe method is to call the Amtrak station one or two stops before yours a few minutes before the train is due there. By then they'll know exactly when the train will be arriving, and the timetable will tell you the running time from there to your station.

Whatever Happens, Do Not Miss Your Train!

Someone once said that the only way to be sure of catching a train is to miss the one before it. Maybe that was true in the good old days, but miss one of Amtrak's long-distance trains and you've got a real problem. Most of them operate just once a day, so in the best-case scenario you'd have to wait 24 hours for the next one. During peak travel times, however, you may find the train sold out for the next day . . . and the next, and the next. That's especially likely if you're riding in a sleeping car.

For heaven's sake, give yourself plenty of time to drive to the station. Any number of things could delay you, so allow for the unexpected. You may end up sitting in the station for a while, but at least you'll be waiting calmly. Don't begin your train trip with anxiety and stress.

It's commonly assumed that times listed on railroad schedules are arrival times. Not so. When only one time is listed for a specific station, that's when the train *departs*. If the train is running on time, it could actually arrive several minutes before that time. Be aware, too, that in many stations the train won't be there very long—sometimes just 60 seconds or less.

The point is, don't be casual about the business of getting to the station and boarding your train. If you miss a train, getting things straightened out is a minor inconvenience at best. At worst, it will be a nightmare.

Things to Know About Boarding

In coach class, a ticket guarantees you a seat on the train, but most of the time no specific seat has your name on it. This is particularly important to remember if you're traveling with friends or family, because you will undoubtedly want to sit together. While there are no guarantees, there are a few things you can do to make sure you board quickly and, hopefully, end up in the seat or seats you want.

If you're boarding the train at its point of origin, you should have no problem. Just make sure you all get to the station early and check in right away with the Amtrak official at the gate. Even if the train is sold out, he or she can arrange for families and small groups to board ahead of the other passengers.

If you're boarding the train en route, however, the train could be nearly full by the time it gets to your station. Here's what to do:

- When you arrive at the station, ask an Amtrak employee where to stand on the platform so you won't find yourself several hundred feet from the coaches when the train comes to a stop. The object is to be among the first to board.

- Better yet, designate someone in your party, unencumbered with kids or baggage, to hop aboard and look for seats as soon as the train stops. (Do not let someone who isn't traveling do this. At most station stops, the train will start as soon as everyone on the platform has boarded.)

- Once onboard, if you cannot find enough seats together, ask the train attendant for help. If he or she is unable to help, ask the conductor who takes your tickets. One of them should be able to accommodate your party.

In a number of cities, Amtrak provides separate lounges and waiting rooms for sleeping-car passengers and those traveling first-class on the high-speed Acela trains along the Northeast Corridor. The Club Acela lounges are found in Boston, New York, Philadelphia, and Washington, DC. There are also very nice waiting rooms called Metropolitan Lounges in the Chicago, Portland, and Los Angeles stations. They are for use by sleeping-car and business-class passengers and for some of the top-tier members of Amtrak's Guest Rewards program. All of these lounges have full-time Amtrak staff and feature complimentary soft drinks, comfortable seating, and wireless Internet connections, among other business-related amenities. (The lounge in Chicago actually has a working fireplace.)

An attendant will ask to see your ticket when you enter; you will be welcomed into the lounge only if you have just arrived or are about to depart in sleeping-car accommodations. Amtrak follows this rule to the letter. I was once refused entry to the lounge in Chicago because the first three-hour leg of my trip—Chicago to Galesburg—was in coach class, notwithstanding the fact that the following day I was traveling in a sleeper from there all the way to Oakland.

A number of other stations have separate waiting areas for sleeping-car passengers. You'll find them at St. Paul/Minneapolis, St. Louis, New Orleans, Raleigh, and Miami. These waiting rooms often have no attendant and the amenities are minimal, but they will get you out of the noisy, crowded main areas of the stations.

Welcome Aboard!

OK, you planned your trip, packed carefully (and light), arrived at the station early, boarded without problems, and have just settled into your seat. The train starts rolling before you realize it, and you're on your way. Now you're ready to experience everything that's relaxing and fun about a rail journey.

6

LIFE ONBOARD

Rule Number One: Don't Sweat the Small Stuff

Today's long-distance trains provide passengers with most of the comforts of home. Despite all the improvements and refinements, however, don't expect things to be perfect. A train is not a cruise ship on wheels. With up to 300 people living together in close quarters for one or two days, there are bound to be some inconveniences. Bear that in mind, and before making an issue out of something, ask yourself if you're being reasonable under the circumstances. I once listened to a woman in an adjoining room berate the train attendant mercilessly because he had been unable to silence a minor rattle somewhere in her room. The poor man had tried several times to find it, and clearly it was time she thanked him for his effort and made the best of things. So, before boarding, why not resolve to lighten up a bit? There's too much to enjoy on the train to let minor things spoil your trip.

Where to Stow Your Baggage

If you're traveling in one of Amtrak's coaches, either one of the single-level cars or a bi-level Superliner, you'll find room for one or two medium-sized suitcases in the rack above your seat. There will be plenty of space for a small carry-on bag in the same rack or on the floor under your feet. Superliner coaches also have a large storage rack for luggage just as you enter on the lower level at the middle of the car.

Viewliner sleepers used on most eastern trains will accommodate some baggage in the rooms, but not much. One carry-on-size bag can be stored on a high shelf in a Viewliner roomette, although it's hard to reach, and the larger bedrooms can handle two such bags.

Roomettes in Superliner sleeping cars really have no place to store baggage conveniently. Like the coaches, however, each bi-level sleeper has a large, easily accessible luggage rack on the lower level. You can stow your baggage there, taking the overnight essentials with you in a small tote bag to your room.

The larger bedrooms in both types of sleeping cars do have more floor space, so there's room to maneuver around one or two small bags during the day. But much of that area disappears when beds are made up for sleeping at night. Again, a better option would be to leave bags on the lower-level storage rack.

Your Onboard Crew

You'll come into contact with a number of crew members during your trip, including your train attendant, the conductor, dining-car staff, and a lounge-car attendant. (For a complete explanation of the duties and responsibilities of each, plus the same for the engineers in the locomotive, see chapter 7, "Who's in Charge Here?")

Traveling in Coach Class

If you're traveling in coach class on one of Amtrak's short-haul trains, you will not have been preassigned a specific seat. That means you should just climb aboard and sit where you want. On long-distance trains, conductors may assign you to a specific seat as you're boarding. Most are quite reasonable about shifting people around, so if you have a problem with your seat assignment, ask if you can be reassigned. Except in very unusual circumstances, families wanting to sit together will always be accommodated. Make sure you speak to the conductor about that at the gate before heading for the platform.

Where to Sit?

For a smoother, quieter ride, you should try to pick seats near the middle of the car and, in the case of the Superliners, on the upper level. Some Superliner coaches do have lower-level seats, but these are usually reserved for handicapped or elderly passengers. Unless you require such accommodations, head upstairs. The view is better from up there anyway.

Be Careful About Changing Seats

When your ticket is recorded electronically by the conductor, he or she slips a cardboard seat check into a slot on the front of the baggage rack over your head. That tells both him or her and the train attendant where you're getting off. Don't change seats without notifying either the conductor or the train attendant or without taking the seat check with you. This is especially important if you're on an overnight trip and have to leave the train in the wee hours. Many a passenger has changed seats during the night and slept through his stop because the train attendant couldn't locate him. When that happens, the train attendant and the conductor are the ones who invariably get the blame—which explains why they can be uptight if you change seats without telling them.

Changing Cars Can Cause Problems

For instance, when the westbound Empire Builder pulls into Spokane, Washington, it's split into two trains. Most of the train continues on to Seattle, but a sleeper and one or two coaches are detached, are hooked to a new locomotive, and head southwest

for Portland, Oregon. This all happens around 2:00 AM, so if
you're sound asleep in one of those big coach seats, it had better
be in the right car!

Traveling in First Class

Actually, Amtrak doesn't commonly use the term "first-class"
anymore. Instead they'll say that you are "in the sleepers." That
means you're comfortably ensconced in private accommodations
in a sleeping car. It also means that the cost of your meals in the
dining car has been included in the sleeping-car surcharge you
paid when you bought your ticket.

Once you're shown to your room, take your time and settle in. The train attendant should come by within minutes after
departure to show you where everything is and how it all works.
If he doesn't, use the call button and ask for that brief orientation. You'll find things in your room to be very compact. In fact,
first-time riders are sometimes startled at how small the accommodations appear. But the rooms are well designed, very efficient,
and generally quite adequate. (You'll find detailed descriptions of
the various accomodations in Amtrak sleeping cars in chapter 9,
"Passenger Train Equipment.")

What to Wear

In another day and time, people dressed up to travel. Cramped
spaces on planes changed all that, and today casual dress is
acceptable, if not always appropriate. Feel free to dress comfortably for your train trip. That's especially good advice if you're
traveling in coach, where you'll be sleeping in your clothes. Jeans
or slacks and a sport shirt are fine for men; a skirt or slacks and
a blouse are equally appropriate for women. My suggestions are
based on personal taste, of course. You will sometimes see shorts,
tank tops, and T-shirts emblazoned with messages of question-

able taste. For the most part, however, passengers comply reasonably well with today's minimum standards.

Smoking Policy

Smoking is not permitted on any Amtrak train, although passengers on long-distance trains are able to step off at certain designated stops for a smoke on the platform. These "smoke stops" will be announced ahead of time over the train's PA system.

A word of warning here to smokers: Amtrak is very strict when it comes to the no-smoking policy. Passengers caught smoking in their rooms, in the lavatories, or even in the vestibules between cars are put off the train. On one of my cross-country trips, a conductor put it very succinctly: "If you're caught smoking on this train, the very next stop will be yours." Trust me, they really mean it!

Problem Passengers

The subject of smoking violations leads me to the issue of passengers who cause problems for train crews or their fellow travelers. Here again, Amtrak has a no-nonsense attitude—passengers causing trouble are put off the train. In some cases, especially if it will be several hours before the train reaches the next stop, the conductor will have the engineer radio ahead and arrange to meet the police at a highway crossing. Either way, passengers causing trouble are given a very short leash, then it's *aloha*. (In this case, *aloha* definitely means *good-bye*!) For more on this subject, see chapter 8, "When Things Go Wrong."

Fido Has to Stay Home

Pets are a no-no. Not at your seat, neither in nor out of a carrier, and not even in the baggage car. At first I thought this policy was awfully severe, but after hearing a number of horror stories from Amtrak crew members about pets running loose on trains, I've come to agree that it's the only practical approach on a long train trip. An exception is made for certified service animals. Note, please, that there has been agitation from some pet owners and from a few publicity-seeking members of Congress to liberalize the no-pets policy, so it's best to check with Amtrak for the lastest information.

Things That Go Bump in the Night

Many a passenger has bedded down for the night in a cozy sleeping-car room, only to become aware of a persistent rattle or squeak coming from somewhere inside the compartment. If you're the type to be bothered by such things, just get up and track it down. Most of the time it's something easily located and fixed—a coat hanger inside the closet swinging with the motion of the train or a ladder in the unused upper berth not stowed quite right. It's amazing how effectively a washcloth wedged into a crack can silence a rattle. If you can't locate that elusive noise, call the train attendant. He or she has found and fixed many a rattle and will probably have better luck.

The Doppler Effect

As your train goes past a grade crossing with flashing lights and a clanging bell, you'll notice that the pitch of the bell will suddenly drop as you pass the intersection. That's the Doppler effect, named for Christian Doppler, an Austrian scientist, who came up with the explanation for this phenomenon in the mid-1800s. The short explanation is that as you reach then continue beyond the grade crossing, the sound waves put out by the clanging bell lengthen and take longer to reach you, which accounts for the drop in pitch. You'll notice the same thing when the engineer of another train is blowing its horn as it passes you.

Security for Your Belongings

Incidents of thievery are quite rare aboard Amtrak trains, but that doesn't mean you can ignore everyday common sense. The best rule is to leave any real valuables at home. If you must bring them aboard, take them with you whenever you leave your seat. That's an essential precaution for coach passengers; however, it's a good rule for sleeping-car passengers too. You can latch the door to your private room once you're inside, but the doors don't lock from the outside. Sleeping-car passengers can feel comfortable about leaving cameras, tote bags, and even handbags in their rooms, but put them someplace out of sight, then pull the drapes and close the door to your room securely when you leave. Notify the train attendant if someone suspicious opens the door to your room. (Don't be overly concerned, however. It's almost always a case of right room, wrong car.)

Personal Food and Drink

Passengers are permitted to bring food and drink aboard the train. Unless you have special dietary issues, however, I recommend eating in the dining car or buying packaged food and snacks from the lounge car. The dining-car food is quite good, and eating there is an opportunity to get up, move around, and meet some of your fellow passengers. Besides, especially in the coaches, foods with strong aromas can be annoying to people seated nearby.

If you're riding in coach, don't bring any alcoholic beverages aboard (you are not permitted to consume them at your seat). Beer, wine, and some mixed drinks are available in the lounge car and must be consumed there. If you're in a sleeping car, you may bring your own alcohol aboard, but it must be consumed in your room. Whether coach or sleeper, however, Amtrak train crews have a very low tolerance for passengers who overindulge and cause problems. As noted earlier, conductors can and do put offenders off the train. Literally a sobering experience, I'm sure.

Dining Onboard

Part of the enjoyment of traveling by train is the unique experience of eating in a rolling restaurant (a pretty good one too). Amtrak is into food service big-time. The systemwide total is impressive: nearly 10,000 meals served every day as a year-round average. That number makes Amtrak one of the major food providers in the country. Considering the long hours and the busy, crowded conditions under which they work, Amtrak's food-service people do an incredible job. As an example, the dining-car crew on the California Zephyr prepares and serves between 350 and 400 meals every day, depending on the time of year.

There are fewer choices on the menu than what you would find in a restaurant because storage space in a dining car's kitchen is limited. Nevertheless, the portions are generous, the food is good, and the service is usually cheerful and efficient. You will find one vegetarian meal on the menu at each meal.

In a full-service dining car, the kitchen crew consists of a chef and at least one food specialist. When real china replaced the disposable plates, an additional person was added to help wash dishes. Then another round of budget cuts was imposed. As of this writing, meals on almost all Amtrak trains are again being served on disposable plastic plates. There are several exceptions where real china is still being used: aboard the Empire Builder, running daily between Chicago and Seattle; on the Coast Starlight, the daily train between Los Angeles and Seattle; on the

Auto Train, operating between Lorton, Virginia, and Sanford, Florida; and in the first-class cars on the Acela trains running in the Northeast Corridor between Boston and Washington, DC. The Amtrak people clearly understand that real china enhances the dining-car experience, and bringing it back on other trains is being seriously discussed. As always, however, money is the issue because real china dishes mean another employee has to be brought aboard to wash them.

Staff in the dining area itself includes someone Amtrak calls a lead service attendant, plus as many as three other servers. That number again depends on the train's equipment and the number of passengers onboard.

The dining car is located near the middle of the train—usually with sleeping cars in front and coaches to the rear. When you enter the diner, wait at the doorway for an attendant to seat you. Meals are family-style, meaning you'll be seated at a table for four. If you're traveling alone, you'll sit with one or more of your fellow passengers. I suggest you take the initiative and break the ice immediately. Introduce yourself and get the conversation started: "Where are you from?" "How far are you traveling?" "Are you enjoying your trip?" I always look forward to mealtimes on the train, because I've met some very interesting people in Amtrak dining cars. Besides, the alternative is to sit in an uncomfortable silence for the better part of an hour.

Kids are welcomed in the dining car. Booster seats are not always available, although they're supposed to be. In some (but not all) of the Superliner dining cars, the top portion of the seat lifts off and can be used for youngsters to sit on. For whatever reason, most dining-car crews either don't know about this feature or don't volunteer it, so you'll have to ask.

In years past, individual chefs were given a fair amount of latitude in what they serve and how it was prepared. More recently, Amtrak has standardized the menus, and you'll see many of the same dishes offered on different trains. There will be different specials, however.

Nevertheless, here's an idea of what you can expect when you enter an Amtrak dining car. (See page 92 later in this chapter for tipping protocol.)

Breakfast

The dining car is usually open for breakfast from 6:30 AM (double-check the exact time with your train attendant) until about 9:30 AM. There are usually no PA announcements from the diner for the first hour in consideration of passengers who may still be sleeping. The busiest times are usually between 7:00 and 8:30. You'll be seated on a first-come, first-served basis. To avoid a wait, get to the diner just when it opens or wait until 8:30 or 9:00. The usual breakfast fare is served: cereal; scrambled eggs or an omelet of some kind; French toast (a tradition of train travel) or pancakes; bacon or sausage; a biscuit or a croissant; and tea, coffee, or fruit juice. Grits are also served on many trains, especially those traveling to or through the South.

Lunch

Dining-car service begins around 11:30 AM and continues until everyone is served, closing usually around 1:30 PM. As with breakfast, there are usually no reservations taken, but PA announcements are made. The lunch menu will probably include soup, a choice of hamburger or veggie burger, chicken sandwich, individual pizza, and a salad plate. For dessert there's pie, cake, or ice cream. Drinks include coffee, tea, milk, soft drinks, beer, and wine.

Dinner

On long-distance trains, dinner in the dining car will be by reservation only. Normal procedure is for one of the dining-car staff to move through the train sometime in the afternoon and to assign passengers to the various seatings, which start at 5:00 or 5:30 PM and run as late as 8:00 PM. Usually (especially if you're in a sleeping car), he or she will be able to seat you when you prefer to eat. Again, PA announcements will tell you when to head for the diner.

The evening menu is more extensive than lunch. There will be several entrees; you will be able to choose from among chicken, fish, a vegetarian pasta dish, steak, and a chef's special. (On one of my recent trips, I had a braised lamb shank that was as good as any I've ever had in a restaurant.) Dessert includes pie, cake, or ice cream; coffee, tea, milk, soft drinks, beer, and wine are the beverages.

You may pay for your meals in the dining car with cash or credit card. As already noted, if you're a sleeping-car passenger, all your meals are included at no additional charge. You will have full choice of the menu and will only have to pay for beverages if you order beer or wine with your meal. (But please do remember to tip the server for your food and to base that amount on the printed menu prices.)

Coach passengers are also welcomed in the dining car, of course, and can choose from the same menu as folks from the sleeping cars. The only difference is that meals are not included in the cost of the coach ticket.

Your train attendant will bring meals from the dining car to your sleeping-car accommodations if you request it. But unless it's difficult for you to move throughout the train, why do that? Part of the train experience is going to the dining car and meeting some of your fellow passengers over a meal. If you do elect to eat in your room, be advised that it could take a while to get there and may not be piping hot when it arrives.

The Lounge Car

The other dining option on long-distance trains with Superliner equipment is the Sightseer Lounge Car, which is available to all passengers, whether traveling in coach or sleepers. There is a snack bar on the lower level where a variety of hot and cold sandwiches, snacks, and drinks are almost always available. The attendant does stop serving several times a day for his or her meal breaks, but generally the lounge car will be open from 6:00 AM until close to midnight. On shorter runs, the lounge car will remain open for the entire trip. Sleeping-car passengers *do* have to pay for their purchases in the lounge car.

The Pacific Parlour Car

The Coast Starlight, which runs daily in both directions between Los Angeles and Seattle, has an additional lounge car that is available only to sleeping-car passengers. It features a section with comfortable easy chairs, and there are several booths where passengers can be served meals from a special menu. There is a full-time attendant in the car who fills drink orders and serves the meals. There is also a small theater on the lower level where feature films are shown in the afternoons and evenings. Needless to say, this is a very popular spot for sleeping-car passengers.

Walking While You Rock and Roll

It takes a while to get used to walking on a moving train. For one thing, the motion of the train changes constantly depending on the speed of the train and the condition of the track—sometimes the motion is nice and smooth, and sometimes it's quite bouncy. When you're walking from car to car, do as the train crew does: place your feet farther apart than normal as you go, and brace yourself by placing your hands against the corridor walls in sleeping cars or by gripping the seat backs of chairs as you move through coaches. In the vestibules between cars there are candy-striped handles to hold onto as you step from one car to another. Use them!

Beware the "Denver Cocktail"

If you're on one of the western trains and would like to have a mixed drink or two in the lounge car or some wine or beer with your meal in the diner, don't forget that altitude increases the effects of alcohol on the human body. For example, the California Zephyr climbs to more than 9,200 feet as it crosses the Continental Divide west of Denver; at that altitude, one glass of wine will have the effect of two. This physiological phenomenon is usually the reason why otherwise sedate passengers are occasionally seen tottering back to their seats from the dining car as the eastbound Zephyr begins its descent into the Denver area.

What About Bathing?

Taking a bath, in the literal sense, can't be done. But you can manage to approximate one with a little effort and some ingenuity. As with almost everything else, a lot depends on what kind of accommodations you have.

Amtrak coaches don't have showers. There are simply too many passengers to convert a much-needed lavatory into a shower, so almost all coach passengers just do without, especially if it's just one overnight. But a practical alternative is a minimal sponge bath, which you can accomplish in one of the lavatories. Just add a washcloth and a small bar of soap in a plastic bag when you pack.

Viewliner sleepers have a shower room at the end of the car, and Superliner sleepers have one on the lower level. You might find them a bit cramped if you're tall, but they work quite well.

There's also a shower in each of the large bedrooms in both Viewliners and Superliners. Actually it's a compartment the size of a phone booth—a *small* phone booth—containing both a toilet and a shower. The shower works like the one on the lower level, except you have even less room to maneuver because of the toilet. I've noted this elsewhere, but it bears repeating: Be careful not to press the "shower" button when you meant to flush the toilet. You'll need a good sense of humor if you do.

Sleeping in Coach Class

Any way you slice it, you'll be sleeping in a chair. That's not nearly as bad as it sounds, though, because Amtrak's coach seats are large and comfortable. They recline and most have leg rests. In fact, they're pretty much like that nice recliner in your living room, the one you fall asleep in while watching late movies. The major difference, of course, is the noise and motion of the train and the other people around you. Some passengers don't seem to manage this part of the train experience very well, but there are some tips that can make it easier:

- Bring a blanket and your own pillow. Another option would be the Comfort Kits available for sale in the lounge car. They include a light blanket and an inflatable pillow.

- Don't eat a huge dinner, and skip the coffee or Coke.

- Change into loose clothing—an extra-large sweatshirt and sweatpants are ideal.

- Don't try to sleep until you're ready for it; read or chat with your seatmate instead.

- Earplugs and a sleep mask could help. These items are included in the Comfort Kits mentioned above.

- Perhaps your doctor will prescribe something to help you sleep before you leave, or you could try one of the over-the-counter pills that are commonly available.

Getting to Sleep in a Sleeper

Not everyone sleeps well on a train, even in a sleeping-car roomette or bedroom. I'm fortunate in that respect: I usually sleep like a baby. Under those clean sheets in my cozy roomette, I have a feeling of contentment that makes that extra fare worth every dime.

Remember that the train attendant has a lot of beds to prepare—30 or 40 of them if you're traveling in a Superliner and the car is full. Try to give him or her as much advance notice as possible when you want to have your beds prepared. Ideally, get one of the later seatings in the diner, then let the attendant know when you're heading off to dinner so he or she can have your beds made up when you return.

Here are a few suggestions to help ensure a good night's rest in your sleeping-car bedroom:

- You won't need to bring a blanket, but you might want to bring a travel pillow—one of those small down-filled kind you can roll up and pack in your suitcase.

- Don't overdo it at dinner, even though your meals are free. Avoid drinking anything caffeinated.

- Stay up reading as late as you can; turn out the light only when you're really sleepy.

- You can easily darken your room, so a sleep mask isn't necessary. However you might consider using earplugs.

Incidentally, do not try to prepare the bed yourself or close it up in the morning, especially if you're going to be occupying the room for another night. There's a right way to do it, and the train attendants would much rather you left that job to them.

Tipping: Whom and How Much?

For some reason, the matter of tipping members of the train's onboard crew is confusing to many travelers. Fear not. Here are the ground rules:

- Do not tip the conductors. (Yes, some people do try.)

- Do tip your car attendant. If he or she directs you to your accommodations, gives you an orientation of where everything is and how it all works, gets your bed ready when you want it and put away promptly in the morning, and is generally pleasant, $10 per day, per person, is about right. But if he or she checks on you periodically, if the bathrooms and shower room are tidied up several times during the day, if he helps with your luggage as the train approaches your destination, and—this pushes *me* over the top—if he tells you which room he will be in during the night should you need him in any emergency, then I think $15 per person per day is appropriate. And, of course, if you ask for any special services—having a meal brought to your compartment, for example—add something for those extras. In coach class, assuming you've been helped with baggage and have received cheerful and friendly attention, my suggestions are $1 or $2 for a one-night trip and $3 or $4 for two nights. Most passengers tip the train attendant as they leave the train at their final destination. (By the way, I've interviewed numerous train attendants during my many travels on Amtrak—and although it's deplorable, all agree that female attendants tend to receive smaller tips than their male counterparts. Please be sensitive to that inequity.)

- Do tip the lounge-car attendant. Extra change left behind on the counter after each purchase is appropriate.

- Do tip the service people in the dining car. Follow the same rules you would in any other restaurant: start with the standard 15 percent and move up for really good service or down for casual or unfriendly service.

Please note that some sleeping-car passengers feel no need to tip dining-car staff because their meals are complimentary. For shame! If you have the means to travel in a sleeping car, you can afford to tip generously where warranted. Please do so. Tip at least 15 percent of what you would be paying if your meals were not included in your fare. I should also mention that the IRS assumes passengers will be tipping these people and requires workers to pay income tax on an estimated amount of income from tipping.

If done right, the jobs on a long-distance train are not easy—tips are truly earned. Train attendants routinely put in 18–20 hour days. The dining-car staff prepares and serves many hundreds of meals a day, starting at 6:00 in the morning and ending as late as 9:00 PM. The lounge-car attendant is on duty almost nonstop for 16 or 17 hours. The onboard crews working cross-country trains put in all those hours for three days and two nights, spend one night in a hotel, then work the same schedule on the same train on their way back home. I would encourage you to recognize and reward people who perform efficiently and cheerfully under those conditions.

Finally, you should be aware that official Amtrak policy says no employee shall solicit tips. I've never once run into it, but should it happen to you, especially if it's flagrant, I would encourage you to report the individual. It's not that the sin is so great; it's just a pretty good indication of a bad employee who should be weeded out. So when you get home, call Amtrak at 1-800-USA-RAIL and ask to be connected with a customer relations agent. Give them the date, the train number, and, if you have it, the employee's name. Likewise for employees who perform poorly or with an obvious bad attitude.

Taking Photographs

If you enjoy taking photographs on your vacation, traveling across the country by train will provide you with a limitless number of photo opportunities, both inside and outside the train. I carry a medium-quality digital camera when I travel; with it, I'm able to cover almost any photo opportunity.

Interior shots on a train are no more difficult than photos taken indoors at home. For shots of a party in the lounge car or of that nice couple from England you met over dinner, set the camera on automatic and blaze away.

Unfortunately, it's not as easy to get really first-rate shots of the scenery passing by outside. Shooting through the tinted train windows is the biggest obstacle to good pictures. Unlike European railroads, the windows in American coaches and sleeping cars cannot be opened (although they can be pushed out in an emergency). Final results may not be perfect, but there are a few things you can do to improve the quality of those important souvenir photos.

- Because the train is moving, slower shutter speeds can result in blurry photographs. Switch to the "TV" setting on your digital camera to take video—or, if your camera is so equipped, switch from automatic to "selective shutter speed"—then set the shutter speed to at least 250.

- Get the camera's lens as close to the window as you can *without* touching it. A lens pressed against the window or a camera body braced against any other part of the train can transmit the train's vibration to the camera. The result: blurry photos.

- If you can control the adjustment, switch your camera from automatic to "selective focus." If the window is at all dirty or spotty, some cameras with the automatic-focus feature will focus on the transparent window pane instead of that gorgeous scene passing beyond it. Controlling the focus yourself will avoid that problem. Usually you won't have time for a lot of adjustment, so if your camera has this feature, the best advice is to set your focus on "infinity" and forget about it.

- If you have time, check for any reflections in the window— that white pillow on the seat behind you—and move them or block them with your body before shooting.

- Don't use the automatic flash for photos taken through the train window. It will likely cause a photo-wrecking reflection. Besides, it's of no use for objects more than 15 or 20 feet away. *Do* use the flash for interior shots, even during daytime hours.

If you take the ultra-simple approach and use one of the so-called idiot-proof cameras exclusively, you probably won't be able to make most of those adjustments. Don't worry about it! Your photos won't be up to *National Geographic* standards anyway, and they'll still make dandy souvenirs.

Please do not try for clearer photos by opening the windows in the top half of the train's exit doors, either in the vestibules or on the lower level of the Superliners. You really do run the risk of injury from flying debris kicked up by the train, from passing trains, or from stationary objects at trackside. If any of the onboard crew sees you doing it, you could be put off the train. Yes, they are that serious about it.

One more thing: Don't feel bad when you get home and find that quite a few of your photos have been ruined by what I call "the green blur"—bushes or trees that suddenly zoom by just as you press the shutter. I'm an expert on green-blur photography and have hundreds of shots to prove it.

Onboard Activities

Any organized activities occur in Superliner lounge cars because they're so much bigger than their single-level counterparts. Movies are shown on two Amtrak trains: in a small theater on the lower level of the Pacific Parlour Car on the Coast Starlight (available for sleeping-car passengers only) and in both the coach and sleeping car lounges on the Auto Train.

Passing the Time

Finding something to do on the train is more of a problem for some passengers than for others. Many people—and I'm one of them—can just ratchet down and dreamily let the hours, along with the miles, roll by. Others need to change their activities frequently. Having something available to do is important, especially at night or when you can't see much outside to hold your attention.

Most kids have a low threshold for scenery watching on long-distance train rides, so bring some games to help occupy their time. PHOTO COURTESY OF THE AUTHOR

Enjoy the Scenery

This, of course, is the main reason for traveling by train, so take full advantage of it. On most long-distance trains, Amtrak provides passengers with printed route guides identifying the major points of interest along the way. These guides include a written description and a schematic map that tells you on which side of the train each feature will appear and about when to start looking for it.

Sometimes, a member of the crew (usually one of the conductors, since they know the route best) will provide commentary about the passing scenery over the PA system. Unfortunately, there really isn't any standard when it comes to this kind of live narration. Some passengers enjoy it; others would prefer not to have to listen to it. Some conductors have a real feel for this kind of thing and do a wonderful job; others don't. Some won't do it at all.

Several of Amtrak's trains feature volunteer lecturers from the National Park Service or from local historical societies who offer commentary over the PA system about the countryside through which the train is passing. Because it's dependent upon volunteers, this extra bonus is usually available during the busy summer months only, and not necessarily on every trip on every long-distance train. Without exception, however, I've found these people to be interesting, articulate, and well informed. All deserve thanks and appreciation for their dedication and effort. Please make it a point to acknowledge them should you be on one of those trains.

Track the Train's Progress

A portable GPS is a lot of fun, because it will tell you where the train is at all times. But for a permanent souvenir of your train trip, bring along a soft-cover road atlas of the United States. As your route takes you from town to town, mark the train's progress on the maps with a colored highlighter. If you don't want to bring the entire atlas, just photocopy the appropriate pages before you leave home.

Compute the Train's Speed

The train's speed varies greatly, of course, depending upon track conditions, grade, the amount of rail traffic, weather, and other factors. Outside of the Northeast Corridor from Washington, DC, to Boston—where Amtrak's high-speed Acela trains can reach speeds of 150 miles per hour—the top speed is 79 miles per hour almost everywhere else in the country. "How fast are we going?" is almost certainly the question kids ask most often, and there's a way to figure it out quickly, easily, and accurately. You'll need a sweep second hand on your watch and a calculator. You can also work out the math yourself. You'll need to be able to see the mileposts passing by outside your train. (Information about mileposts can be found in chapter 10, "How It All Works.")

The formula is simple: Divide 3,600 (the number of seconds in an hour) by the number of seconds it takes you to travel one mile (the distance between two mileposts). Thus, if it takes the train 53 seconds to travel one mile, you're going 67.92 mph. The engineer in the locomotive cab carries a stopwatch for the same purpose, by the way. He or she is required to operate right at the speed limit and will regularly check the accuracy of the speedometer in the cab using this same method.

If you're not interested in doing the math, the table on the following page will shortcut the process.

There is another way to compute the train's speed, but it's a lot less accurate. Count the number of "telephone" poles passing by in a 15-second period and multiply that number by six. Most of the time, that will give you a rough idea of the speed. (Incidentally, those are not really telephone poles. They were originally installed by the railroad to bring electricity to its signals and switches.)

Time Between Mileposts	Speed (mph)
2:00.0	30
1:43.0	35
1:30.0	40
1:20.0	45
1:12.0	50
1:00.0	60
:55.4	65
:51.4	70
:48.0	75
:45.0	80

Estimate Your Arrival Time

I enjoy figuring out whether we're gaining or losing time along our route. It's quite easy to do since departure times for each stop are listed on the Amtrak timetable. You can go to the Amtrak website and print one out before you leave, or you can get one at the station before you depart or from the train attendant or conductor once onboard. Sleeping-car passengers may even find one in their rooms when they board. Just for fun, I use this means to log our progress and to maintain an ongoing estimate of when we'll arrive at our final destination. One of the little things you discover through this exercise is where the schedule has been padded, which allows a train that's been delayed to make up time.

Take a Walk

At least once after each stop, the conductor "walks the train," literally passing through every car from one end of the train to the other. He does it to collect tickets from passengers who have just boarded or just to satisfy himself that there are no problems. You should do it occasionally to get the juices flowing a bit. After all, before you know it you'll be back in the dining car for another meal! You'll find it's more exercise than you might think, since you'll be working more than normal to keep your balance in the moving train.

Read a Book

Most of us have any number of books we haven't been able to get to because of our busy daily schedules. Here's the perfect opportunity to start on that tome you've been holding onto. I try to save most of my reading for the evening, when there's little or nothing to see outside.

Listen to or Watch Electronic Gizmos

All sorts of audio and video materials are now available and can be watched or listened to using any number of devices—everything from children's stories to classic literature to old radio shows from the '40s and '50s. This can be the best of both worlds. I once sat gazing out the window of the Empire Builder as it rolled through the farm country of Minnesota and I listened to an audio tape of Garrison Keillor spinning some of his wonderful yarns about Lake Wobegon. (Note: Amtrak requires that you use earphones with these devices.)

Do Puzzles or Play Games

Bring along a book of crossword puzzles. Most also include other games: anacrostics, cryptograms, and other diabolical word games. Bring a deck of cards (or buy a souvenir deck in the lounge car) for solitaire or other card games with your traveling companion or the new friends you made in the lounge car. If you're traveling with children, by all means pick up a book of games for kids in your hometown bookstore before you leave. There are many available, and all will give you lots of new ideas for games and other diversions you'll all enjoy.

Listen In on Train Talk

You can do this with a device called a scanner, a radio receiver that picks up conversations among members of the operating crew (usually the engineer and the conductor). These little devices rapidly scan across radio frequencies used by police, fire departments, civil defense, railroads, taxi companies, and others, and they automatically stop whenever they come across a channel in use. For years I thought only the real hard-core train nuts carried these little electronic toys, but I must confess that I bought one some years ago and have enjoyed using it whenever I travel by train. You not only hear conversations between members of your train crew, but you also pick up those from yard workers, passing trains, dispatchers, and the recorded voices of the automatic detectors you pass. Scanners provide a fascinating look at railroad operations and are perfectly legal, although there are a couple of things to remember:

- Use the earphones that come with the scanner so the periodic squawking won't disturb other passengers. As a matter of fact, earphones are required for all audio devices on Amtrak trains.

- I suggest being judicious about displaying your scanner or passing along anything you hear to other passengers. There's no law against using one, but train crews will be a little more guarded in their conversations if they notice someone with a scanner.

You can buy a serviceable scanner in most any electronics store for around $150. They run on batteries but can also be operated by being plugged into the electric receptacle in your room (if you're traveling in a sleeping car). Just be sure the model you buy will pick up the frequencies commonly used by the railroads (160.215 to 161.565 megahertz). You can find a listing of specific frequencies on all the various Amtrak routes at www .on-track-on-line.com.

There's Romance on the Rails—Literally

For some passengers, an overnight train trip seems to have a direct effect on the libido. Train crews grin and shake their heads when asked about some of the more inventive means taken by passengers to have sex onboard a long-distance train. Amorous couples have been discovered in the baggage car, in vestibules, in the lounge car, in the washrooms (quite a trick, given the cramped quarters), and anywhere else where opportunity, desire, and, I suspect, a sense of mischief or daring collide.

Because of the lack of privacy at their assigned seats, coach passengers are most often the ones who seek somewhat more secluded locations for these activities. But not always. Sleeping-car passengers are occasionally discovered having sex outside of their rooms in other parts of the train. And it's not unknown for couples safely ensconced in private accommodations to deliberately leave their window shades up during their lovemaking as the train flashes—sorry, I couldn't resist that—through small towns.

For the most part, Amtrak crews try to look the other way when encountering these situations. This unofficial common-sense attitude has a lot to do with whether other passengers are being disturbed or offended.

By the way, those who successfully engage in these amorous onboard activities are said to have joined the 80-mile-an-hour club, the rail equivalent to the mile-high club of the airline industry.

A Few Do's and Don'ts

Most of these suggestions probably apply more to coach passengers because of the communal seating arrangement, but whether you're sitting in coach or a sleeper, you're still living with a lot of other people in fairly confined circumstances. Being a good neighbor is really just a matter of common sense and basic courtesy, so remember the following:

- Use earphones with radios, electronic devices, and scanners. (Amtrak will enforce this.)

- Loud conversations, even in private sleeping-car accommodations, can be very disturbing to people located nearby, many of whom will be relaxing, trying to read, or dozing.

- Tidy up after yourself in the washroom. One train attendant cannot possibly keep all of them clean all of the time.

- Let your train attendant know right away if you find something wrong—a malfunctioning toilet, for example. Early attention to these problems will minimize inconvenience to fellow passengers and can frequently prevent things from getting worse.

- Don't hog a seat hour after hour in the Superliner lounge car if other passengers are obviously waiting for a chance to enjoy the views.

- As pleasant as it may be, don't linger in conversation for more than a few minutes over coffee after your meal in the dining car. There's either another seating scheduled or the dining-car crew is ready for a well-earned break.

- Unless it's truly important, don't bother a member of the crew who's on a meal break in the dining car. It's a tough job, and he deserves that short time to himself.

- If you're traveling with children, don't let them run around the train without supervision. It's dangerous, especially in the vestibules between cars, and it can be very annoying to other passengers.

One last word on the subject of behavior: Some passengers
are under the impression that there are no laws onboard a train.
They actually think they can indulge in drugs, liquor to excess,
and any number of other illegal activities with impunity. Wrong!
Wherever the train happens to be, the laws of that particular state
apply to everyone onboard. Passengers can be removed from the
train and arrested in exactly the same way they can be kicked out
of a hotel or restaurant and into the waiting arms of the law. It
can and does happen.

7

WHO'S IN CHARGE HERE?

The success of any company, whether it's a manufacturing firm or a railroad, depends on its employees and how well they perform their jobs. When Amtrak came into existence in 1971, it inherited thousands of employees from private railroads. Along with all those people came a kind of compendium of pecking orders, systems, and procedures that somehow had to be forged into one way of doing things. In many respects it didn't work out very well; change for the better took years.

Amtrak has reorganized its systems over the years and introduced newer and better management techniques. Happily, that has included the granting of more authority to frontline employees. Today, at least in theory, key members of the onboard crew can take action on the spot to rectify most problems.

A Word About Race and Gender

Although there are no doubt inequities remaining in some areas, Amtrak has rather consistently demonstrated a progressive approach to the problem of discrimination by race or gender. The most obvious example is that of train attendant. In the days of the Pullman porter, these jobs were limited to black males. Today, passengers are just as likely to find that their attendant is a white woman—or any other person, for that matter.

This enlightened attitude also extends to giving women an opportunity to work in other railroad jobs that were traditionally the exclusive province of men. Women are now serving in every capacity on both freight and passenger trains, including as engineers up there in the head end. For traditionalists, not to mention sexists, that change has taken some getting used to. My brother Pete was on a short-haul trip in the Midwest a number of years ago when a rail fan, seated across the aisle from him, turned on his scanner to listen in on chatter among the crew. The man suddenly sat bolt upright in his seat and blurted to everyone within a 20-foot radius, "Holy crap! The engineer's a girl!"

Like Snowflakes, No Two Railroad Jobs Are Alike

First, you should know that a distinction is made between *operating crew* (the engineers and the conductors) and *service crew* or *onboard crew* (everyone else working onboard). As those terms imply, the operating crew is responsible for actually running the train, while the service crew looks after the needs of passengers. There is another significant difference: the service crew usually stays with the train for the entire trip, while the engineers and conductors, who are restricted by federal law to working no more than 12 hours in a row, are replaced at regular intervals along the way.

Most Amtrak crews tend to become quite close and treat each other like family. For instance, train attendants will switch off, with one looking after two cars through a couple of stops while the other takes a meal break. If one of the dining-car crew becomes ill, it's not unusual for one of the train attendants to pitch in and help out. Once, while I was traveling eastbound on the Southwest Chief, our train slowed to a stop when we met our westbound counterpart so that several cases of soft drinks and a bag of ice could be handed from our lounge car to theirs.

Being able to get along with people is certainly a prerequisite for anyone considering a job with Amtrak. By the time someone gets to be a veteran employee, he or she has seen it all and can deal with most of it pretty darn well.

There are, of course, many other key jobs in the operational structure of a railroad, but the emphasis in this chapter is on those employees who are directly responsible for getting you to your destination safely and comfortably.

Dispatcher

Wherever the train may be, its progress is controlled every inch of the way by a dispatcher. The airline equivalent is the air-traffic controller, but there is an important difference: Railroad dispatchers are employees of the individual railroads, while air-traffic controllers are employed by the Federal Aviation Administration (FAA), an agency of the US Department of Transportation. (The FAA is one more hidden government subsidy of the airline industry not enjoyed by Amtrak, by the way.) Dispatchers who control trains traveling in the Northeast Corridor between Washington, DC, and Boston are Amtrak employees, because those tracks are owned by Amtrak. Elsewhere throughout the country, the movement of Amtrak trains is controlled by dispatchers employed by the host railroads—that is, the railroads over whose tracks the Amtrak train travels.

Like their aviation counterparts, dispatchers are critical to the safe operation of the nation's railroads. Typically, they work in darkened rooms, monitoring the progress of trains on an illuminated display of the tracks for which they are responsible. The job requires complete concentration, and their fellow employees take pains not to interrupt or distract them.

Dispatchers communicate directly with a train's engineer by radio. They also control the signals seen by the engineer along the route. The dispatcher's main and constant concern is knowing exactly where each train is at all times. To assist the dispatcher, the engineer checks in by radio regularly—when the train passes specific checkpoints, when it leaves each station, and at other times along the way.

There is other, more specific communication between the train crew and dispatcher, of course. The dispatcher frequently directs the train to slow down, stop, or resume normal speed. He may remind the engineer that there are workers on the track at a certain location or instruct him to reduce speed between two specific mileposts because that track has recently been laid. When receiving such instructions, the engineer will acknowledge the call and carefully repeat the message so the dispatcher will be sure it was heard correctly. The engineer will often conclude his part of the transmission by verbally noting the time and the train number and then identifying himself by name. For important matters, the dispatcher is also the train's link to the rest of the world. If a passenger becomes seriously ill, for instance, the engineer can call the dispatcher and ask her to arrange for paramedics to meet the train at the next station stop.

Engineer

This is the job we all wanted when we were kids. If you've ever been one of the privileged few to get a ride in the cab of a locomotive, you'll know why. It's quite a thrill to sit up there with all that horsepower, grandly acknowledging the waves from kids of all ages as you thunder past. But make no mistake: it's a demanding job, and while it's generally agreed that being a freight engineer is more difficult, the men and women hauling Amtrak trains around the country are acutely aware that they're responsible for the lives of several hundred passengers.

Becoming a locomotive engineer isn't easy. It's particularly difficult if your goal is the head end of a passenger train, but it's not quite so hard if you're after a job as a freight engineer. Basically, it boils down to supply and demand. Most engineers, or at least the older, married ones, seem to prefer working for Amtrak because of convenience. An Amtrak engineer works a set schedule and thus has the luxury of knowing in advance when he'll be at home and when he'll be away. A freight engineer, however, is usually on call and goes whenever and wherever he's needed.

Then there's the matter of training. Before someone can even be considered for an engineer's job, he or she has to spend ten weeks in a classroom. One section covers instruction in the mechanical aspects of the equipment, another deals exclusively with air brakes (reflecting the obvious importance of knowing the hows and whys of stopping a train weighing many thousands of tons), and the third is a detailed review of the operational rules of railroading. From the classroom, an engineer trainee moves into the cab of a locomotive working with a qualified engineer for a full year of on-the-job training. Even after the classroom and on-the-job experience, there's still no guarantee that the trainee will be selected. Some would-be engineers are rejected because, according to one veteran engineer, they "just don't seem to have a *feel* for it." No matter how long they've been on the job, every engineer goes through refresher training periodically and must take regular exams to qualify and requalify for the specific territory he or she works.

Of course, the engineer is the person who controls the locomotive that pulls the train. She alternately operates the throttle to start the train in motion and keep it moving and operates the brakes to slow or stop the train. She also controls the whistle and constantly uses the radio to communicate with the conductor and the dispatcher.

To start the train, the engineer opens the throttle, which causes the diesel motors to run faster, generating more electricity and increasing the flow of power to the traction motors on each of the locomotive's axles. As that happens, most engineers lean out of the window and look straight down at the ground. In that way, they can tell the instant the train starts to move and can adjust the throttle accordingly to keep the wheels from slipping. That's a real no-no, because it can cause a jerk to be felt throughout the train. Passenger-train engineers pride themselves on their smooth starts, so to start with a small jerk is mildly embarrassing. It will probably subject the engineer to some friendly razzing from the conductors, too.

Freight trains are much longer than passenger trains, and there is a lot more slack, or "play," built into the coupling mechanism hooking each car together. As a freight train starts moving, the slack is taken up in one car after another down the length of the train. In years past, brakemen in the cabooses would hear the jolt coming toward them and brace for it. As the slack is taken up in car after car, it builds in intensity; by the time it gets to the last car of a long freight train, it can literally knock you off your feet.

As strange as it may seem, freight engineers must handle their trains very gently. Taking up slack abruptly while a freight train is rolling can literally snap a coupling and break the train in two. In fact, to prevent massive derailments, the knuckle in the coupling device is deliberately designed to be the weakest link in the chain and to break under severe stress. How many times one "breaks" a train is one way of measuring the performance and abilities of a freight engineer. Sometimes it happens because the engineer caused it, but other times a knuckle gives way from metal fatigue or because it's old and rusted. When that happens, the engineer will replace the defective knuckle (spares are carried in freight locomotive cabs) and keep it to show his superiors as proof that the break was not his fault.

Once under way, the engineer's attention is almost always directed toward the track ahead. She's on the lookout for obstructions but is also watching for signals, speed-limit signs, whistle posts (warning her to blow the whistle for an approaching grade crossing), and other trackside markings. The locomotive cab is equipped with two large side mirrors, and the engineer uses them to check the rest of the train on curves and look for any problems, such as smoke from an overheated bearing or shifting loads. The assistant engineer does the same on the other side of the cab. Traditionally, the engineer sits on the right side of the locomotive cab because that's the side of the tracks where all the signs and signals are usually placed.

The visual inspection was also an important function performed by railroad personnel riding in cabooses at the end of freight trains, but both the cabooses and the people who rode them have been replaced by an electronic device mounted at the end of the rear car. Called FRED by railroad people—an acronym for "flashing rear-end device"—it picks up reports from the automatic detectors alongside the track and relays them by radio to the engineer in the head end.

Unlike the smooth ride passengers are treated to, it's pretty bouncy in the cab of a locomotive, and the rough ride can affect the accuracy of the speedometer. Because trains must run at or close to the prescribed speed for any given stretch of track, most engineers carry a stopwatch, which they use regularly to determine precisely how fast the train is moving. This is done by recording the exact time it takes the train to pass between two mileposts and computing the speed from that. (See the table on page 99.)

Many Amtrak engineers came to the job with freight experience, and all agree that being a freight engineer is the more difficult of the two jobs. Because freight trains are so long—a 150-car train can be over a mile and a half from end to end—the engineer of a freight train often has one part of the train coming up a hill and the other part heading down the other side, all at the same time. Just to complicate things, the number of cars doing either is constantly changing as the train passes over the crest of the hill. That's very tricky because the engineer must make sure he's pulling *all* the cars *all* the time. Now suppose there's a curve in that stretch of track. That means he also has to think about centrifugal force affecting the part of the train that's going around the curve. Veteran engineers will tell you that in many ways their job is tougher and more demanding than that of an airline pilot. The cockpit of a modern jet certainly looks complicated, but, says one engineer I spoke to, "Those are all fancy gadgets to help the pilot do his job. We don't have any of that stuff to help us." And he's quite right. In that sense there is indeed a greater burden placed on the crew of a locomotive. If the train is running in fog or snow, there is no radar to help the head-end crew. The engineer must be so familiar with his route that he can "see" the track ahead in his mind's eye.

There's another similarity between the locomotive engineer and an airline pilot: Both are expected to operate their machines in a manner that will minimize the use of fuel. The pilot does it by adjusting the attitude of the aircraft in flight so it passes through the air with the least possible resistance. The locomotive engineer conserves fuel in much the same way the driver of a car does—with a delicate touch, both with the throttle and the brakes.

Federal law permits an engineer to be on duty for no more than 12 hours; for that reason one pair of engineers does not stay with a long-distance train for the entire route. For instance, along the westbound route of the California Zephyr, operating crews change in Galesburg, Illinois; in Lincoln, Nebraska; in both Denver and Grand Junction, Colorado; in Salt Lake City, Utah; and so on all the way to Emeryville, California. Usually, a crew coming off duty will overnight at one of those points, then the next day take the eastbound train back to where they started. Under no circumstances is an engineer permitted to continue operating a train after she reaches the 12-hour limit. If a train has an unexpected delay en route, and it appears that an operating crew will "go dead" before reaching its scheduled crew-change stop, Amtrak must anticipate the problem and arrange for a fresh crew to meet the train somewhere along the route before that happens.

Engineers are intimately familiar with the track in their territories—that is, with the stretch of track over which they operate their trains. They know that track the same way a commuter knows the roads between home and work. They *have* to, and they must take regular tests to prove it. In many cases, they also get to know some of the people who live along their regular routes. These folks sit in their windows or step out into their backyards to wave as the trains go by. They frequently get a wave and a friendly whistle toot in response.

One more little tidbit that I found interesting: unlike the airlines, where meals are provided for the cockpit crews, head-end crews on Amtrak trains bring their own food in lunch pails. The only thing they're permitted to get from the dining car is coffee. On occasion, however, a chef will bend the rules and send up food that would otherwise spoil and be thrown out. But the steak or half chicken that can be used another day stays in the diner's freezer.

As with almost any job, there is a downside to being a railroad engineer. The first thing a visitor to the head end discovers is that it's noisy up there. That fact shouldn't be surprising, because you're sitting just a few feet from the equivalent of 4,000 horses. All that power makes quite a racket, and it's magnified several times whenever the train enters a tunnel. Another culprit is the whistle. It's blown constantly, and while the volume can be controlled to a degree, it still ranges from loud to damn near unbearable. Earplugs are provided but really aren't practical, since there's a lot of necessary conversation going on. The noise factor improved in the early '90s when Amtrak phased in a new generation of locomotives that feature a fully-enclosed, air-conditioned cab.

There is, however, one serious negative to the job, and it's a big one. Many engineers, whether working freight or passenger trains, have struck and killed someone while at the controls of the locomotive. Perhaps it's a truck driver who thought he had plenty of time to drive across the tracks before the train reached the crossing. Maybe it's a teenager playing chicken with the train on a dare. And maybe it's a poor soul who's decided it would be a quick way to end his or her life. Whatever the circumstances, they're all equally tough on the person who happens to be at the controls of the locomotive at the time. Spend a few hours riding in a locomotive cab and you somehow sense a touch of uneasiness as every grade crossing is approached. Most engineers manage to keep it in perspective. One told me, "As long as I've done everything possible—if I wasn't speeding, if I used the whistle, and if I applied the brakes—I can't allow myself to take it personally." There is, of course, no way in the world to stop in time, although the engineers always try.

Once upon a time, even after steam locomotives had been taken out of service, the second person in the locomotive cab was called a fireman. Today, both are considered engineers. The one not actually operating the locomotive sits on the left side of the locomotive cab and provides a second set of eyes and ears, calling out the signals as they're passed, noting any change in the speed limit, sending and receiving messages on the radio, and generally assisting with the many details and allowing the other engineer to focus on the primary task of operating the locomotive. Assistant engineers are fully qualified to operate the locomotive, and they can and do take over the controls from time to time to provide their colleagues with some relief. Two engineers are used on all long-distance trains, but on short-distance runs, there is only one engineer in the cab. Union regulations do not permit only one person in the locomotive cab for trips lasting more than six hours.

Conductor

There is a conductor on every train—whether passenger or freight, whether long or short, and whether it's traveling 1,000 miles or 1,000 yards. This is the person actually in charge of the train, who is roughly equivalent to the captain of a ship at sea. That means the conductor has to be thoroughly familiar with both railroad operations and the train itself.

Anyone who's an Amtrak conductor has worked his or her way up the ladder and knows a lot about railroad operations. Every new conductor goes through an initial eight-week training program, which includes train operations, emergency procedures, passenger relations, and all of the procedures necessary for the handling of tickets. Assuming the applicant is hired, he or she becomes an assistant conductor, working in that capacity for at least six months before becoming eligible for promotion. All conductors are required to take refresher courses periodically.

As do the engineers, each conductor works a specific territory, usually a section of the route just a few hundred miles long. He or she knows every switch and every crossover intimately. Conductors are required to take an annual test on the operating rules, and that test is based on the specific territory they work. If a conductor moves her residence, a new test must be taken and passed before she can begin working the new territory. By the way, it takes a grade of 85 percent or better to pass those tests. Conductors are also required to pass a physical exam every two years.

The conductor is in regular contact with the engineer by radio throughout the trip and, in this manner, stays up to date on the train's progress, track conditions, other rail traffic, and any number of other details. If there's some kind of mechanical problem with the locomotive, it's the conductor (in consultation with the engineer) who decides when or if the train can continue on its way. While the train is en route, it's the conductor who can be called upon to deal with all of the little idiosyncrasies that are found in every car: a bedroom door that comes off its track, a circuit breaker that trips for no obvious reason, and who knows what else. Finally, and it's the most obvious of the duties, she's also responsible for collecting tickets and for supervising the loading and unloading of passengers and baggage. Even when there's nothing apparent going on, most conductors "walk the train" every hour or so, just to keep an eye on things.

The conductor also has the authority to deal with any other problem if it involves the safety or well-being of the passengers. If a passenger becomes ill, the conductor can arrange for an ambulance to meet the train at an upcoming stop. If a passenger becomes disorderly, the conductor has the authority to stop the train and put him off.

Because he's so thoroughly familiar with the train's route, it's usually the conductor who makes periodic announcements over the public-address system about points of interest along the way. It's also the conductor's responsibility to inform passengers as to the reasons for any delays that may occur. (Too many conductors just don't do that, however, and it's a real sore point with many frequent passengers. In my opinion, there is simply no excuse for not informing passengers about delays that are longer than a few minutes.)

Finally, there is also paperwork to do. The conductor officially notes all arrival and departure times (which he confirms by radio with the engineer, who passes that information along to the dispatcher). Should the train be late, the conductor is responsible for filling out a delay report, which includes both the length of the delay and the reason it occurred.

By the way, the assistant conductor used to be called a trainman, flagman, or brakeman. Today this person has the same duties and responsibilities as the conductor but is in a subordinate role. One vestige of the old job remains, however, because the assistant conductor is often assigned to look after the rear portion of the train.

Coming back to the issue of gender once again, if the assistant conductor happens to be female, many passengers assume that she has little or no responsibility other than taking tickets. Not so. She takes the same tests, meets the same requirements, and must have the same knowledge of railroad operations. Usually the only real difference between the two jobs is length of time on the job.

Conductors are subject to the same 12-hour limit of service time that applies to the head-end crew; so if the train is delayed by a winter storm and they hit their 12-hour limit in the middle of a Nebraska cornfield, that's where the train stops and waits for new conductors and engineers.

Train Attendant

These are the folks who look after the comfort of passengers on all of Amtrak's long-distance trains. There are no train attendants on short-haul trains or on trains that may cover a lot of distance but don't operate overnight.

Note that the correct term is *train attendant* or *car attendant* and not *porter*. It's not a major issue with most people, but in the minds of some, *porter* is a term that carries with it a reminder of another time. Its origins date back to the days when virtually all sleeping cars were manufactured, owned, and operated by the Pullman Company and only black males were hired to staff those cars. The jobs were highly prized, especially during the Great Depression, and those who got them took justifiable pride in the quality of their work. Not surprisingly, however, a good deal of latent racism came with the territory. It became the unfortunate custom for many passengers to call every porter "George," after the company's founder, George M. Pullman. Hearing that every day from passengers who neither knew nor cared what their porter's given name was had to be a humiliating and dehumanizing experience for many of the Pullman porters. Incidentally, that bit of history is one of the reasons Amtrak has made a point of providing all employees with name badges.

New hires go through a thorough training program and have periodic refreshers. As with all new hires, they'll have to take a number of "student trips" and perform up to expected standards before becoming permanent employees.

I had always assumed that brand-new attendants start out working in coaches and gradually work their way up to sleeping cars, but that's not necessarily true. Amtrak people bid for their assignments, and whether or not their requests are granted is determined in part by seniority and in part by how popular the particular trip is. Whether an attendant works in coaches or sleepers seems to be pretty much a matter of choice; in fact, many attendants prefer the coaches. Sleeping-car attendants make more money because of tips, but even under normal circumstances, they work a lot harder and their passengers can be much more demanding.

Amtrak assigns one train attendant to every sleeping car, no matter if it's one of the single-level Viewliner sleepers or a bi-level Superliner. Not so with coaches. You'll usually find one attendant for every three coaches on single-level eastern trains, while one attendant looks after two coaches out west in the Superliners. (By the way, in Amtrak slang, these folks are known as "tacos," an acronym for "*t*rain *a*ttendant, *co*ach.")

Many of the attendant's duties are the same, whether working in coach or sleeper: boarding passengers, helping to stow their baggage, maintaining a seating chart, keeping the car orderly and the bathrooms clean, making sure each passenger gets off at the right stop, and generally doing whatever is necessary to make sure the trip goes pleasantly for everyone.

Sleeping-car attendants have fewer people to look after but much more to do. I once had a wonderful conversation with a longtime train attendant who provided the best description of the job I've ever heard. "This sleeper," he said, "is just like a small hotel—and I'm the only employee!" That's just about right, too. The attendant is doorman, receptionist, bellhop, cleaner, server, and concierge all rolled into one. Spend 48 hours watching a good one in action, and you'll have a real appreciation of what a demanding job it is.

A sleeping-car attendant reports for duty about three hours prior to the train's departure. He makes sure every room is in order and has towels, face cloths, soap, a route guide and time-table, bottled water, and anything else that's supposed to be there. He cleans mirrors, removes any dirty linen, stocks and cleans the restrooms, and looks for anything that may not be in working order. (If a toilet doesn't function properly, now is the time to find out and get it fixed!) He also checks to be sure all bedding has been made up ahead of time and is neatly stored in the upper berths. Most of the time everything's shipshape, but not always— in those cases, he'll have to make it right by himself. Even if he does find everything in order, there's a whole lot of bed making in the life of a sleeping-car attendant. When a passenger is ready to retire for the evening, the berth has to be lowered into position and arranged for sleeping, and on two-night trips, it must be made up again the next day. Often there is as much as a 50-percent turnover on a 48-hour trip, meaning half of the bedrooms could be occupied by different individuals on successive nights. The first passenger may ride overnight from Chicago to Denver with the second traveler boarding in Salt Lake City for the trip from there to Oakland. The attendant must pull off the old sheets and remake the bed before the new arrival boards and is ready for a good night's sleep. There's even more bed making to do on turn-around trips. The California Zephyr, for instance, originates in Chicago and is turned around in Emeryville for the return trip. The car attendant makes up all the beds in the car for the train's trip back to Chicago the next day. In a Superliner sleeper booked to capacity, that's a total of 44 beds.

You'll first meet your attendant on the platform where she will check your name off against her passenger manifest and direct you to your room. Once the train is underway, she should also look in on you to make sure you understand where everything is in your room and how it all works.

Some sleeping-car passengers enjoy the idea of room service and ask the attendant for beverages or meals served in their rooms. Strange as it may seem, because the dining-car experience is one of the unique and enjoyable experiences in train travel, it's not that unusual for a sleeping-car passenger to have *all* meals brought to the room for the entire trip. Of course, that's the norm for passengers who have difficulty moving about the train.

The sleeping-car attendant will also give you a wake-up call if you would like one or if you're going to be leaving the train at an early morning stop. He'll offer to bring juice or hot coffee to your room at whatever time you wish.

The train attendant is the person you should first contact with any problem or need. Whatever it may be, you can be sure that the attendant has heard it before and will take it in stride. (I always make it a point to ask the attendant in my car to tell me about some of the unusual experience he or she has had. They all have dozens of stories, some so bizarre they couldn't possibly have been invented.)

Coach attendants usually occupy one of the rear seats in their car. Depending on how full the train is, sleeping-car attendants will either be in roomette 1 or, on one of the Superliner trains, in the "transition sleeper" or "dorm car" up front, just behind the baggage car. Some will make a point of telling you which room they're in should you need something during the night. If your attendant doesn't volunteer that information, by all means, ask. But please, be considerate. Don't roust the poor soul in the middle of the night for some trivial request. By the same token, don't hesitate to call if you have a legitimate need—if you fall ill, for example.

The typical workday for a train attendant is 16–18 hours long. It would be worse than that, but they help each other out. Typically one attendant will handle the boarding of passengers for several cars in the middle of the night so a colleague can get a bit more sleep. The upside is the time off, and every attendant I've ever talked to lists this as a major benefit to the job. It varies according to the schedule of the employee, but on average a train attendant will get four days off for every three he or she works.

Lead Service Attendant

Amtrak dining cars used to be headed up by a steward, which was someone in a neat blue uniform who greeted passengers and ushered them to a seat at one of the tables. Stewards were also responsible for taking payment, making change, and supervising the serving part of the dining-car procedures. Because of cost cutting, those days are gone; personally, I think that's a pity. Being greeted by a polished maitre d' as you enter the dining car certainly added to the overall experience. Today, the steward's job is performed by someone called the lead service attendant (LSA), who also waits on tables.

The LSA is responsible for the quality of the service in the dining car. He or she seats people, distributes the meal checks on which an order is noted, records the complimentary meals of sleeping-car passengers, and collects payment from the coach passengers. He or she is also responsible for all of the cash collected in the dining car. Over the duration of a two-day trip, that amount can add up to many thousands of dollars. The accounts had better balance at the end of the trip, too, because the LSA could be required to make up any difference from his or her own pocket.

Because the LSA also pitches in and waits on tables, however, there just isn't much time to spend on the niceties of dining. Without stewards on the trains, the emphasis is necessarily more on getting people seated and served in a reasonable amount of time.

Whether it's a steward or an LSA, this is the person responsible for making sure everyone gets fed, whatever it takes. Years ago, I was on the Coast Starlight headed for Seattle when a power failure knocked out all the ovens in the diner's kitchen. The steward hopped off the train at the next stop, dashed to a telephone, and arranged for delivery of hot meals to the train at a station up ahead. (I've often tried to imagine the scene in a KFC restaurant when the phone is answered by a 20-year-old assistant manager, and on the other end is an Amtrak LSA wanting 250 chicken dinners delivered to the local train station in 90 minutes. Sounds just like a Bob Newhart or Bill Cosby routine, doesn't it!)

Service Attendant

This is Amtrak's gender-neutral term for *waiter* or *waitress*. Call it what you will—on a long-distance train, it's really a tough job. Each day he or she will start serving breakfast in the dining car as early as 6:30 in the morning, while the final seating for dinner often lasts until 9:00 PM. In between, the service attendants could have served as many as 450 meals. It's quite true that the chef and his or her assistants in the kitchen had to prepare all those meals, but the service people had the added responsibility of maintaining a cheerful disposition throughout that 16-hour day. It's especially grueling on the western trains that take two nights to reach the West Coast. After a scheduled 50-hour trip from Chicago to Emeryville, crews working the California Zephyr spend one night in a hotel, then depart the next morning for the trip back home—two more tough 16-hour days. A compensating factor, usually the most important one for Amtrak crews, is that they'll get anywhere from five to eight days off before their next trip.

In addition to waiting on tables, each member of the service crew has other specific duties: setting the tables, filling the salt shakers, sorting and stocking the packaged condiments, and a host of other tasks. They're pretty much the same things you would be doing in your home to prepare for a dinner party.

In Amtrak's early days, most crew members were veterans of the railroad; many were third or even fourth generation. A handful of those folks remain, but through normal attrition, their numbers have diminished.

Chef

Once you enter the kitchen of an Amtrak dining car, you're on the chef's turf. A good one keeps a sharp eye on everything that happens within his or her domain. The chef boards the dining car several hours before the train departs to make sure the kitchen has been left in proper order by the previous crew. Occasionally things are not shipshape, and in those cases a long trip begins by cleaning up after someone else.

An Amtrak computer determines in advance the amount of food and supplies that should be put aboard a dining car before each trip. The first order of business for the chef is to check supplies against that list to be sure he or she has received everything the computer ordered. That's important because every steak and piece of chicken must be accounted for at the end of the trip—anything missing might have to be paid for out of the chef's own pocket. Some food is prepared or cooked ahead of time. Bacon, for example, is precooked, then heated prior to serving.

Amtrak chefs are permitted some latitude within the framework of the current menu. For example, the chicken dish can take many savory forms, depending on how the chef chooses to prepare it. The "chef's special" offers another outlet for some culinary creativity. Although there isn't a lot of variety on the menu because of limited storage space, many chefs bring their own personal collection of spices onboard to give several of the items on the bill of fare an additional bit of individuality.

Once the trip is underway and mealtime begins to approach, activity in the diner's kitchen increases to a pace that's somehow frenzied and orderly at the same time. The chef is still clearly the one in charge and handles most of the actual cooking. Orders come in, are filled, and are sent out (or up via dumbwaiter, in the case of Superliners, where the kitchen is on the lower level) with amazing dispatch. And they'd better be organized! On some of the more popular trains, as many as 300 meals will have to be prepared and served at several sittings over a three-hour period. Meals have to be prepared and served efficiently or the dinner hour will stretch into bedtime—which is annoying to passengers and exhausting for the dining-car crew.

One veteran Amtrak supervisor, who has worked his way up through the ranks, says that a chef has the toughest job on a passenger train. I absolutely believe it!

Food Specialist

These are the people who work in the kitchen under the supervision of the chef. Responsibilities are divided but include all of the tasks we perform at home in our own kitchens, from putting the groceries away to cleaning up the pots and pans after the last meal is served. Depending on the train, there will be one or two of these people working down on the lower level of the dining car with the chef. The days are long and the work is hard. As with many other onboard employees, what makes it all worthwhile is good pay for the hours you work and lots of time off for leisure or, in many cases, another job for additional income. Newly hired food specialists go through an extensive initial training program of about 80 hours and must take a number of trips, totaling about 60 hours, and perform satisfactorily under the watchful and usually very critical eye of a veteran chef.

Lounge-Car Attendant

The specifics of this job vary somewhat according to the kind of equipment involved. On eastern trains, especially the short-haul trains without a dining car, it's a particularly busy job. The attendant operates behind a counter in a galley located in the middle of the lounge car and provides hot and cold sandwiches and a variety of beverages for passengers. On western trains, the attendant is located in a similar facility on the lower level of the Superliner lounge car.

The lounge-car attendant's schedule is a killer: On the long-distance trains, he or she will be up at 5:30 AM, making coffee and preparing the little galley to open at 6:00. The attendant takes three 45-minute meal breaks during the day and finally closes down around midnight. For most of that 18-hour day, the lounge-car attendant is on his or her feet serving a constant stream of passengers and performing a variety of tasks: heating packaged meals in the galley's microwave oven, serving potato chips and other snacks, pouring cold drinks, selling decks of cards or coloring books, and making change. All the while a cheerful disposition must be maintained.

Before outlawing it altogether, Amtrak permitted smoking only in the lower level of Superliner lounge cars. Most passengers were glad to have the rest of the train be nonsmoking, but it made life miserable for the lounge-car attendants, who found themselves working that grueling schedule in a constant haze of tobacco smoke. When the total ban on smoking took effect, no one was happier than the lounge-car attendants.

Station Agent

While not part of the onboard crew, these people deserve at least some mention since they're often the first Amtrak employee a passengers encounters. Depending on the size of the station, the station agent's job may or may not be full-time. Basic responsibilities include keeping the station clean, selling tickets, and handling baggage. They'll also direct you to the spot on the platform to wait so you'll be near your car when the train stops. Frequently, however, they're called on for other things. For instance, if the lounge car on an incoming train is running low on ice, a radio message may be sent from the train asking the station agent to have several bags of crushed ice waiting when the train pulls in.

Yard Workers

As your train passes through major stations around the country, you'll see railroad employees in hard hats working around the trains—both freight and passenger. This is tough, dangerous work. You'll see them hanging onto ladders on the sides of rolling cars and working in between railcars for the coupling and uncoupling process. They talk with the engineer by radio and help direct him when he's backing up to add more cars to the train. They'll do this by calling out car lengths ("Two cars . . . one car") then switching to feet ("Twenty feet . . . ten . . . five"). Finally, and this is a curious railroad tradition, they will all call out, "That'll do!" just before the cars bump together.

8

WHEN THINGS GO WRONG

Amtrak ridership has been increasing every year. The railroad is now carrying some 32 million passengers annually over nearly 21,000 miles of track on trips ranging from short commuter runs to cross-country odysseys. It's an immensely complex operation, and usually everything goes according to plan—a real testament to Amtrak's 20,000-plus employees. Sometimes, however, things do go wrong. Knowing what could happen can help avoid a problem or help you deal with the situation if it does occur. Not knowing and being unprepared, mentally or otherwise, can turn a minor inconvenience into a much bigger problem.

To Whom Do You Turn for Help?

When a problem occurs, the best advice is to ask for help calmly, politely, and early. Since areas of responsibility are divided, knowing which of the onboard crew to talk to is helpful too.

- The train attendant has primary responsibility for your comfort and safety. See him or her about problems within your car. If he or she can't help, take your problem to the conductor.

- The conductor is responsible for problems of an operational nature, and, like the captain of a ship at sea, the conductor is the ultimate authority aboard a train.

Some years back, Amtrak streamlined its chain of command and gave more authority to onboard employees. Conductors can now waive penalties for passengers who purchase their tickets after they board the train and can upgrade passengers into sleeping-car accommodations if, in their judgment, the circumstances warrant it (and, of course, if spaces are available). Conductors can also issue Amtrak travel vouchers on the spot in order to help compensate people for problems. The amounts involved are rather small, but just about everyone concerned applauds the management principle involved.

What If You Get Sick?

If you experience some kind of a health problem while onboard, inform your train attendant right away. An unexpected illness can happen to anyone, so don't be embarrassed. And don't wait until you're in a real emergency situation before asking for assistance. For one thing, the sooner you notify the crew, the more time they'll have to consider the options and make the appropriate arrangements.

Start by giving the car attendant your best assessment of what's happening. If it's something you've experienced before, tell him what you think you'll need. He'll probably alert the conductor.

Sometimes the conductor or train attendant will use the train's public-address system to ask if there is a physician onboard who can take a look at you. The conductor may also decide to radio ahead and arrange for paramedics to meet the train at the next station. They'll evaluate your condition and take the appropriate action. Sometimes that means providing medication, or that might mean you'll leave the train and make a trip to a local hospital. Whatever the circumstance, take comfort in the knowledge that a passenger's becoming ill is not an unusual occurrence for Amtrak crews. You'll find them concerned, sympathetic, and capable.

Missed Connections, Everyone's Number-One Problem

Trains running behind schedule are the single biggest recurring headache Amtrak has to deal with, at least in terms of their day-to-day operations. Trains can be late for any number of reasons—bad weather or equipment problems, for example—but the most common cause is freight traffic. Amtrak's long-distance trains operate over track owned by one of the freight railroads, and the dispatchers for those railroads often give priority to their freight trains at Amtrak's expense.

When trains run late, passengers miss connections. Then it becomes Amtrak's responsibility to make things right. Unfortunately, it's almost a certain lose-lose situation for Amtrak. Missed connections, or "misconnects" as they're called, cost the railroad a lot of money—the most recent figure I heard was $140 million a year. No matter what kind of a solution is worked out, the affected passengers will not be happy.

Regular riders, and people who understand the unique complexities of a long-distance railroad operation, are usually much more tolerant of delays than the infrequent or first-time traveler. Veteran rail travelers also take the likelihood of delays into consideration when they make their travel plans, allowing plenty of time between connecting trains. When working out a rail itinerary, my rule of thumb is to figure that the train could be as much as three hours late for each night I'm aboard and to schedule my connections accordingly. For example, if I'm traveling between New York and Chicago (one night onboard), I make sure the second train departs at least three hours after my scheduled arrival. If I'm traveling from Los Angeles to Chicago (two nights onboard), I'll allow no less than six hours in Chicago before connecting with a train going on to the East Coast. In fact, more often than not I will spend the night in a hotel and continue my train trip the following day. It's far better to play it safe than to find yourself finishing your journey on an Amtrak bus.

As a passenger, you'll probably be aware that your train is running late. If it looks like you may miss a connecting train, buttonhole a conductor before you arrive to get his advice on your options. Once you pull into the station—it will most probably be New York City; Washington, DC; Chicago; or Los Angeles; since most scheduled connections take place at one of those stations—go immediately to Amtrak's passenger-service desk in the station. And by that, *I mean run if you can!* A hundred or so other passengers from your train will be in the same situation, so the object is to be one of the first problems solved instead of one of the last. The Amtrak employee at the desk will already be aware that a connection was missed and will probably have some tentative answers for you by the time you show up.

The important thing is to let them know what you want. Be reasonable, however. Amtrak may be willing to meet your request but unable to because of the time of year, the weather, the time of day, the number of people involved, the number of vacancies at nearby hotels, and many other factors. Through it all, keep your cool. The person you're dealing with is the *answer* to your problem, not the cause, and is no doubt doing his or her best to help you.

Problems with Accommodations

Occasionally passengers with sleeping-car tickets find themselves in the wrong type of room or, more typically, *think* they are in the wrong room. Some first-time travelers—especially if traveling as a couple—take one look at a roomette on a Viewliner or Superliner and are convinced they can't possibly spend two days in a room that small. (You can, of course.) But sometimes real mix-ups do indeed occur. Whatever the problem, if you want to change your sleeping-car accommodations, start with the train attendant. If he or she can't help, speak with the conductor. Bedroom space is very tight, especially in the summer months, but sometimes a last-minute cancellation or no-show will enable him or her to put you into a different accommodation.

Plan for a Late Arrival

If your train runs late, that can cause a real inconvenience for someone planning to meet you at your destination. When you make those pickup arrangements, by all means instruct the person to call Amtrak at 1-800-USA-RAIL or go online to www .amtrak.com to get the latest arrival time before leaving for the station. It's a basic precaution that could keep your ride from having to sit in a station parking lot—perhaps in the middle of the night—waiting for a train that's running two or more hours late.

Poor Service

In any organization of 20,000 or more employees, there will be some sour apples, even rotten ones. That certainly doesn't excuse poor service, but it should serve to remind us all that maintaining a high level of competent service is an ongoing effort for any company, large or small.

It helps to be a little understanding yourself. For instance, if you're traveling in a sleeper and ask for a meal to be served in your room, remember that your attendant is looking after the needs of 30 or 40 people. He has to go to the dining car to place your order, go back when it's ready, and then bring it to your room. In the meantime, other passengers are asking to have their beds made up, and there may be a station stop coming up where he has to board new passengers. Cut the attendant some slack if you can. Train attendants and serving personnel in the dining cars have very tough jobs, and sometimes even the best of them will get cranky. Try to keep things in perspective, and don't let one person having a bad day spoil your trip. In the unlikely event that you run into a real problem employee, seek out the conductor. If you're not satisfied with the action taken, note the employee's name and, after you get home, contact Amtrak about the problem. (How-to details are at the end of this chapter.) But do it! Amtrak can't deal with problem employees if you don't go to that trouble.

Rattles and Squeaks

As mentioned in an earlier chapter, the railcar in which you're riding has probably been around a long time. The constant motion of the train can cause strange noises to develop, and some can drive you crazy when you're trying to sleep. Usually it's something easy to find and simple to fix—slamming a washcloth in a rattling cabinet door, for instance—so at least make the effort. The next step is to call your attendant, who will probably be able to locate the problem and take care of it quickly. On rare occasions, mysterious squeaks and rattles just can't be silenced. When that happens, it may be possible to change rooms. Otherwise you'll just have to tough it out. Heck, if a rattle will bother you that much, you won't be sleeping much anyway. (I must confess that the myriad sounds produced by a moving sleeping car is like a lullaby for me.)

Problem Passengers

Occasionally the stranger sitting next to you can turn out to be something of a problem—a constant talker, for instance. When it happens on a plane, most of us just suffer through it for three or four hours. On a long-distance train, however, a chatterbox can become a 48-hour ordeal. At the very least, you can get up and retreat to the lounge car for a while.

But if your seatmate or someone nearby turns out to be something significantly more than just an annoyance—making sexual advances or being drunk or quarrelsome, for instance—you can and should ask for help. First you should notify your train attendant, then the conductor. Amtrak personnel are more than willing to take firm action against the occasional serious troublemaker—to the point of putting the person off the train, bag and baggage.

The conductor is the ultimate authority in these matters. One told me with a smile, "Occasionally there'll be a group in the lounge car that gets rowdy from drinking too much. I tell 'em pretty firmly to settle down and if they don't, I'll just put the ringleader off the train. When that happens, his pals are like little lambs the rest of the way."

In extreme cases, the local state police are contacted by radio and a patrol car meets the train where the tracks cross a major highway. I was once aboard the Desert Wind (a train that, alas, no longer operates) when it stopped at a grade crossing somewhere near the Nevada-Utah state line. An obnoxious character, who had staggered aboard the train in Las Vegas and had been drinking steadily ever since, was suddenly confronted at his seat by two state troopers and hustled off the train to the enthusiastic applause of several dozen of his fellow passengers. When last seen, he was twisted around looking back at us through the rear window of the police car, on his way to at least one night in the Caliente, Nevada, jail. Incidentally, in order to avoid a loud argument or worse, a disorderly passenger is told once to shape up but is given no second warning before actually being put off the train.

Equipment Failures

Mechanical breakdowns occur and can be very disruptive, depending on how and when they happen. Things are improving, but for many years severe budget restraints forced Amtrak to keep a limited amount of equipment in more or less constant use and to stretch out the time between equipment maintenance and overhauls.

The most significant problems, as you might expect, occur when locomotives break down. Even a partial loss of power at the head end can disrupt an entire schedule. For instance, if you're on the California Zephyr heading out of Denver and up into the Rocky Mountains and one of the engines fails, it could be enough to delay the entire train until a replacement unit arrives.

The most common equipment problem is the breakdown of one or more of the toilets. Sometimes it's mechanical, sometimes they're clogged, and occasionally in the winter they freeze. Whatever the reason, it's unpleasant and inconvenient for all concerned, passengers and crew alike. (For more than 50 years, toilets in the older cars simply emptied onto the tracks. Because they were so simple, they almost never failed. Many train-travel veterans still say the federal mandate to require all Amtrak cars to have self-contained toilets was expensive and unnecessary. There are good arguments on both sides of that issue, as you would expect.)

Electrical problems in the dining car can be bad news for the entire train. When the ovens or grills go down, the kitchen crew has to improvise. Sometimes the only answer is a frantic phone call to a fast-food restaurant near the next scheduled stop. One way or another, however, they always manage to make sure folks get fed.

Follow Up on Your Complaint

There may be a certain amount of nostalgia attached to the image of the grizzled old railroad veteran, one who was brought up on steam and has railroading in his blood. The odds were against Amtrak in its early days, and hard-nosed railroad people were necessary to make it all work and keep things running. The trouble is, many of those old timers thought of passengers as a necessary evil—just a particularly bothersome type of freight—and that attitude was felt by passengers.

With the passing years, the old-time railroad men left Amtrak, and a new crop of younger executives took their places. As a result, there is a much broader understanding that, first and foremost, Amtrak is in the service business. So should you follow up by reporting problems you might encounter? You bet! How else can someone in a position of authority improve or correct things? You should know that Amtrak takes all complaints seriously. The complaints are categorized, the source of the problem is tracked down, and, in my experience anyway, a reasonable effort is made to take corrective action.

Amtrak wants to deal with problems quickly, so the preferred means is to make your complaint or comment by phone. Call Amtrak's main number, 1-800-USA-RAIL, and ask to be connected with customer relations. They are available weekdays (except holidays) from 7:00 AM to 10:00 PM EST.

You can also use e-mail. Go to www.amtrak.com and click on "Contact Us," then follow the instructions. Of course, there's always snail mail. Write to Amtrak Customer Relations, 60 Massachusetts Avenue NE, Washington, DC 20002.

To help Amtrak pursue your complaint most effectively, be prepared to provide specific details, stick to the facts, and be as brief as possible. Avoid the temptation to gripe about relatively trivial problems. Most important, be polite and keep things unemotional. Remember, the folks you're talking to are on your side.

Whichever way you choose to make contact, remember that Amtrak is a very large organization, and it performs a complex service for millions of people. Things are bound to go wrong from time to time. Give them a reasonable amount of time to investigate and make things right. Above all, don't just take your grievance home and bad-mouth the entire Amtrak system to all your friends. Outraged letters to the editor won't solve anything either, and complaining to your representatives in Washington could have a negative effect on what is already inadequate federal-government funding. In other words, by all means go ahead and complain, but try to keep things constructive.

9

PASSENGER TRAIN EQUIPMENT

As you will notice, both Amtrak across the United States and VIA Rail in Canada use a variety of equipment. We'll get into some specifics later in this chapter, but first let's focus on the basic standards that are common to all or most railcars.

Most passenger cars are about 85 feet long, give or take a foot or two, and no more than 10.5 feet wide. The traditional single-level railcar is about 13.5 feet high, but newer cars are taller. The bi-level Superliners, which Amtrak began adding to its fleet in the 1970s, measure 16 feet, 2 inches from the rails to the top of the car itself. The single-level Viewliner sleeping cars are 14 feet high. Dome cars, still being used on Canada's premier trains, have a glass viewing dome mounted on top of a standard railcar, which increases the height to 16 feet. Height is an important consideration when determining which type of car will be assigned to any given train. For example, on a number of eastern routes, Superliners can't be used because they're just too tall for some of the bridges and tunnels along the way.

Each railcar has a total of eight wheels, four at each end. Those four wheels form a single unit called a truck. (In Europe, it's called a *bogie*.) The number of wheels on a locomotive varies depending on what it's used for. Some have eight wheels, others have twelve, and some of the really heavy-duty freight locomotives can have as many as sixteen wheels.

Locomotives

All told, Amtrak has more than 330 passenger locomotives in its fleet. Most Amtrak trains are pulled by one of three basic types, but others are used for specialized jobs.

Amtrak's Southwest Chief, with two P-42 locomotives at the head end, pauses for a crew change in Albuquerque, New Mexico. PHOTO COURTESY OF THE AUTHOR

The workhorse of the Amtrak fleet is the diesel-electric P-42 locomotive, first put into service in the late 1990s. You can't miss these brawny machines. They look big and powerful, as indeed they are, and can reach speeds of 100 miles per hour. Each produces 4,250 horsepower, meaning that two of these units can haul a train that previously would have required three engines. To provide an example in another context, one P-42 locomotive can produce enough electrical power to run more than 700 homes. Unlike its predecessors, the P-42 has a modular design, so a faulty component can be pulled out and replaced in much less time than a similar repair in one of the older engines. P-42s are used throughout the Amtrak system, with the exception of the Northeast Corridor between Boston and Washington, DC, which is electrically powered.

There is a power car—it's not called a "locomotive"—at each end of a high-speed Acela trainset. PHOTO BY GENO DAILEY

Amtrak's high-speed Acela trains have what is called a "power car" at each end of the trainset, which is the term used to describe the entire consist. Once assembled, these trainsets are treated as a single unit, and cars are rarely added or removed. Both of the Acela power cars are driving the train when it's moving, with the engineer controlling both with one set of controls. The all-electric Acelas draw their power from an overhead wire, the *catenary*, and only operate on the Northeast Corridor, where they reach speeds of 150 miles per hour along several stretches of track.

Amtrak's regional service trains running in the Northeast Corridor (Boston–New York–Washington, DC) are hauled by these powerful new ACS-64 all-electric engines, known as "Sprinters." PHOTO BY CHRISTOPHER BLASZCZYK

The newest engines added to the Amtrak fleet are the all-electric ACS-64s, built by Siemens. Seventy were ordered and, as deliveries began in late 2013, they replaced older engines being used along the Northeast Corridor (Boston–New York–Washington, DC) and on the Keystone service (New York–Philadelphia–Harrisburg). Nicknamed "Sprinter," this engine generates as much as 8,600 horsepower and is among the more powerful engines in the world. (For reasons best known to old-time railroaders, these all-electric machines are referred to as "engines" or "motors" but not as "locomotives.")

In addition to the Acela trainsets and trains pulled by the Sprinters, two other types of all-electric engines have been used

Many of Amtrak's regional trains running between Boston and Washington, DC, have been hauled by these powerful all-electric HHP-8 engines. PHOTO BY CHAO-HWA CHEN

in the Northeast Corridor. The HHP-8s are easily recognized because they have a sleek, sloped-nose styling similar to that of an Acela power car, but they pull standard Amfleet coaches. The HHP-8 trains don't run quite as fast as the Acelas, and some of them make a few more stops.

For years, the AEM-7 engines hauled trains along the Northeast Corridor at speeds in excess of 100 miles per hour. PHOTO BY GENO DAILY

The other engine is the venerable AEM-7, which looks like an old shoebox. By the time you read this, most of them will probably have been retired, replaced by the new Sprinters as they've been delivered and put into service. I always liked the AEM-7s, though, probably because they had a brute-strength look about them and the same general appearance as a lot of the European locomotives.

Other locomotives in Amtrak's fleet are smaller and less powerful and are used in various rail yards around the country to assemble long-distance trains.

If you're traveling in the Pacific Northwest, you may ride in one of Amtrak's Talgo trainsets. These Spanish-built trains provide what Amtrak calls its Cascades service between Eugene or Portland, Oregon, and Seattle, Washington. An additional two

A sleek Talgo trainset en route to Seattle waits in the Portland, Oregon, station for passengers to load. PHOTO COURTESY OF THE AUTHOR

daily trains using Talgo equipment make the run between Seattle and Vancouver, British Columbia. The very first look at a Talgo can be a bit startling. The power car at each end of the trainset is much taller than all the cars in between, and the whole package can appear a bit out of balance at first. But these trains can get up and go. The roadbed won't yet allow the Talgo equipment to run at the speeds for which they were designed, but they are very comfortable and have proven to be popular with the traveling public.

Talgo trainsets include coaches—both standard and business-class services—and a Bistro car, which provides a variety of drinks, snacks, and simple meals heated in an onboard microwave oven.

Information on how locomotives operate can be found in chapter 10, "How It All Works." For a description of the engineer's job, see chapter 7, "Who's in Charge Here?"

Baggage Cars

There is one baggage car on every long-distance train, and it's located immediately behind the locomotive and in front of the first passenger car. This is where Amtrak carries baggage (including bicycles) that has been checked by passengers. Amtrak's own company material is also carried there: cartons of printed timetables to resupply stations along the route, bulk paper goods, and sometimes nonperishable supplies for the dining car.

Amfleet Coaches

There are two kinds of Amfleet cars. Amfleet I coaches are used for short-haul runs, have a vestibule at each end of the car, and will seat 72 passengers. They're used on all-coach trains that run in the Northeast Corridor, plus on short-haul trains operating in the East and the Midwest. The other version—Amtrak refers to them as Amfleet II cars—is used on the overnight trains running in the eastern part of the United States, specifically the Silver Meteor and the Silver Star, which operate between New York

Amfleet coaches are used on most Amtrak trains running east of the Mississippi River.
PHOTO BY GENO DAILEY

and Florida; the Crescent, which runs between New Orleans and New York; the Cardinal, which runs from New York through West Virginia and Kentucky to Chicago; and the Lake Shore Limited, operating daily between Chicago and New York/Boston. These coaches were designed to accommodate 59 passengers and are more spacious, offering passengers more legroom and leg rests on each seat.

You'll be able to identify either type right away, because the exterior shape is more rounded than the classic passenger railcar. You may also notice that the windows in Amfleet I cars are rather small compared to newer equipment. When these railcars were being designed during the late 1960s, there was some concern that the windows might pop out from the vacuum created when two trains, each traveling at 125 miles per hour, passed each other on adjacent tracks. Hence the smaller windows, and the problem never occurred.

Amfleet coaches have two comfortable seats on each side of a center aisle. The seats recline and an airline-type tray folds down from the back of the seat in front of you. There's an overhead reading light and a luggage rack above every seat. Each car has two lavatories, one of which is designed to accommodate a wheelchair.

Amfleet Café Lounge Cars

These are the cars that provide food service on Amtrak's all-coach trains. There are several versions of this car in service in the Northeast Corridor and on other short-haul routes in the East and the Midwest. They are also on the overnight trains in the East, which also carry a full-service dining car. But they all offer some kind of seating arrangement at either end, with a snack bar in the center of the car staffed by an attendant. The usual fare includes a variety of salads and sandwiches, some served cold and some that are heated in a microwave, plus an assortment of other snacks and drinks, including beer and wine.

High-Speed Acela Service

The Acela trains operate along the Northeast Corridor and represent Amtrak's entry into the world of high-speed rail travel. The trainsets are streamlined and ultramodern, and they certainly look the part. However, for a number of reasons, most of which have to do with the track over which they operate, the Acelas manage to reach their top speed of 150 miles per hour on only a few rather short stretches. In fact, it takes the regional service trains only 30 to 40 minutes longer than the Acelas to make the run between Washington, DC, and New York City.

As you would expect, the fare for an Acela ticket is higher than the cost to ride the slower regional trains. For me, the extra exhilaration that comes from riding in one of these sleek trains is worth the difference.

Amtrak considers any seat on one of the Acela trains to be business class. Indeed, the seats are wide and comfortable and, as in business class on regional trains, you get free nonalcoholic drinks in the cafe car when you present your business-class ticket stub. The upgrade available on an Acela train is to a first-class car, which gets you a meal served at your seat, as well as the free soft drinks. You pay for that perk, of course: the cost of the upgrade is about a hundred dollars.

Check Out the Quiet Car

Quite a few Amtrak trains now include quiet cars, where the rules prohibit cell phone use and loud conversations. You'll find these safe havens from the din of today's world on both the Acelas and the regional service trains running in the Northeast Corridor between Boston and Washington, DC; on the Hiawatha service between Chicago and Milwaukee; on the Keystone service in Pennsylvania; and on several of the Midwest corridor trains. There is no extra charge to sit in a quiet car, but please note that seating in the quiet car is unreserved. My advice? If you have to trample a little old lady to get a seat in the quiet car, do it!

Short-Haul Trains in California

Amtrak's Capitol Corridor service runs from San Jose, California, north through the Bay Area to Oakland and Berkeley, where it swings eastward to Davis and Sacramento, with additional limited service going on to Auburn at the base of the Sierra Nevada mountains. These trains feature bi-level coaches and a cafe car. The entire route takes a bit over three hours to complete.

Similar equipment is found on the Pacific Surfliner trains, which run over a 350-mile route in the southern part of the state from San Luis Obispo by way of Los Angeles and Santa Barbara to San Diego. The most frequent service is between L.A. and San Diego.

Amtrak also operates what's known as the San Joaquin service; its trains run from Sacramento through the Bay Area, the vast San Joaquin Valley, and Fresno to Bakersfield. These all-coach trains, which include cafe cars, use bi-level railcars known as "California Cars."

The Capitol Corridor, San Joaquin, and Pacific Surfliner trains all operate under the Amtrak banner, but all three systems are subsidized by the State of California. It should be noted here that Amtrak also operates quite an extensive system of bus connections in California, which allow passengers from the various trains to reach a great many cities and towns not served by rail.

Viewliner Sleeping Cars

These are the single-level sleepers in Amtrak's fleet, and they were the first passenger cars that Amtrak was able to create from square one. These cars were designed for use on overnight trains running in the eastern part of the United States. There are now

50 Viewliners in service, and another 25 sleepers and 25 dining cars are being built and put into service. Viewliner sleeping cars are used on the Lake Shore Limited, running daily between Chicago and both Boston and New York; on the Silver Meteor and the Silver Star, which are the two trains running daily between New York City and Florida; on the Crescent, which operates daily between New York and New Orleans; and on the Cardinal, which runs three days a week between New York and Chicago on a southern route through Washington, DC, and over the Blue Ridge. (There are no Viewliner coaches; Amfleet II equipment is used to provide coach service on those trains.)

A Viewliner sleeping car, part of the Crescent's consist, awaits passengers before departing from New Orleans. PHOTO COURTESY OF THE AUTHOR

The most obvious innovation found in the Viewliner sleepers is the second row of windows, which provides viewing (and helps to minimize the claustrophobia) for passengers in the upper berths. Each Viewliner sleeper can accommodate up to 30 people in 15 different rooms.

Every Viewliner includes three large two-person bedrooms, one of which is designed to accommodate a person with a disability and a companion. The other two bedrooms can connect to form a large suite with plenty of room for four people. Each bedroom includes a washbasin, a toilet, and a shower. There is also a small clothes closet and space for storing two small- or medium-sized suitcases.

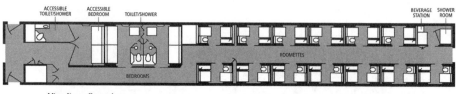

Viewliner floorplan.

The twelve roomettes are smaller—a lot smaller—but will also accommodate two people. Because the roomettes are much narrower than the bedrooms, whoever draws the upper berth will especially appreciate that second window. Each roomette includes a fold-down washbasin and a toilet. There is a very high shelf that will take two small suitcases, although they will be hard to reach when the upper berth is lowered. Passengers in the roomettes have access to a shower that's located at the end of the car.

The Superliner Fleet

These bi-level cars are used on all of Amtrak's long-distance western trains and on three trains running in the east: the City of New Orleans, the Capitol Limited, and the Auto Train. Superliners are larger and heavier than Amfleet or Viewliner cars, so the ride is generally smoother and more comfortable. Passengers move from car to car on the upper level only.

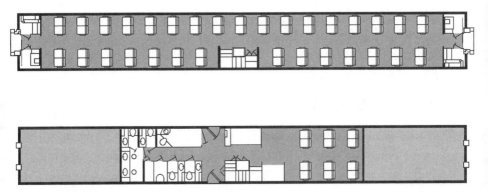

Upper- and lower-level floorplans for a Superliner coach.

Superliner Coaches

There are minor variations in the way these cars are laid out, but a typical Superliner coach can accommodate 70 or more passengers. Most of the seating is on the upper level, although many of the coaches have seats on the lower level usually reserved for disabled or elderly passengers who would have trouble climbing the narrow stairway. There is plenty of room for baggage. Stash your big suitcases in the large storage racks near the lower-level entrance to the car. Don't worry about leaving your big bags there. Just be sure that each one is clearly identified so someone with a similar-looking piece doesn't take yours by mistake. There is also a luggage rack above the seats running the full length of the car. This is the place for smaller bags and for other items you'll want close by when you're in your seat.

The coach seats are wide and comfortable. Most will recline as much as 35 degrees, and each comes with a fold-out leg rest.

If you have to sleep sitting up, this is definitely the way to do it. Assuming you're not assigned to a specific seat, pick one close to the middle of the car where the ride will be quieter and a little smoother. Don't choose a seat in the last row, because they're in front of a wall and won't recline as far. And, because they face a wall, avoid seats in the first row, too. Not a big deal, but they have just a bit less legroom.

Superliner Sleepers

If it's full to capacity, a Superliner sleeping car will handle as many as 44 people in four distinct types of accommodations. As do the coaches, these sleeping cars have a large luggage rack located on the lower level of the car where you enter. This is where you should store most of your luggage—everything but the personal items you'll be using in your compartment. You will have access to your luggage at any time during the trip, but it's just a lot easier to separate out the necessities and take only those into your room. Don't worry about leaving your bags on the storage rack; problems with thievery are quite uncommon. Just be sure your luggage is locked and clearly and securely tagged with your name and address.

There are fourteen roomettes in each Superliner sleeping car: four on the lower level and ten on the upper. They are small but very comfortable for one person, though they are designed to accommodate two. Facing seats slide together and flatten out to form the lower berth, and the second bed folds down from the wall above the window. Since the upper berth is just 24 inches wide (by comparison, a standard twin bed is 38 inches) and rather close to the ceiling, I don't recommend it for large passengers. There are no toilets or washing facilities in the room, so you'll have to use one of the four lavatories in the car—one on the upper level and three on the lower level. There is also a shower with a changing room on the lower level.

If two people are occupying the roomette, you'll have to leave your luggage in the lower-level storage racks, bringing only toiletries and the bare essentials into the room. If you're in a roomette by yourself, there is a small shelf (it's actually a step up to the upper berth) that will accommodate a small airline-sized carry-on bag. There is a place to hang a couple of garments (coat hangers are provided). Yes, the roomettes are small, but because you pay for sleeping-car accommodations by the room and not per person, this is by far the most economical way for two people to enjoy the privacy and comfort that sleeping cars offer. Remember, too, that all meals for both people are included in the fare.

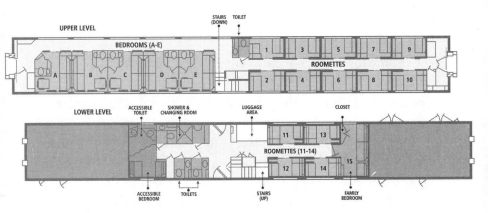

Floorplans for upper and lower levels of a Superliner sleeping car.

The five large bedrooms are all located on the upper level and are very adequate for two adults. By day, there's a long upholstered benchlike seat facing a comfortable chair. The large seat flattens out at night to form a lower berth that's wider than a standard twin bed and can accommodate an adult and a small child. (Two adults will find it either crowded or cozy, depending on the couple's priorities at the time.) The upper berth folds down and is

32 inches wide—a good deal roomier than the upper bunk in the roomettes. There is a washbasin and a lighted vanity mirror in the room, as well as an enclosed combination toilet-shower. (The shower works well, but it's rather awkward with the toilet in the same small phone-booth-sized compartment. If I'm traveling in one of these bedrooms, I use the shower on the lower level.) A small closet provides space for two or three hanging garments. Theoretically, there's room for one or two suitcases, but you'll have to keep them on the seat or on the floor. Either way, it'll be awkward negotiating around them, so, as with the roomettes, it's a lot easier in the long run to leave your bags on the lower-level storage rack and bring essentials in a couple of shoulder bags into these rooms. As with the Viewliner bedrooms, two pairs of these rooms have a folding partition between them that can be opened for a large four-person suite.

On the lower level of each Superliner sleeping car is one family bedroom. They are designed for two adults and two small children, and they do the job quite well. Two of the berths are full-size and will handle moms and dads quite nicely. The other two—one upper and one lower—are definitely for kids, since each is just four feet nine inches long. There is a washbasin, a mirror, and a changing table for infants. There's no toilet, but three lavatories and a shower room are just a few feet from the door. If you need to have luggage in the room because of the kids, it's less of a problem here because there's a lot of space on the seats and floor. As a practical matter, however, I'd keep all your bags on the luggage racks, which are right outside in the corridor.

These family bedrooms offer two big advantages. First, they extend the entire width of the car, providing a look at the scenery on both sides of the train. The other plus is the cost. These bedrooms will sleep four—two adults and two kids—and Amtrak often (but not always) prices these rooms below the cost of the bedrooms, which will only accommodate two adults comfortably. Remember too that all four of you will get complimentary meals in the dining car when you travel in the family bedroom. However, there is only one of these rooms in each Superliner—one more reason to make your reservations as far in advance as possible.

There is also one "special bedroom" in each of these sleeping cars. This is really just a politically correct term meaning that the room is designed for a passenger with disabilities plus a companion. The room is well designed and handles a wheelchair quite neatly. There are two beds, a toilet, a washbasin and mirror, a little closet, and—ta-da!—a storage rack for two suitcases. Like the family bedroom, this room runs the entire width of the car, and there is only one in each Superliner. These rooms may be sold to nondisabled passengers within 72 hours of departure if the rest of the accommodations are sold out.

All Superliner rooms include a small built-in, fold-out table for playing cards or games. There is also a temperature control, and you can adjust the flow of air through a vent in the ceiling. (Note: It's common for these vents not to close all the way, so be prepared to deal with chilly conditions at night.)

There is another quirky little thing about Superliner sleepers. In some of the cars (but not all), you summon the car attendant by pulling, not pushing, the call button. When the button is pulled, a bell rings and a small light goes on outside your door. Don't push the button back in until the attendant arrives. If you do, the light will go out and he or she won't know which passenger rang.

Lounge cars on trains with Superliner equipment are open to both coach and sleeping-car passengers. PHOTO COURTESY OF THE AUTHOR

Superliner Lounge Cars

On any Amtrak train using Superliner equipment, this is the place to be for the best look at the passing scenery. The upper level features comfortable chairs that face huge windows extending halfway up the roof of the car. On the lower level there are booths with tables and a snack bar where you can buy sandwiches, chips, candy bars, and a variety of juice and beverages, nonalcoholic and otherwise. There is also a limited selection of souvenir items: playing cards, postcards, coloring books for the kids, and the like. The lounge-car attendant opens up very early in the morning and, except for well-deserved 45-minute meal breaks during the day, will serve passengers until midnight or close to it. The upper level of the lounge car is for all passengers, whether traveling in coach or sleeping car, and is open and available all night.

All meals are family-style in Amtrak dining cars, which is a great opportunity to get to know other passengers. In this case, however, *family-style* meant one big family.
PHOTO COURTESY OF THE AUTHOR

Superliner Dining Cars

The diner is located in the middle of the train next to the lounge car so that no passenger is too far from either car. Food is prepared in a gleaming stainless-steel kitchen on the lower level and sent up in a dumbwaiter. The menu offerings change periodically but are pretty much the same on all trains. One or two regional dishes are often featured: for instance, on Southern and most Western trains, grits are usually an option at breakfast, along with hash brown potatoes. (There's a lot more about dining-car procedures and protocol in chapter 6, "Life Onboard.")

Pacific Parlour Car

These cars are only found on the Coast Starlight on the run between Los Angeles and Seattle, but what a delight they are!

The upper level includes a small kitchen and bar, table seating for a dozen or so passengers, and a lounge area with comfortable, overstuffed seating. There is a large flat-screen TV set up in a mini-theater on the lower level. These cars are for the exclusive use of sleeping-car passengers, who can choose to take their meals here or in the adjacent dining car.

Superliner Cross Country Café Cars

The basic idea behind the Cross Country Café was to combine both dining facilities and the amenities of a lounge all in one railcar. It was a good idea in theory, but the new configuration was never really accepted by passengers or the crews that staffed these cars. The design was modern and stylish—quite attractive, really—but somehow it just wasn't as comfortable and inviting. Interestingly, Amtrak crews seemed to find the set-up somehow inefficient and that, they felt, affected the quality of service they were able to provide. Amtrak quickly got the message and has wisely reconverted the dining area in these cars to the traditional arrangement with tables for four.

Superliner Transition Sleepers

Also referred to sometimes as "the dorm car" by Amtrak crews, this is always the first bi-level car in a Superliner consist, located right behind the baggage car. As the name implies, this car provides sleeping quarters for most of the onboard crew members. There are no large bedrooms in this car; all the sleeping accommodations are roomettes. Sleeping-car attendants sometimes occupy roomette number 1 in their cars, but they'll use the dorm car if all the regular rooms are sold, which is the case much of the time. The lower level includes toilets and a shower for the conductors and other crew members. Amtrak has also begun selling some of the roomettes in this car to regular passengers. In fact, I found myself in one of those rooms on a recent trip from Chicago to Seattle on the Empire Builder. Frankly, I liked it: there was a lavatory very near my room, and because the crew was working throughout the train, it was nice and quiet both day and night.

10

HOW IT ALL WORKS

Back in the late 1990s, Amtrak was carrying about 20 million passengers a year. In the decade that followed, that number increased to almost 29 million in 2008, and by the end of 2013, it was up again—to 31.6 million. About the only thing that will limit continued growth in ridership is a lack of seats and beds in which to put passengers. People are turning to trains due mostly to high gas prices, more and more automobile congestion, the higher cost of flying (not to mention the increase in delays, security hassles, and other aggravations), and a greater awareness of the environmental benefits of rail travel.

The Amtrak system includes a total of some 21,000 miles stretching coast-to-coast. Amtrak itself owns only about 750 miles of that track, most of it along what is called the Northeast Corridor, which is the route running between Boston and Washington, DC, by way of New York City. Most everywhere else, Amtrak trains are operating over track owned and maintained by private freight railroads, usually referred to as "contract" or "host" railroads.

Hauling that many people all over the country, not to mention feeding and providing beds for many of them along the way, is a complicated business, and it takes a lot of people and equipment to make it happen.

For example, it sounds simple to say that the California Zephyr runs between Chicago and the San Francisco area. But remember that the train runs every day in each direction, and it's a two-night trip. So, at any given moment, Amtrak needs *six* complete trains to operate the California Zephyr: two are en route heading west, another two are heading east, and two more are getting ready to depart at either end of the route. Each of those six trains requires nine cars and two (sometimes three) locomotives. That means, at a minimum, Amtrak needs 54 railcars and a dozen locomotives just to run that one long-distance train. Then, of course, there are three other western trains that run two-night trips: the Sunset Limited, the Southwest Chief, and the Empire Builder. In addition, there are eleven other trains that operate over routes that require one overnight to complete. Amtrak also has what they call "protect locomotives" located in strategic places around the country and ready to be pressed into emergency service—there are some in Denver, for example, in case one of the Zephyr's locomotives should fail.

There are some obvious differences between passenger and freight operations, but the basic technology and operating procedures are pretty much the same—whether it's an Amtrak train carrying 300 people from Seattle to Los Angeles or a freight train hauling coal from a Wyoming mine to a power plant near Chicago.

The Track

When you stop and think about it, it's the track that makes rail travel different from every other form of transportation. Railroads spend a lot of time and money on the construction and maintenance of their track. It's important too, because poor track means trains must run at slower speeds; that in turn means reduced revenues for the railroad.

The first step in laying track is to carve the path (it's called the *subgrade*) out of the terrain and, as much as possible, level it off. This is done by removing earth from the high spots and using it to fill in the low areas. Look for this as you travel. You'll immediately be aware of the terrain rising and falling as it passes your window while the actual roadbed remains more or less level.

Once this subgrade has been prepared, two layers of ballast are added. The first is coarse gravel; the second is crushed rock or crushed slag. These two layers of ballast can be as much as 2.5 feet deep, depending on the condition of the subgrade.

Next come the cross ties—traditionally wood, but more and more made from concrete—which are embedded in the top ballast. Wooden ties are placed a foot apart (3,000 for every mile of track); concrete ties are larger and heavier and are placed two feet apart. Concrete ties are used more in areas where there is heavy or high-speed train traffic. They also should last up to 25 years before needing to be replaced. Under the same conditions, a wooden tie, even when it has been chemically treated to resist rotting, will only last for about seven years.

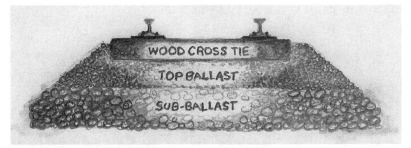

Railroad track is laid by fastening rails to wood or concrete cross ties on top of two layers of gravel or crushed rock.

When wooden ties are used, heavy metal plates, called *tie plates*, are placed on the ties. The rails are laid over the tie plates, then both are fastened to the ties with track spikes, which are really just huge nails. Tie plates are embedded in the concrete ties when they're formed, and the rails are fastened to the ties with heavy metal clips. There are minor variations, but generally that's the way all track is laid.

The two rails are laid exactly four feet, eight-and-a-half inches apart, which is known as *standard gauge*. The importance of establishing a standard width for track is obvious: It means an individual freight car can be hauled virtually anywhere in North or Central America. Parallel tracks are laid 14 feet apart—that's the distance from the center of one track to the center of the adjacent track.

There are a number of narrow-gauge railroads in this country. These rails are just three feet apart to accommodate smaller locomotives and cars designed for operating on steep grades and around tight curves in mountainous terrain. Most of these narrow-gauge railroads have become tourist attractions and provide excellent opportunities to experience railroad operations typical of another era—not to mention a chance to view spectacular scenery up close. (You'll find more information about scenic excursion trains in the back of this book.)

Traditional 39-foot rails are bolted together using a metal plate. See the small space between the rails? That's what produces the clickety-clack sound. PHOTO COURTESY OF THE AUTHOR

For years, individual rails have been 39 feet long—not really an odd number, since they were originally hauled on standard 40-foot flatcars. They're laid end to end and bolted together at the joints. It's this joint that makes the clickety-clack sound when the car's wheels pass over it. Today, when track has to be replaced, quarter-mile lengths of welded rail are most often used. It goes down much faster, and because the joints are some 1,300 feet apart and are welded together, the clickety-clack sound is gone. That, of course, is how you can tell when your train passes onto a stretch of welded rail.

The rails themselves vary in size, weighing anywhere from 112 to 145 pounds per yard. The size of the rail used depends on the amount, weight, and speed of traffic it's going to get. Heavy-duty rails are found on main lines, with lighter-weight track used for spurs and sidings.

You'll probably notice track work going on in many locations during your train trips. The equipment used is fascinating to watch. One machine (actually, it's several machines mounted on a number of articulated railcars) will remove the old wooden ties, level the ballast rock, put new concrete ties into position, and install welded rail—all in one operation. In fact, as this incredible machine is functioning, the front part is rolling on the old rails, while the rear is actually riding on the new rails it has just installed.

It's also amazing to remember that for years, railroad workers laid track using only hand tools. Incidentally, back in the late 1800s, most of those tools were made by the Gandy Manufacturing Company. The word *Gandy* was stamped on the handle of every pick, shovel, and hammer. That's why, even today, track workers are still called *gandy dancers*.

Every so often you may see one or more of the wooden cross ties smeared with white paint. That means those ties have either been marked for replacement or for treatment with a chemical preservative. Occasionally you'll also see one cross tie painted bright yellow. That tells the engineer where to stop the train so he or she won't activate crossing lights and barricades at a grade crossing up ahead. There's no sense in stopping all that automobile traffic if the train isn't ready to proceed across the intersection.

The Wheel

More precisely, perhaps, it's the *flange* on the wheel that's the important element and what makes a train's wheel different from all others. The flange is that one-inch ridge projecting from the inside edge of the wheel. In combination with the flange on the wheel at the other end of the axle, it's what keeps the wheel on the rail and the train on the track.

Here's something else unique about the way a train works: the wheels of a railcar are press fit onto the axles with powerful

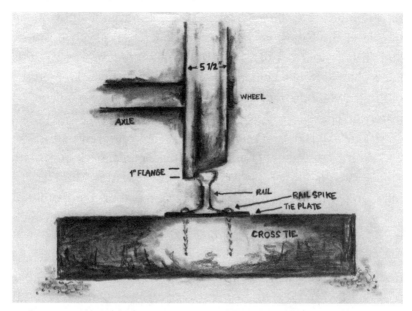

Two things make a railroad different from other forms of transportation: the flange on the inner edge of the wheel and the fastening of the wheel to the axle.

hydraulic presses, and the entire unit turns. You'll notice it immediately if you look carefully at the wheels of a train rolling by at
a slow speed. It's done that way to ensure that the wheels stay
on the rails, and it provides better distribution of the immense
weight of the railcar.

I found that quite interesting, but it immediately raised
another question: as the train proceeds through a curve, even I
can understand that the outside wheel has to travel a somewhat
greater distance than the wheel on the inside of the curve. But
how is that possible if both wheels are fastened to the axle and
are turning at exactly the same rate? Why isn't the outside wheel
skidding to keep up with the inside wheel?

There are two unusual things about a railcar's wheel set: (1) the wheels are, in effect,
welded to the axle so all three parts turn as one unit, and (2) the wheels aren't flat
where they sit on the rail.

In the illustration above, notice that the part of the wheel
touching the rail has been fashioned at an angle. (It's been exag-
gerated here to help illustrate the point.) As the train travels
through a right-hand curve, centrifugal force pushes each railcar
to the left. That causes the outside wheel to have a slightly greater
diameter *where it rests on the rail* than does the wheel on the

inside of the curve. And *that* means the outside wheel covers that small extra distance through the curve with the same number of revolutions as the other wheel. And no skidding.

It All Starts with the Locomotive

The proper term for this monster is indeed *locomotive*, but railroad people also use the terms *engine* and sometimes *moto*.

When it rolls off the production line, every locomotive is assigned a number that is unique all across the country. No two have the same number, regardless of which railroad may own them.

When speaking about a modern railroad locomotive, most people refer to it as a "diesel." Well, they're half right. Technically, it's a *diesel-electric* locomotive. Its diesel motors (there can be several in one locomotive) are not actually used to move the train but to power electric alternators that generate direct current (DC), which is sent to traction motors on each of the locomotive's axles. That's what makes the train go. In addition to powering the traction motors, a locomotive's generators run fans for removing heat and the air compressor for the braking system, and they provide electricity for the rest of the train.

There are also all-electric locomotives. Instead of producing their own electricity, they draw it directly from an overhead wire, called a *catenary*. These locomotives are much more powerful than the diesel-electrics, and they're faster too.

In any discussion of railroad locomotives, *traction* is the key word. That's why locomotives are heavy—deliberately weighted—to provide as much traction as possible. Traditionally, traction motors have used DC, but that's changing. Some newer locomotives now have AC (alternating current) traction motors because they use less electricity and are therefore more fuel efficient. AC locomotives also have more pulling power—three AC locomotives can replace five DCs—and they require less maintenance.

Unlike with automobiles or airplanes, the engineer sits on the right side of the cab when he's operating the locomotive. A second engineer occupies the left-hand seat. This second engineer is fully capable of operating the locomotive and, in fact, frequently relieves the engineer at the controls. Short-haul trains often have only one engineer.

The only set of controls is on the right side of the locomotive cab in front of the engineer. There's a throttle to increase or reduce power to the traction motors, a control for the air brakes, and a little handle or button that blows the whistle. Of course there are a number of gauges that allow the engineer to monitor all the machinery, the fuel reserves, and the train's speed.

The engineer blows the whistle as the train approaches grade crossings where automobile traffic crosses the tracks. On many locomotives, the loudness of the whistle can be adjusted according to how hard the handle is pulled. Engineers will often ease up a bit at night when passing through a residential area, when they can clearly see that there is no traffic near the grade crossing, or when the train is moving at slow speeds. Pull that handle all the way, however, and the whistle will make your ears ring!

A built-in device called an *alerter* is found in all locomotives. If, over a period of 20–25 seconds, the engineer doesn't adjust the throttle, apply the brakes, or blow the whistle, a loud horn sounds and a bright light starts flashing in the cab. It pretty well guarantees that the engineer won't become distracted from his duties or fall asleep. If the engineer fails to respond by touching one of those controls or pressing a special button after the horn and light have been activated for a few seconds, the brakes will be applied automatically and the train will come to a safe stop. These devices are in place should the engineer become unable to operate the locomotive for any reason.

Head-End Power

Most of us take electricity for granted around the house and at work. Flip a switch and the light goes on just about every time. That's true on a train, too, but making sure it happens every time is a bit more complicated. A fully-loaded passenger train requires a lot of electric power. In the coaches and sleepers, electricity powers the air conditioning, the lights, and the outlets for electric razors and hair dryers. It provides hot water for washing up and showering. In the lounge car there is a microwave oven and refrigerators—all are run by electricity. And, of course, there are all those passengers watching movies and playing games on their various electronic devices. The biggest user of electricity in the consist is, as you would expect, the dining car with its ovens, ranges, grills, freezers, refrigerators, dishwashers, and water heater. There's even a dumbwaiter in the Superliner diners to carry food from the kitchen on the lower level up to the hungry passengers on the upper level. It, too, is run by electricity.

We've already talked about how diesel motors in the locomotive run generators to produce the electricity that moves the train. The electric power to run all those lights and appliances comes from the same source: from a special generator used just for that purpose in the locomotive. It's referred to as *head-end power* by the crew; you'll frequently see it abbreviated simply as HEP.

Long before passengers arrive, the service crew is onboard preparing the train for departure. They all need to see what they're doing, of course. In particular, the dining-car crews need to have all of their appliances working to store perishable food and to start preparing food. Before the locomotive is attached to the train, that electricity comes from a cable provided at the station. It's called *hotel power.*

Coupling

The coupling device that joins one car to another has two principal features: a drawbar and a knuckle on the end of that drawbar. The drawbar is attached to the car's frame and is constructed so it will slide forward or backward some five or six inches to provide slack. The knuckle looks like a cupped hand that grips and locks

The coupling mechanism between two freight cars. The knuckles make the connection and the drawbars provide the slack that allows a locomotive to move a freight train's massive weight. PHOTO COURTESY OF THE AUTHOR

with the knuckle on the other car. The cars are also connected by hoses to provide air pressure for the braking system and by cables to carry electricity from the locomotive throughout the train. The knuckles hook together automatically when two cars are pushed firmly together, but the complete coupling process requires a railroad worker to manually connect the air hoses and electric cables. When *uncoupling* cars, the worker simply releases a lever on the knuckles and the cars are pulled apart, while the hoses and cables part by themselves.

Train Orders

Immediately before departing from the train's point of origin, or wherever the engineer boards the train en route, he or she is given a set of train orders. These are a sheaf of papers which authorize that specific trip and notify the operating crew of any changes from normal track conditions along the way. These could include locations where crews are working on the track or *slow orders* for other sections of track. Trains operate at slow speeds over new track until it has had a chance to stabilize. Train orders can also be called *track warrants*.

Starting to Move

Smooth starts are much easier with a passenger train, because there are a lot fewer cars and little or no slack between them. Engineers pride themselves on smooth starts, which, with practice, can be done consistently.

Starting a freight train of 100 or more cars is quite another matter. Theoretically, it's just not possible for a locomotive to move all that weight. It does, though, and the secret is in the coupling mechanisms on all those freight cars. There's roughly a foot of slack between each car in the train. When the freight engineer wants to start the train moving, he or she first gets rid of all the slack by backing up enough to compress the entire train. Then, when the engineer starts the locomotive moving forward, the slack is gradually taken up and the train starts moving literally one car at a time. Once all the cars are moving, the locomotive can keep them rolling and even speed up and slow down. But it was the *slack* that got them all started.

Stopping a Train

Being able to stop a train is critically important and can be a tricky thing to do. It is, after all, a massive amount of moving weight and sometimes moving at high speed. For example, an eight-car passenger train traveling at 80 miles per hour requires a minimum of three-fourths of a mile to stop, even under emergency braking conditions. Much greater weights are involved with freights; as would be expected, they are that much more difficult to stop. A 100-car freight train can weigh more than 10,000 tons and, even traveling at just 30 mph, will simply not be able to stop in less than one mile.

There's really only one way to stop any rolling vehicle—by applying pressure against the wheels. That's the way we stop cars, and it's the way trains are stopped too. There is a brake on every wheel of every car of every train.

Braking was done manually on the earliest trains, but it wasn't until about 1900 that air brakes became standard equipment on all railroad cars, whether freight or passenger. The air brakes on every car in the train are controlled by the engineer from the locomotive cab, although, in an emergency, the conductor can activate the brakes from anywhere on the train.

The brakes are operated by using compressed air carried throughout the train by hoses that are connected when any two cars are coupled together. The first air brakes used the compressed air to force the brake shoes against the wheels. That method worked well as long as nothing went wrong. But if the air compressor failed or if a hose broke anywhere along the train, the resulting loss of air pressure meant the entire braking system failed, leading rather quickly to spectacularly unpleasant consequences. Then in 1887 in Burlington, Iowa, George Westinghouse had a very simple but very bright idea: instead of using the air pressure to force the brake shoes against the wheels, use it to hold them *away* from the wheels. In that manner, the brakes would automatically be applied if the system failed for any reason, and the train would stop. There have been frequent changes and improvements ever since, but the basic principle behind the air brake still works—and it's still the way trains are stopped.

There is another braking system worth mentioning. *Dynamic braking* is used to very gradually slow the train without applying the air brakes. In the simplest terms, instead of sending electricity to the traction motors to move the train, the whole process is reversed. The turning wheels are used to power the traction motors and generate electricity. The resulting drag causes the train to slow gradually. That electricity has to be used in some way, so it's put to work operating blowers that cool the traction motors. Any excess is dissipated through giant grids on the roof of the locomotive, like the coils on top of your electric stove. A rough—*very* rough—equivalent is slowing your family car by slipping it into second gear.

As a passenger, you can frequently tell whether the engineer is using the dynamic brakes or the air brakes. For one thing, air brakes slow the train much more rapidly. You can also hear them quite clearly—not the escaping air pressure but the sound of the brake shoes being applied to the wheels beneath your car. There is no noticeable sound when the dynamic brakes are applied, but you can usually feel a very slight bump just before the train begins losing speed—it's the slack between the engine and the baggage cars being compressed.

"Spotting" the Train

The tricky part to stopping a passenger train is more the where than the how. The object is to stop the train at just the right spot so that passengers waiting on the platform can step right into their coaches or sleepers and boxes, crates, and heavy suitcases can be unloaded right out of the baggage car onto the waiting carts. The engineer often gets some help in spotting the train by radio from the conductor, the baggage handler, or the station agent. If the train is longer than the platform—often the case in small-town stations—the engineer will have to "double-spot" the train, meaning the train will stop to unload and board passengers into the sleepers, then pull ahead to repeat the process for passengers riding in coaches on the rear.

Hills and Curves

When it comes to railroading, flatter is better. (That is, in fact, why railroad tracks were often built along the banks of rivers.) Hills, referred to as *grades*, can be a problem. Because of the train's immense weight, the steeper the grade, the more difficult it is to negotiate. The engineer's main concern is to keep the locomotive's wheels from slipping, causing a sudden loss of traction. To keep that from happening, he must apply just enough power to do the job, reducing speed gradually if necessary. Driving your family car up a slope in icy conditions is a pretty good comparison. Speaking of ice, poor weather conditions just make an engineer's job that much tougher. Most locomotives are equipped with sanders, which sprinkle sand on the rails just ahead of the locomotive's driving wheels to give them better traction. Take a close look at the wheels of a locomotive when you next have the opportunity, and you'll see what looks like a small metal tube pointing right down at the track directly in front of the wheel. That's it—that's the sander.

Railroad people measure the steepness of a grade in terms of percent. A one-percent grade means that the track rises (or falls) one foot for every 100 feet of rail. For a typical Amtrak passenger train, grades of two percent can be handled without any particular problem. Operating a freight train up such a grade is more complicated, because they're a lot heavier and a lot longer. The steepest grade on any mainline track in the United States is 4.7 percent. That's crossing the Blue Ridge Mountains near Melrose, North Carolina. How steep is that? Well, railroaders consider anything more than 1.8 percent to be *mountain grade.*

With a train, *down* can often be a much bigger problem than *up*. The whole principle of a steel wheel on a steel rail is to reduce friction to a minimum in order to move those massive weights.

That's well and good, but the result is what's called a lack of rolling resistance—it simply means that once a train gets rolling, it can be hard to stop. If it's coming downhill, even a hill that would be unnoticed by the driver of an automobile, a train can react like a roller coaster and accelerate. As I've mentioned elsewhere, an engineer can frequently find him- or herself at the head of a long train that's actually going downhill and uphill—trying to speed up and trying to slow down—all at the same time. So how does a freight engineer handle a train? The same way a porcupine makes love: very carefully.

Keep to the Right

Where there is double track—that is, two tracks running parallel to each other—trains usually stay to the right. There are exceptions, as you will probably notice, but they are usually caused by track work of some kind.

Speed Limits

In most parts of the country, the maximum speed allowed for Amtrak trains is 79 mph. Why 79 and not 80, you ask? Well, federal regulations require that any train operating at 80 mph or faster must have a device in the locomotive cab that picks up and visually displays trackside signals for the engineer. Since most Amtrak locomotives outside of the Northeast Corridor have not been so equipped, their speed has been limited to 79 mph.

That is changing however. In 2009, the Federal Railroad Administration directed that all US railroads begin to implement a system known as positive train control (PTC). The PTC technology can, if necessary, automatically override actions by a train's engineer—if, for example, he or she should fail to stop before passing a red signal. The new system will be in place on all trains by 2015. For Amtrak, the net result will be greater safety and higher speeds where track conditions permit.

This is certainly not to say that many trains don't go faster than 79 mph today. On the Northeast Corridor between Boston and Washington, DC, Amtrak trains routinely travel between 105 and 125 mph, with the high-speed Acelas reaching 150 mph along a few stretches. In parts of Illinois, Missouri, Michigan, Pennsylvania, and upstate New York, Amtrak trains travel at speeds up to 110 mph. Apart from the speed limits, how fast the train goes depends on several factors, including track conditions, the weight of the train (meaning the number of cars), the type and number of locomotives pulling the train, and whether that automatic signaling device has been installed in the engine cab.

Communication

In the old days, members of the train crew communicated among themselves with visual signals, such as waving their arms or, at night, lanterns. Today it's all done by handheld radios, linking the conductors with the crew in the head end. The most powerful radio on the train is in the locomotive cab, and with it the engineer can communicate with the railroad's dispatcher, who may be hundreds of miles away. The engineer can also receive radio messages from the crews of other trains, from Amtrak personnel at stations they pass, from work gangs laying new track, and from other official sources using the railroad frequency.

When members of the onboard service crew need to communicate among themselves, they most often use a closed-circuit intercom or the train's public-address system. Sometimes they use both, as when you hear something like the following over the train's PA system: "Conductor to the IC, please." That could be just about anything—perhaps a passenger in one of the coaches has asked to be upgraded into a sleeping car and the car attendant there needs to ask the conductor if there are any unoccupied roomettes.

Trackside Signs

During your railroad journey, you'll see a lot of signs beside the track, obviously meant to communicate information to the crew in the head end. Once explained, the meanings are pretty obvious. I found that knowing what those signs mean added to the interest and enjoyment of my train trips.

While all railroads use signs at trackside to convey the same information to the engineer, there are some differences in the appearance of those signs from one railroad to another—just another reason why engineers have to qualify on each route. Here's a rundown on the most common railroad signs.

Mileposts

These are the most common—and, in many ways, the most important—of all railroad signs. It might take you a few minutes to spot them because they don't all look the same. But as the name implies, there will be one every mile. Some are white posts imprinted with black numerals; others will just be numbers the size of postcards fastened to a metal stake; still others may simply be stenciled onto square sheets of metal and fastened to one of the "telephone poles" running alongside the tracks. Most mile-

Three typical examples of railroad mileposts.

posts are positioned right next to the track, so you'll need to get close up to the window to see them. In any event, you'll quickly be able to identify them because they're numbered in sequence, indicating the number of miles from that spot to a major terminus. Depending on which direction you're traveling, the numbers will get bigger or smaller, one mile at a time.

Mileposts are important because they enable the railroad to pinpoint a location along a route. For example, before starting out on the day's run, the engineer might be given train orders telling him he can expect to find work crews on the track between mileposts 745 and 749. It works the other way, too. If the engineer notices any kind of problem en route, he can radio the dispatcher and refer to a specific milepost.

You can make use of the mileposts to figure out how fast the train is moving. There's a simple formula for that in chapter 6, "Life Onboard." On some routes, curves in the track may have been straightened to permit higher speeds; when that happens, the old mileposts might not be exactly one mile apart. If you want to be really accurate, check the speed several times over any given stretch of track.

Whistle Posts

You'll notice these right away, because there are a lot of them—a black "W" on a small white sign right at trackside. They tell the engineer to blow the whistle because there is a grade crossing ahead—that is, a place where automobile traffic crosses over the tracks. These signs are placed at varying distances from the grade crossing so that trains traveling at the maximum speed

This sign lets the engineer know that there is a grade crossing up ahead and that he or she must blow the whistle to warn automobile traffic.

limit for that stretch of track will give adequate advance warning of its approach. Slower trains will either wait a few seconds after they pass the whistle post before sounding the whistle or they will whistle several times. In some parts of the country, these signs look very different, like a paddle stuck in the ground. On the paddle's blade there are three horizontal stripes and a dot. This is a visual reminder to the engineer of the traditional whistle signal at grade crossings: long, long, short, long. (See "Whistle Signals" on page 182.)

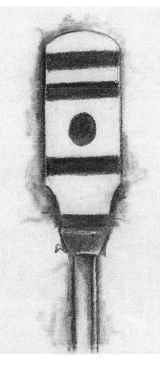

This is also a whistle post, but it's a visual depiction of the traditional warning whistle used for grade crossings: long, long, short, long.

Flags

These come in four colors: red, yellow, green, and blue. Originally, flags were used as warning signals. Three of the colors mean exactly what you would think: red for "stop," yellow for "slow," and green for "resume normal speed." Their purpose is to alert the engineer to something ahead that's on or near the track. Usually a work crew is involved, perhaps clearing a rockslide from the track or simply doing normal track maintenance. Whatever the reason, these flags are a visual warning to the engineer. Blue flags are placed at the front and rear of a standing car or several cars or an entire train, and they alert all concerned that people are working around or under the cars. Although still called "flags" by railroad people, these signs are usually colored squares of metal attached to a little metal pole. (At least they still *look* like flags.) It's easy to miss these flags. They're pretty small, perhaps a foot or so square. Usually you'll see them stuck into the ballast rock alongside the track just next to the rail. At night, electric lanterns in the appropriate color are used.

Speed Limit Signs

You'll also notice a lot of these. As the name implies, they tell the engineer how fast she's allowed to travel. Most of the time there are two numbers posted. The top number is the speed limit for passenger trains; the bottom number applies to freight trains. There is an exact equivalent on many of our highways, where there are sometimes two posted speed limits, one for passenger cars and another for trucks. The principal difference is that signs along a highway tell drivers what the speed limit is between that exact spot and the next sign, while most speed limit signs on a railroad tell the engineer how fast he should be traveling two miles ahead. The reason for that difference, of course, is that it can take that distance for the engineer to reduce his speed gradually from, say, 70 to 40 miles per hour. If the number shown on the sign means the engineer can *increase* the speed of the train, he may do so as soon as the entire train passes the sign. Train crews often refer to these signs as "speed boards." Just to confuse you, on some railroads there are two kinds of speed limit signs: black numbers on yellow signs mounted diagonally on the pole indicate the speed limit two miles ahead; black numerals on white signs mounted level indicate the speed limit at that spot.

There are a number of variations for railroad speed limit signs, but this message is clear: passenger trains may go 70 mph, but freights cannot exceed 50 mph.

Exceeding the posted speed limit is a big no-no in railroading. Inspectors from the Federal Railway Administration are responsible for enforcing speed limits and other safety rules, and they do so by checking train speeds with radar guns. One or two speeding offenses by an engineer, even a few miles an hour over the limit, and he or she will be looking for a new career.

Crossing Ahead

This is a black "X" on a white sign and tells the engineer that the tracks his train is on will be crossing another set of tracks up ahead. (Just to confuse us, some railroads use this sign to warn the engineer that there is a grade crossing ahead.)

Derail Signs

You'll often see these little signs, usually black letters on yellow or orange signs, along sidings as you enter or leave rail yards or stations. Most of the time, the signs spell out DERAIL, but sometimes it's just a large letter "D." Near these signs, you'll see a metal device, often painted bright yellow or orange, attached to a rail. It's designed to deliberately derail a freight car that might otherwise roll out onto the main line and become a safety hazard.

Other Signage

Unfortunately, there is some variation in signage from one railroad to another. For instance, in some parts of the East you may see signs that are shaped like small yellow pyramids. These simply tell the head-end crew that there's a "break" in the rail ahead—meaning a switch or another track is crossing the main line. In Canada, you'll see a lot of small black signs with two white dots, like eyeballs. These tell the engineer to pay attention—there's something just ahead of which he or she should be aware. Most of the other signs that you'll occasionally see along rail routes are there to let the head-end crew know when the method used by dispatchers to control their progress has changed. For instance, "Begin CTC" tells the engineer that the train is now under Centralized Traffic Control; "Begin ABS" means an Automatic Block Signal system is in use from that point on.

Signals and Traffic Controls

You can see a lot of these during any train ride, although you really have to be looking for them because they're placed either right alongside or directly over the tracks. There are a number of different kinds, but whatever the shape, almost all use green, yellow, and red lights to communicate with the engineer. These signals are used to keep proper spacing between trains running on the same track. In almost all cases, they operate automatically. Each signal has a number prominently displayed on it that corresponds to the last mile marker, plus however many additional tenths of a mile. If the train comes up to a red signal en route and the engineer is unaware of the reason he is being told to stop, he can call the dispatcher and say, "I've got a red signal at milepost 172 dot 7."

The track over which your train is running is divided into sections, called *blocks*. There's a signal located at the beginning of each block to control the rail traffic moving through that block. Sometimes the distance between signals can be many miles, while at other times it might be just a matter of a few hundred yards. How frequently the signals appear depends on how far ahead the engineer can see, where another track joins the main line, the location of a switch, and other factors. Generally, signals are set to keep a following train at least two blocks apart from the train up ahead.

For many years, signal lights were operated by electricity carried through wires strung on poles running alongside the track. In many areas, you can still see those poles passing by outside the train window. More recently, especially since welded rail is used more commonly, the electric impulses used to operate the signals are actually carried to them through the rails themselves.

In most cases it's pretty obvious, but here's what those signals mean:

- **Green** (also called a *clear* signal): Proceed at normal speed.

- **Yellow**: Approach (meaning pass the signal) and be prepared to stop at the next signal.

- **Red**: Stop and proceed at slow speed (usually 15 mph).

- **Absolute Red**: Stop and do not proceed.

There are a number of ways to distinguish an absolute red from a normal red signal—typically a second red light will be illuminated or a single red light will be flashing.

Whistle Signals

If you're traveling in a railcar close enough to the engine to hear the whistle, you'll soon notice that there are several different whistle patterns being used. Here's what they mean:

- Long, long, short, long: This signal is used when approaching a grade crossing and is blown when the locomotive passes a whistle post. (I've asked several engineers and many conductors about this particular whistle pattern, and while it is specifically included in the engineer's manual, no one can tell me about its origin. The consensus seems to be "railroad tradition.")

- Short, short: The train is about to move forward.

- Short, short, short: The train is about to back up.

- Long: This means the engineer is going to set—meaning to test—the brakes. This is done when the train is stopped and members of the train crew are outside to visually inspect the application of the brakes.

- One long blast: You'll hear this at a station where the train has been stopped for several minutes and passengers are wandering around on the platform or in the station. It means "Get back on board immediately." Do it! They aren't kidding.

By the way, *whistle*—both as a verb and as a noun—is still used, even though the term comes from the days of steam locomotives. Today, technically, it's an air horn.

Hot-Box Detectors

These remarkable electronic gadgets are an important safety feature for our modern railroads. They're located in metal cases on either side of the track and equipped with sensors that look for overheated journal bearings, referred to as *hot boxes* by the railroads. Potentially, a hot box is big trouble. These bearings connect the railcar to the axle—when one goes bad, it means steel is in contact with steel at high speed. The axle and wheel become hot and, left undetected, can fracture, causing an instant derailment.

As soon as the train has passed over one of these detectors, an automated spoken message is broadcast on the train's radio frequency and heard by both the crew in the head end and the conductors, wherever they are within the train. Here's a typical transmission from a detector, along with an explanation of what it all means:

"UP detector"	The detector belongs to the Union Pacific railroad.
"Milepost one, six, two"	This identifies the train's location.
"Train speed: six four"	We're traveling within the 65-mph speed limit.
"Track one"	Where there's double track, this eliminates any confusion in case there's another train passing on the second track at the same time.
"Number of axles: four, eight"	Yes, it's talking about us; and furthermore we're now sure the detector is functioning properly.
"No defects"	Good! Our train has no hot boxes and nothing is dragging on the track.
"Repeat: no defects"	Just making sure we got the critical information.
"Detector: out"	The message is over.

The conductor will usually radio the engineer following a detector's report just to be sure the message was heard in the head end. The following is typical:

"No defects, number seven"	The conductor tells the engineer that the detector reported no defects. The reference to the train number is to be certain the engineer knows the message is directed at him or her. (In this case, it's the westbound Empire Builder.)
"Highball, seven"	The engineer acknowledges the conductor's message and tells him or her we're proceeding at track speed, the maximum permissible.

Sometimes the engineer will acknowledge the conductor by simply opening and closing his microphone a couple of times. Those two *click-clicks* are very disappointing to a rail fan listening on his scanner.

Although it's rare that a detector discovers a hot box on a passenger train, the electronic voice leaves little doubt about what to do: *"You have a defect. Stop your train! Stop your train!"*

If this does occur, there is almost always a set-out track—you and I would call it a *siding*—near most hot-box detectors where the train can be diverted while the crew assesses the problem. The car with the hot box is usually cut out and left on the siding while the rest of the train continues on its way—a minor inconvenience in the case of freight trains, but clearly a much bigger problem if it's a passenger car full of people. When *that* happens, Amtrak people really earn their pay. The onboard crew tries to accommodate the displaced people throughout the rest of the train. If that's not possible—and frequently it isn't—they'll arrange for alternate transportation and, if necessary, pick up the cost of meals and overnight lodging, too. But, let me emphasize, this is an *extremely* rare occurrence with passenger equipment, which is carefully inspected after each trip and checked periodically along the way.

Other High-Tech Equipment

Every so often, while passing through a rail yard, you may notice a pair of posts on each side of a track with what appear to be floodlights mounted on each. This is a good example of the use of modern technology in the railroad industry. These lights are actually scanners, pretty much like the ones you're used to in the checkout lines at the supermarket. As a freight train passes slowly between these posts, the scanner is used to identify, count, and sort specific freight cars from coded numbers on their sides.

Delays and Why They Happen

Unlike most of the railroads in Europe, passenger trains in North America are required to operate within a system primarily designed to handle freight trains. When an Amtrak train is running on track owned by one of the host railroads, that company and not Amtrak becomes responsible for the train's progress. Amtrak has incentive contracts with many of these railroads, paying bonuses to them for keeping Amtrak trains on time and withholding those payments for poor records. In spite of these arrangements, Amtrak trains can be delayed when dispatchers for these host railroads give priority to their own freight trains. Unfortunately, sometimes that happens—and with some railroads more than others.

The long-distance passenger trains are more likely to experience delays than those on the shorter runs, and that's simply because there's more time for something to interfere with the train's progress. An Acela running between New York and Washington, DC, is on 225 miles of track owned and controlled by Amtrak. It's far more likely to run on time than the California Zephyr, which travels the 2,400 miles between Chicago and Oakland over tracks controlled by two different railroads—Burlington Northern Santa Fe and Union Pacific.

Delays are a fact of life in rail travel, but it will ease the aggravation if you know something about why they occur. Amtrak makes a distinction between *inbound* delays (late arrival) and *outbound* delays (late departure), but they're closely related. In fact, the most common cause of an outbound delay is the late arrival of an inbound train. Amtrak will often hold up a departure if there are passengers on the arriving train who are expecting to make that connection. (You can see how this puts Amtrak in a no-win situation: passengers on the Southwest Chief will be unhappy if their departure from Chicago is delayed waiting for the Texas Eagle to arrive. But if Amtrak doesn't hold the Chief, 15 or 20 passengers on the Eagle will miss their connection and then *they* will be unhappy.)

Inbound delays can cause other major problems for Amtrak too. Arriving trains must be "turned" for the return trip, and if the trains are significantly late, Amtrak crews have less time than they need for that process. And there are a lot of other things to do. The train has to be cleaned, of course, and a mind-boggling variety of supplies have to be checked and restocked: food, fresh linens, and clean tableware for the dining car; ice, snacks, and drinks for the lounge car; fresh pillows for the coaches; and clean sheets, pillowcases, and towels for the sleepers. Most of those beds have to be made up too. There's also a lot going on outside the train, because every arriving train must be inspected before it can go out again.

Once en route, trains can be delayed for any number of reasons, and they often are. An engine can break down with the closest replacement unit hours away. Perhaps there's an electrical problem in the dining car, and an Amtrak electrician has to come aboard somewhere along the way to fix it. If it's unusually hot outside, perhaps there are heat kinks in the rails caused by the steel expanding; under those conditions the train could be poking along under a "slow order." Maybe it's nothing more than an unusually heavy amount of freight traffic that slows the train's progress. Causes for delays seem to come in an endless variety. Here are just a few I've experienced over a number of years while gathering material for this book:

- The westbound California Zephyr is delayed three hours when a Union Pacific freight ahead of us breaks a wheel and the track has to be repaired.

- The northbound Silver Meteor is delayed 30 minutes in Savannah, Georgia, while paramedics come aboard to examine a sick passenger. (He's finally removed from the train and driven off in an ambulance.)

- The southbound Silver Star's departure from Washington, DC, is delayed four hours when a flash flood washes out a section of track 20 miles south of the city.

- The eastbound Empire Builder is delayed a total of 2 hours and 40 minutes after waiting on sidings to allow four other trains to pass (three freights and the westbound Builder).

- The northbound Montrealer is delayed 45 minutes while the train crew removes an old refrigerator and a mattress placed on the track by vandals. (This train no longer operates— although, I hasten to add, not for that reason.)

- The westbound Capitol Limited is delayed 90 minutes just outside Harpers Ferry when the train loses head-end power from one of the locomotives.

- The northbound Coast Starlight is delayed 20 minutes in Oakland where the tracks ran down the middle of a main street fronting Jack London Square. Someone parked a car on the tracks, locked it, and went off shopping. (Yes, of course it's true. No one could make up something like that!)

It's interesting to note that of those seven delays, only one— the equipment failure near Harpers Ferry—can be laid directly at Amtrak's door. The others were caused by weather, one of the freight railroads, or quirky human beings. The delays experienced by the Empire Builder are fairly typical; this one occurred because the BNSF dispatcher gave priority to the other trains.

By the way, if the train is delayed for more than just a few minutes, the conductor should provide an explanation over the PA system. (One of my pet peeves: they often don't do that.) Don't bother asking one of the service crew, your car attendant, or one of the servers in the dining car—they're usually too busy with their duties and probably won't know why the train has stopped anyway.

Hard-core rail fans traveling with their scanners (see chapter 6, "Life Onboard") can usually find out why the train has stopped by eavesdropping while the engineer and the conductor discuss the delay on their radios.

Even when a train is late, it can still be considered "on time." Most airlines record a flight as having left on time if the plane pushes away from the gate within 15 minutes of its scheduled departure time. In much the same way, Amtrak determines if a train has arrived on time by establishing what are called *on-time tolerances*. They vary according to the length of the trip, but if a train's arrival falls within this grace period, it's still considered to be on time.

AMTRAK ON-TIME TOLERANCES	
Length of Trip	Grace Period
0–250 miles	10 minutes
251–350 miles	15 minutes
351–450 miles	20 minutes
451–500 miles	25 minutes
501 or more miles	30 minutes

Making Up Time

Contrary to popular belief, the engineer can't really make up lost time by increasing the speed of the train. The schedule assumes the train will be running right at the posted speeds, and the penalties for exceeding those speeds are severe.

Once a train falls behind schedule, there are really only two ways to make up the time. The first is by hurrying up the loading and unloading of passengers and baggage at station stops along the way; the second is through padding in the schedule itself.

Padding is extra time built into the schedule. It's like a family having a little emergency stash in a savings account to cover unexpected expenses. If a train is delayed for 20 minutes because of track work somewhere along the route, a little padding in the schedule here and there helps get it back on schedule.

For example, take a look at this excerpt from a recent Amtrak timetable:

Train 29	Capitol Limited	Train 30
4:05 PM	Washington, DC	1:10 PM
4:29 PM	Rockville, MD	12:10 PM

According to the timetable, when train 29, the Capitol Limited, starts out on its route from Washington, DC, en route to Chicago, it will take 24 minutes to cover the 13 miles to its first stop, Rockville, Maryland. But for train 30, the *eastbound* Capitol Limited that's completing its overnight trip from Chicago to Washington, that same Amtrak timetable allows a full hour for the train to travel those same 13 miles. That extra 36 minutes is padding to cover any delays that might have occurred in the 764 miles between Chicago and Rockville.

Weather Problems

Trains are usually bothered less by weather conditions than cars or planes, but rain, snow, or cold can and do cause problems for railroads. Heavy rain can wash out track, or, more precisely, the roadbed on which the rails and cross ties have been laid. Steel rails contract and occasionally break in cold weather, and drifting snow can slow or even stop a train. Railroads have special locomotives equipped with snowplows or snowblowers that are constantly on standby when heavy snows are forecast. Prolonged periods of subzero temperatures can freeze switches. And fog sometimes causes delays because it can severely reduce visibility for the head-end crew.

Whatever the cause, and whether it's passengers or freight, railroads will go to great extremes to keep rolling or, failing that,

Giant snowblowers like these are used to clear tracks through mountainous areas where heavy winter snows can block tracks and stall trains. This would make short work of your driveway, wouldn't it! PHOTO BY JEFF TERRY

to resume service as quickly as possible. Washed-out track can usually be repaired in a relatively short time, but not always. In the summer of 1993, for instance, there was such severe and widespread flooding throughout the Midwest that service on Amtrak's western trains was disrupted for several weeks. And in January of 2008, heavy rains in the Cascades caused a massive landslide north of Chemult, Oregon, that buried tracks and diverted or shut down rail service for almost five months.

There are also safety procedures that automatically go into effect when the weather turns dicey. For instance, it's standard procedure for crews to reduce speeds once the temperature drops below 0 degrees Fahrenheit for more than a few hours. Preventative measures are also taken. If you're traveling on a mountain route or in areas that are very cold in the winter, look for cylindrical tanks located next to switches. They contain propane used to feed gas burners—very similar to the burners on the top of a gas stove—which fire up automatically to heat the switches and prevent them from freezing in bitterly cold weather.

Delays or interruptions in train service can also be caused by other natural events. Earthquakes can twist rails out of alignment. In mountainous areas, rock- or snowslides can obstruct tracks. Look for "slide fences" in many mountain passes. These are several horizontal rows of wire strung on posts located beside the tracks in slide-prone areas. Their function is not as a barrier for falling rocks—rather, the instant one or more of the wires is broken by a rockslide, a signal is automatically sent to the operating railroad. Trains are warned by radio about a possible obstruction at that location, and a crew is dispatched to clear the track.

Courtesy from Crew to Crew

The headlights of a locomotive—which are very bright, as you might expect—can be dimmed in much the same way you dim the lights on your car. Depending on circumstances, most engineers will dim or even turn off their headlights when meeting or overtaking another train.

Train crews help each other out and will look carefully at a passing train for any sign of a problem, such as smoke coming from an axle under one of the cars or a shifting load on one of the flatcars. If a freight train is waiting on a siding as your train goes by, the engineer of the freight will usually radio your crew to say something like, "Good run-by, Amtrak," when you've passed. The foreman of a track repair crew will do the same.

Split Trains

Some trains separate into two trains part way through their route. For instance, the Empire Builder leaves Chicago as one consist but divides into two trains two nights later in Spokane, Washington. The main section continues on to Seattle, while a new engine hauls a sleeper and a couple of coaches off to the Southwest and terminates in Portland, Oregon. Three days a week, the Sunset Limited and the Texas Eagle depart from Los Angeles as one long train, but they split apart in San Antonio where the Eagle heads north to Chicago and the Sunset continues east to New Orleans. The Lake Shore Limited begins its westbound run in two sections: one departs from New York City's Pennsylvania Station, the other from South Station in Boston. They join together at Albany and continue on to Chicago as one long train. In each of these examples, the whole process is reversed when those trains make their return trips.

Passenger Manifest

A few hours before a train's departure time, Amtrak's computer prints out a list of all passengers booked on that trip. The printout provides the conductor and car attendants with the names of all passengers, the stations where they will be boarding, their destinations, and, in the case of sleeping-car passengers, their car and room numbers. The manifest will also note if a particular passenger is elderly, handicapped, or might need some special service.

Clean Windows, Please!

Before each trip, most long-distance trains are taken through an automatic car wash (a supersized version of the one around the corner where you take the family car). Keeping the train windows clean is not easy, however. A brief rain squall followed by a dusty stretch of track can undo all that effort within minutes. So can passing through a lot of tunnels. You'll see a lot of blackened freight locomotives operating on the California Zephyr's route west of Denver. That's the result of the heat and smoke from the diesel motors in all those mountain tunnels. Finally, if a train is

Clean windows are important on scenic train rides. In major rail yards, passenger trains are run through giant car washes, but in Jasper, Alberta, before continuing its journey through the Rocky Mountains, VIA Rail's westbound Canadian gets its windows washed the old-fashioned way. PHOTO COURTESY OF THE AUTHOR

late arriving at its destination, there just may not be time to wash the consist before it gets serviced and sent off on its return trip.

Whatever the problems, clean windows should be a priority on all passenger trains. Amtrak justifiably sells itself as the best way to see America, but who wants to see the country through dirty windows? In recent years, Amtrak has started paying much closer attention to what had long been a nagging problem. Ideally, windows should be washed somewhere around the midpoint of the long-distance routes, especially the really scenic ones. And give Amtrak its due: assuming time permits, the California Zephyr gets its windows washed in Denver, and the Southwest Chief gets the same treatment in Albuquerque. It takes time and it's an added expense—but it's important.

Private Railcars

Occasionally you'll find that a private railcar has been added to the rear of your Amtrak train. Most have been lovingly restored and refurbished by wealthy individuals who use them as land-going yachts. Others belong to railroads and other companies that use them as rolling conference rooms. On at least several occasions, inventive companies have used private railcars as the venue for new business presentations to potential clients. Now that's a creative approach!

The railroad expression for these cars is *private varnish,* a reference to the luxurious wood trim once commonly found in such equipment. Amtrak charges $2.75 a mile for hauling these cars around the country, plus additional charges for switching, coupling, or storing these cars en route.

Traveling in a private railcar falls into the everyone-should-do-it-once category, and it may not be as far-fetched as you might think. There are several companies that specialize in running rail tours using these wonderful vintage railcars. For more information, see Appendix C on page 385.

Rail Fans

Finally, a word about the folks who have turned their fascination for trains into a hobby—sometimes a consuming one. They call themselves *rail fans* but are often referred to as *foamers* by railroad employees, meaning that they supposedly begin to foam at the mouth whenever they see a train. For some of these folks, the interest is broad and general; for others, it gets pretty narrow. There are people who collect old railroad timetables, dining-car menus, tickets, posters, or other memorabilia.

During almost any train ride, you'll see rail-fan photographers by the tracks taking your picture as you roll past. Others are train spotters who spend their free time checking off locomotive numbers in notebooks, the object being to have spotted every locomotive of a certain series or all the locomotives owned by a certain railroad.

A few rail fans allow their passion to get in the way of their good judgment. They'll be found wandering around in areas of rail yards that are restricted to railroad employees only. And some "collect" the builders' plates that are attached to every railcar by the manufacturer. The sad fact is, very few passenger railcars still have the original plates in place. Most have been—let's use the right word—*stolen*.

Largely because a very few participate in these illegal or unauthorized activities, rail fans occasionally run into open hostility from some railroad people. More typically, however, they're treated with friendly—and maybe a weary—tolerance. More and more, however, rail fans have become genuinely appreciated. After all, as one veteran Amtrak road foreman pointed out, it's the rail fans who write all those impassioned letters to members of Congress supporting rail travel in general and Amtrak in particular. (Good for them, too!)

11

WHAT ABOUT ALL THOSE FREIGHT TRAINS?

There are more than 560 freight railroads in the United States, although the vast majority serves very specific and usually very small geographical areas. In fact, these local railroads only operate an average of just over 50 miles of track. At the other end of the spectrum, we have what are called the Class I railroads. There are only seven of them, but their trains run over nearly 100,000 miles of track around the country and employ almost 160,000 people. Class I railroads rang up just over $65 billion in revenues for the freight they carried in 2011. Here's a list of those companies (you'll see their identifying logos on locomotives and freight cars everywhere as you ride around the country):

- Burlington Northern Santa Fe (BNSF)

- Canadian National

- Canadian Pacific

- CSX

- Kansas City Southern

- Norfolk Southern

- Union Pacific

Both Canadian National and Canadian Pacific are large enough to be considered Class I railroads by US definition. Together they employ some 38,000 people and operate over nearly 40,000 miles of track in both Canada and the United States, with 3,500 locomotives hauling more than 125,000 freight cars on a typical day. South of our border, two big railroads—Ferromex and Kansas City Southern de México—operate throughout Mexico, and both of them also meet the Class I standard for the size and scope of their operations. These are the only large freight railroads remaining after the financial wreckage and bankruptcies of the late '60s and the mergers and acquisitions that occurred over the last 25 years or so.

It really takes a cross-country train trip before most of us realize how extensive the country's system of freight railroads really is. Freight trains haul every conceivable type of commodity, but coal is still number one. It accounts for about 20 percent of all freight revenues. From just one huge mine in Wyoming, a train pulling 110 cars loaded with coal for Midwestern power plants travels east to the Chicago area every single day of the year. You'll see a number of these trains on almost any of Amtrak's long-distance routes. You'll also begin to appreciate the immense capacity of the grain-producing areas of this continent when you pass trains pulling a hundred or more hopper cars filled with wheat or corn. A special "express freight" runs several times a week carrying California's fresh produce in refrigerated cars direct to a distribution center in New York. Then there are the trains hauling chemicals, frozen food, motor vehicles, petroleum, minerals, lumber, paper, scrap metal, and—well, you name it, and it moves by rail.

Freight Locomotives

Hauling all those freight cars around the country are some 25,000 diesel-electric locomotives. America's railroads take delivery of about 1,400 new locomotives every year. That may sound like a lot—and, of course, it is—but back in 1930 there were more than 57,000 locomotives in service. All but about 600 of those were steam engines.

A pair of freight locomotives hauling hopper cars filled with grain. PHOTO COURTESY OF CSX

The appearance and design of freight locomotives varies tremendously—by weight, horsepower, number of axles, type of traction motor (AC or DC), air-brake configuration, presence or lack of dynamic braking, and so forth. It's no matter, because they're all fundamentally the same underneath: big, powerful diesel motors mounted on a rolling platform. (A more detailed description of how a locomotive operates may be found in chapter 10, "How It All Works.")

There are really only two factors that determine the type of job for which any given locomotive is best suited: *horsepower* and *tractive force.* Horsepower is simply the common way of measuring how powerful the locomotive is, which is exactly the way we measure our cars' engines. Another term for *tractive force*, and certainly more familiar to the layperson, would be *traction.* Whether it's an automobile or a locomotive, all that power can become almost useless if the wheels start slipping. That's what tractive force is all about, and that's why railroad locomotives are so heavy—to increase the tractive force and keep the wheels from slipping on the rails.

Depending on the gross weight of a train, additional "helper" locomotives are usually added to provide more horsepower and more tractive force. The train's weight is determined by the number of cars in the consist and what's in those cars. Obviously, 100 cars loaded with coal will weigh much more than 100 cars loaded with wood chips, but the average capacity of a freight car is about 89 tons.

Passenger trains weigh much less than freight trains, but they need to go faster. That's why passenger locomotives can afford to sacrifice tractive force in favor of more horsepower. It's an oversimplification, but generally speaking freight locomotives are designed to pull very heavy weights at relatively slow speeds, while passenger locomotives are designed to pull less weight but go faster. Until Amtrak's P-40s and P-42s entered service, most of the locomotives used to pull passenger trains were freight engines modified to operate at higher speeds.

Freight Cars

There are about 1.4 million freight cars of all types traveling back and forth across the country. About a third of those are owned by the Class I railroads; the rest are owned by independent railroad car companies, the shippers themselves, and the small regional and local railroads. Somewhere between 50,000 and 70,000 freight cars of all types are built every year to increase the size of fleets and to replace cars that wear out and are scrapped.

The average freight train is about 70 cars long, and many will have well over 100 cars in the consist. In terms of the physics involved, there is almost no limit to how many locomotives a long freight train might be given. There are a number of practical considerations, however. Probably the most obvious is how much of a train's capacity has been sold by the railroad's sales department. But long freight trains can block busy city intersections for a very long time and generate very serious public relations problems. Extralong trains can even cause the railroad itself problems if they block important switches in the rail yard. As it is, freight trains run through many towns across the country. In many cases, those towns have to build and staff duplicate police, fire, and ambulance facilities to make sure that one of those emergency responders won't be delayed by having to wait for a slow freight.

You'll see thousands of freight cars from the window of your train. Part of what's interesting about a train ride is knowing what all those cars are for and what's inside them. There is an almost infinite variety of sizes and designs, but it all starts to take shape if we break them down into a few simple categories.

Boxcars

This is what most of us mean when we say "freight car." It's an enclosed car with a roof and sliding doors on both sides. Boxcars are used to carry a whole variety of general merchandise, particularly items that must be protected from the weather. If your local hardware distributor orders 200 power lawn mowers from a manufacturer, chances are those mowers rode across the country in one of these railroad cars.

A typical boxcar, used for general cargo of all kinds that must be protected from the weather. PHOTO COURTESY OF ORANGE EMPIRE RAILWAY MUSEUM

A lot of boxcars are specially equipped in one way or another. For example, special refrigerated boxcars are used to carry fresh produce from California all over the country. These refrigerator cars have to be equipped to maintain a constant, cool temperature so the fruits and vegetables inside won't spoil in the summer. In the winter, shippers have the opposite problem—fresh produce crosses the country in heated cars to keep it from freezing.

Gondola Cars

Take a common boxcar, cut it in half horizontally, and—voila!—you've got a gondola car, or "gonnie" as the train crews call them. Gondola cars have low sides and ends, a solid floor (meaning the contents can't be unloaded through a trapdoor in the bottom),

There are four openings underneath this hopper car through which its cargo of grain is unloaded. PHOTO COURTESY OF THE AUTHOR

and no top. Depending on the weight of the material they were designed to carry, some gondola cars have higher sides than others. You'll see all sorts of things being hauled in these cars: scrap metal, iron and steel products, and almost anything else that's heavy and doesn't need protection from the weather.

Hopper Cars

These look a lot like gondola cars, except they all have high sides and many are covered. But all hopper cars have one thing in common: the interior walls slope toward trapdoors in the bottom of the car through which the contents are unloaded. These cars are used to carry such things as coal and grain in bulk.

A train of tanker cars. PHOTO COURTESY OF CSX

Tanker Cars

You can identify these cars very easily. They're basically long cylinders with a dome on top through which they're filled. Tanker cars are used for carrying liquids that range all the way from milk to petroleum to some pretty dangerous materials—chemicals, primarily. Many of these cars are pressurized to carry such things as carbon dioxide, which we think of as a gas (providing the bubbles in soft drinks, for example) but which turns into a liquid when it's compressed.

Flatcars

As the name implies, these cars are really nothing more than rolling platforms with no sides or top. The basic flatcar traditionally has been used to carry things such as logs (to sawmills), lumber (from sawmills), and other commodities that can be stacked flat and wrapped or don't need to be covered from the weather. Some flatcars have high reinforced panels at each end, designed to keep loads from shifting either forward or backward with the movement of the train. The military uses flatcars to move tanks, trucks, and other heavy vehicles. You'll often see very large pieces of machinery being carried in this manner.

There's also an entire subgroup of flatcars that are known as *intermodal cars*. They were first designed to carry truck trailers, which are driven to the railroad yard, unhooked, and simply swung aboard this special flatcar. At its destination, the trailer is lifted off the flatcar, hooked to the cab portion of a semitrailer, and driven straight to its destination. Railroad people refer to this arrangement as "TOFC" ("trailer on flatcar") or "piggyback." To the everlasting confusion of the general population, the trains themselves are called "pig trains." Shipping containers are also carried on flatcars, and you will see a great many of these as you travel around the country by train.

A simple idea at work: the stacking of two shipping containers doubles the carrying capacity of a train. PHOTO COURTESY OF THE AUTHOR

Double-Stack Cars

A double-stack railcar is actually a modified flatcar that features a sunken bed, allowing it to carry two stacked shipping containers and still remain under the normal height limit of about 20 feet. The benefits to these stack trains are obvious: trains that could formerly haul 120 trailers in a piggyback configuration can now carry up to 240 containers without adding to the length of the train. These double-stack cars are certainly easy to spot, and you'll see them almost exclusively on western routes. When loaded with two nine-foot-high containers, they are too tall to run on many eastern routes, which run under low bridges and through tunnels without adequate clearances.

Many of these flatcars are now articulated—that is, permanently linked together—so that each set of wheels actually serves two flatcars. The net effect of this ingenious arrangement is to reduce the total number of wheels touching the track, meaning there is a corresponding reduction in drag. That, in turn, translates into a significant savings in fuel costs.

Auto-Rack Cars

You soon get to recognize these cars quickly. First of all, they're high—a full 16 feet. Automobiles and small trucks are driven inside and tied down into position on one of the two or three levels. The sides of these railcars are very distinctive, too. They're made from panels of lightweight aluminum, which are designed to protect the cars and trucks inside from being damaged by material swirling up from the roadbed or—more commonly, I'm sorry to say—from stones thrown by youngsters from the sides of the tracks.

New cars are shipped across the country in special multilevel railcars.
PHOTO COURTESY OF CSX

Huge blades for wind turbines are hauled on flatcars designed for this use.
PHOTO COURTESY OF BNSF RAILWAY

Specialty Cars

If you want to ship some strange kind of cargo by rail, there will either be a specially built car that already exists and can accommodate it, or, if you're going to ship a lot of those things, someone will build a car just for you. For instance, Boeing has some special "high-wide" cars they use to transport airplane fuselages. With the increasing number of wind farms around the country, special cars have been designed to carry the huge blades used on wind turbines.

When it comes to moving freight, time is money. The freight railroads certainly know that and will go to great lengths to keep their trains moving. Crews and heavy equipment are located around the country to go quickly to the site of any derailments, and many millions of dollars are spent every year upgrading track to allow more constant and higher speeds. When a massive landslide closed several miles of track north of Chemult, Oregon, in 2008, heavy equipment and hundreds of men were rushed to the area and worked almost literally without stopping for several months until the tracks were reopened. The freight (like the mail) must go through!

12

SAFETY IS PRIORITY NUMBER ONE

If you spend any time around railroad people, you'll soon become aware that safety is constantly on everyone's mind. And with good reason: with massive weights moving at high speeds, railroading is an inherently dangerous business. The consequences of poor safety practices can mean wrecks, which are hugely expensive. They can potentially cost millions of dollars in damage to equipment and freight, not to mention additional millions when people are hurt or killed.

Every railroad employee is responsible for safe operations and, if necessary, is empowered to override orders from superiors. For example, if an engineer receives confusing or garbled radio instructions from a dispatcher, he can refuse to move the train until he's satisfied that he clearly understands the instructions.

Maintenance

Regular maintenance is just as important to a railroad as it is to an airline. Amtrak performs maintenance and repair work at a dozen facilities located around the country: Albany, New York; Boston; New York City; Wilmington, Delaware; Washington, DC; Chicago; Miami; New Orleans; Los Angeles; Oakland,

California; Seattle; and Beech Grove, Indiana, near Indianapolis. Every locomotive is inspected every day to make sure it's functioning properly. As with airplanes, locomotives are pulled out of service for prescribed maintenance at regular intervals: every 15, 60, and 90 days, and all the way up to complete overhauls every 4 years. Passenger cars go through similar checks and overhauls, although not as often as the locomotives do.

Safety Procedures

Whether it's a railroad, an airline, or a steel mill, the key to safety lies in establishing and rigidly sticking to prescribed systems and procedures. For every function or task in railroad operations, there is one right way to perform it. Regardless of the job, railroad workers know that to deviate from proper procedures is to court disaster.

Speed Limits

Individual railroads set the speed limits for their tracks. How fast a train is permitted to go is determined by the "level of sophistication in the track," meaning the quality of the roadbed and the "superelevation." (That's what you would call the banking or tilting of the track, which counteracts centrifugal force and permits higher speeds around curves.) Once set by the railroads, speed limits are then enforced by Federal Railroad Administration inspectors who randomly monitor selected areas of track with radar guns to make sure limits are observed. There are circumstances when a train might exceed the maximum authorized speed (going downhill, for example), but a horn will sound in the locomotive cab, and if the engineer doesn't use the brakes they are automatically applied. In railroad lingo, that's called a *penalty application*.

Time Off

Every member of the operating crew—meaning the engineers and conductors—has a limit to the number of on-duty hours he or she is permitted to work. The employee is not allowed to work for more than 12 hours, and after that he or she must break for at least 8 hours before beginning another 12-hour shift. This rule is strictly enforced. Once that limit is reached, an engineer or a conductor "goes dead" and cannot continue to operate the train. That's true even if bad weather or mechanical problems have delayed the train so much that time runs out before it reaches a station. In those cases, the crew must stop the train wherever it is and wait for a new crew to be put aboard. Usually Amtrak will have been alerted to the problem in advance by radio and will arrange for a fresh crew to meet the train somewhere en route.

Drug Testing

Railroads have always had strict rules against the use of alcohol or drugs, but they were self-policed. That all changed a number of years ago when an accident occurred in Chase, Maryland. A Conrail engineer, Ricky Gates, ran his locomotive onto the main line and into an Amtrak train, killing a number of people. A subsequent investigation found there were several contributing causes for the accident, but Gates tested positive for marijuana. As a direct result, the federal government began pressing for a universal policy of random drug testing. Those tests are now administered by the railroads to their conductors, engineers, and dispatchers.

There has been an additional if somewhat ironic benefit to come from that accident. The railroad unions and various companies realized that if they didn't work closely and productively together to find an acceptable and meaningful drug testing policy, the federal government would probably do it for them. From this improved relationship between the two traditional adversaries has come Operation Red Block, an anti–drug and alcohol program. It's run by the unions, supported by management, and thought to be effective by all.

Also as a result of what railroad people now refer to simply as "Chase, Maryland," every American railroad must meet specific federal guidelines for the certification of engineers. Before that accident, each company had its own standards and requirements for training, knowledge of rules, and physical exams. Today, however, minimum standards are consistent throughout the industry, and engineers are recertified every three years.

There are lots of other safety procedures unique to railroad operations, but here are a few typical examples to illustrate their variety and depth.

- When preparing to move a locomotive, the engineer will (1) start the bell ringing to indicate a locomotive is about to move and (2) blow the whistle to indicate the direction of movement: two toots, forward; three toots, back.

- Whenever a "civilian"—meaning you or me—rides in the cab of a locomotive, an additional railroad employee must be present to minimize possible distractions for the engineer.

- Radio messages from the dispatcher to the engineer are acknowledged and carefully repeated to be certain that every detail of the message was understood.

- When a blue flag (or light) is placed at the front and rear of a train to indicate that people are working under or around the train, the only person permitted to remove the flag is the one who put it there.

- When backing into a station, the train will come to a "safety stop" 50 to 100 feet from the bumper post, then continue backing slowly before coming to a final stop.

- The second engineer in the locomotive calls out passing signals to be certain they have been seen and noted by the engineer. One of the two will relay that information to the conductor by radio, and the conductor will acknowledge it.

- A train may not leave its point of origin without train orders, which provide the engineer with the latest information about track conditions and contain formal permission to depart.

Safety Equipment

Railroading is still very much a hands-on business, but more and more automation is being introduced, particularly in the area of safety devices. Again, it's impossible to list all of these gadgets, but a good sampling should give you the idea.

- As mentioned elsewhere, in every locomotive cab there's something called an *alerter*, which is designed to make sure the engineer is always in command of the train. If the engineer doesn't change the throttle position, touch the brakes, or blow the whistle (on some locomotives a special button must be pushed) for 20–25 seconds, a strobe light will begin to flash in the cab and a loud horn will sound. At that point the engineer has just a few seconds to perform one of those tasks (as if to say, "Yes, I'm still here and still in control"). If he or she doesn't, the brakes will be applied automatically and the train will come to a stop.

- Located beside the tracks are electronic detectors that broadcast warnings to the train crew if the detectors sense overheated journal bearings (called hot boxes) or any kind of dragging gear. For more information about these devices, see chapter 10, "How It All Works."

- Every locomotive is equipped with an event recorder just like the black box carried in an airplane. Throughout the trip, it records the train's motion and speed and the engineer's use of controls. In the event of an accident, the information from this device will be used to help determine the cause.

- Amtrak is installing video cameras in all of their road engines, meaning locomotives that operate between cities. In the event of a grade-crossing accident, a video record can help determine if the warning lights were flashing and the gates were down when the accident occurred. These video records have other uses, but the reality is that this information is most often used by the railroad to disprove charges of negligence in the lawsuit almost inevitably brought by the victim's family— a sign of the litigious times in which we live, I'm afraid.

- Where trains traveling through mountain passes run close to canyon walls, wire fences are installed along sections where rockslides could obstruct the tracks. When you spot one, you'll realize immediately that these flimsy slide fences couldn't hold back any falling rocks. On the contrary, they're intended to break. When that happens, a warning signal is triggered, and the railroad's dispatcher is immediately alerted.

- Supplementing direct voice communication between the locomotive engineer and the railroad's dispatcher is a whole sophisticated and complex system of signals to control the movement and location of every train. A key element in all of these systems is the implementation of Positive Train Control.

Positive Train Control

By far, the most significant advancement in the area of railroad safety will be the introduction of Positive Train Control, known as PTC. Using global positioning technology and lots of highly sophisticated sensors and computers, PTC will know the exact location and speed of every train anywhere in the country. That information can be used by the system to override an engineer who, for whatever reason, may exceed a speed limit or go through a red signal.

Positive Train Control has been on the wish list of the National Transportation Safety Board for many years, but it was given priority in 2008 following a terrible accident in Chatsworth, California, when a commuter train ran through a red signal and collided with an oncoming train. The engineer, who was one of 24 people killed in the collision, was apparently texting at the time and failed to see the red light. PTC would have automatically stopped that train.

In the aftermath of that tragedy, Congress passed legislation mandating the implementation of PTC by all of the nation's rail lines that carry passengers or hazardous materials. The law also included a mandatory completion deadline: December 31, 2015.

Everyone acknowledged that PTC would be a good idea, but as the railroads began to implement the technology, they realized that the new system was complicated and, of course, expensive. So some of the freight and commuter railroads began pressing for new legislation to extend the deadline, claiming it was simply not possible to have PTC up and running by the end of 2015. Other freight and commuter railroads said they *would* be able to meet the deadline. To address these mixed responses, it was recommended that Congress amend the law to give the Federal Railway Administration the authority to extend the deadline on a case-by-case basis.

Then, in November 2013, a few miles up the Hudson River from New York City, a Metro-North commuter train, heading into a curve at an excessive speed, derailed. Four people died and more than 100 were injured in another accident that PTC would probably have prevented. As of this writing, however, it's uncertain how Congress may respond to any request to extend the PTC implementation deadline.

Grade-Crossing Accidents

This is probably the single biggest safety problem facing America's railroads. Without doubt, it's the most frequent one. On city streets, main highways, and dirt roads, cars cross over train tracks at thousands of locations from one end of the country to the other, and every crossing has the potential for tragedy. Motor vehicles of all kinds are hit by trains with a frequency that is astounding—averaging about once a day, every day. The circumstances vary, but the outcome doesn't: the train always wins. Do you want a graphic analogy? An Amtrak engineer told me that a train hitting a car is roughly comparable to your family car running over a mailbox.

Most of these accidents occur during broad daylight with good visibility and with the warning signals working perfectly. Furthermore, most of the time the driver of the car involved is sober.

Even more surprising, in about a third of all the car-train collisions that occur at night, the car drives smack into the side of a moving train. Speed is almost always the critical factor in these accidents because the driver of the car is "overdriving" his headlights—that is, by the time his headlights reveal the train, he's going so fast that he's unable to stop before reaching the crossing.

An increasing number of deaths occur when a train strikes someone walking on the tracks. Many of these are young people listening to loud music through earbuds or headphones.

Whether the person is in a vehicle or on foot, it's clear that a certain percentage of these incidents are actually suicides or attempts at suicide. Even so, I think we could agree that those deaths and injuries are all equally unnecessary.

It's rare to find a railroad engineer who hasn't been involved in a grade-crossing accident. It's a traumatic experience for all of them, of course. Some handle it philosophically, realizing that they can't feel responsible for the death of someone who drove around a gate and into the path of their train. For others, that's easier said than done. Most railroads recognize that and provide time off and professional counseling to crews involved in fatal accidents. For a very few, however, the experience is enough to force them out of their chosen profession. (More on this very serious problem can be found in chapter 7, "Who's in Charge Here?")

Here are a few commonsense rules for automobile drivers:

- Always assume a train is coming (the same way you would anticipate another car coming if you were crossing a highway).

- Slow down, roll down the window, and listen. You can't hear the train if your window's closed or the radio's blaring.

- Never, ever ignore active warning signals or drive around lowered gates. (This isn't as obvious as it sounds. A driver may see a switch engine parked a hundred yards down the track to the left and assume that's what brought the gate down. Big mistake! It could be another train approaching at high speed from the right.)

- Where there's more than one track, wait a bit when the train passes and watch out for a second train that could be coming from the opposite direction behind the first one.

- Don't be tempted to race a train to the crossing, even if it looks like a safe bet. Because of their enormous size, trains appear to be traveling much slower than they really are. Have you ever watched a big passenger jet on its final approach to an airport? It looks like it's just floating lazily along when, in fact, the plane is probably moving at more than 150 miles per hour.

- Don't ever stop your car on a train track. If traffic's backed up, wait until there's room on the other side before you cross over. If your car happens to stall on the track, get everyone out immediately and call the police. They'll contact the railroad's dispatcher, who will alert the engineer of any approaching train by radio.

Operation Lifesaver

In the early 1970s, the problem of grade-crossing accidents had reached near epidemic proportions, with collisions occurring at the rate of one every 45 minutes around the clock. That's when Operation Lifesaver was started. Operation Lifesaver is a program of information and education aimed at reducing the number of these awful accidents. It's funded by federal, state, and local governments and the nation's railroads. And it has worked—the number of fatalities has been cut in half, although some of the credit certainly goes to the railroads, including Amtrak, for installing warning lights and gates at more and more crossings. State and local governments share in the cost, but improved safety doesn't come cheap. The average cost of one of these gate installations comes in at about a quarter million dollars.

More recently, the industry has started a new campaign to promote safety around railroad tracks. A key element is its website: www.CommonSenseUseIt.com.

Derailments

As the term implies, a derailment occurs when the wheels of one or more cars come off the rails. A number of things can cause derailments. If an overheated journal bearing (a hot box) goes undetected long enough, the wheel and axle will get red-hot and finally break. Sometimes very hot weather can cause "sun kinks," which push the rails out of alignment. Sometimes there's an obstruction on the track that causes the train to come off the rails. Whatever the reason, derailments are a major headache for railroads. When they do occur, particularly if it happens at high speed, there can be a lot of damage to the track and the equipment. Railcars are very heavy, and it takes special know-how and equipment to get them back on the track. There could also be several hundred yards of track to repair. And all of this could be happening many miles from the nearest available manpower or equipment.

The chances of an Amtrak or a VIA Rail passenger train ever experiencing a derailment are remote. In freight operations, however, derailments are not so uncommon. Because they interrupt the flow of freight, derailments can mean big-time loss of revenue to a railroad. It's essential, therefore, that operations get back to normal as quickly as possible. Some railroads have their own crews and equipment on standby for this purpose. Others use one of several companies who are on call around the clock and who specialize in handling derailments.

Safety Rules for You

Some of these warnings may not have occurred to you, and others may seem obvious, but you would be absolutely amazed at some of the really dumb things people do in and around trains.

- When crossing tracks, step *over* the rails, not on them. Railroad workers never step on a rail because they're slippery, particularly if wet, and it's a very easy way to twist or break an ankle.

- Don't walk right next to the locomotive, especially if it's off the station platform. Every so often there's an automatic "blow down," which clears the air brake reservoir with 140 pounds of pressure. Accumulated water, sometimes mixed with just a tad of fuel oil, can spray on anyone who happens to be standing too close at the time. All that pressure can also cause small ballast rocks to fly. Please note that a blow down is an automatic function and is not controlled by the head-end crew. People standing close to the engine are startled when a blow down occurs and sometimes, when they see an engineer laughing, mistakenly think it was done deliberately as a practical joke. Not so.

- Don't try to get to the other side of the train by walking around the rear car. The train could move unexpectedly or another train could be passing on the adjacent track. In either case, you're history.

- Once onboard and walking through the railcars—to and from the dining car, for instance—place your feet wider apart than normal. It will give you better balance. Hold onto seat backs, railings, and the walls of corridors as you go.

- Don't leave your seat without shoes on, and for heaven's sake, don't let your kids run around without shoes. Amtrak makes an announcement about this, but in my opinion, it often isn't given enough emphasis. The principal danger is the moving, overlapping metal plates that passengers walk across when passing between cars. Get one of your tootsies caught in there and the next thing you know, the conductor will be calling ahead for an ambulance to meet the train at the next station.

- Even with their shoes on, kids running around loose onboard or on the station platform cause real heartburn for Amtrak people. A lot can happen to an uncontrolled youngster, and none of it is good. Keep them on a tight leash. (See chapter

6, "Life Onboard," for some ideas on how to keep them occupied.)

- If you find yourself in the upper berth in a sleeping car, hook up the restraining straps designed to keep you from falling out. After all, you're sleeping on a moving train, and it's a long way down.

- Most people don't think so, but it really can be dangerous to open the hinged window in a vestibule door to look out of the train or to take pictures, particularly at high speeds. Dust and debris from the track often flies up into the vacuum created by the moving train, and there can be very little clearance between the train and objects it passes.

- As you ought to do on a plane or when spending the night in a hotel, be sure you know how to get out of the railcar in a hurry if you should have to do so. A number of windows in every car serve as emergency exits. Each is clearly marked and will have a red handle on it. Pull on that handle to remove the rubber gasket holding the window in place, then push the glass out.

Bottom line for all this talk about safety: the railroads have their acts together pretty well. All it really takes for the rest of us to be safe is common sense.

13

TAKING THE TRAIN IN CANADA

Some decades ago, you could cross the entire breadth of Canada on just one train, all the way from Halifax on the Atlantic Coast to Vancouver on the shores of the Pacific. A single-train trip is no longer possible, but you can still undertake that rail odyssey and only have to change trains a couple of times.

Some wonderfully scenic rail journeys, including one I rate among the ten best in the entire world, are offered by VIA Rail, Canada's equivalent to Amtrak and the company operating Canada's nationwide system of passenger trains.

Although it's a huge country covering millions and millions of square miles, 90 percent of the Canadian population lives within 200 miles of its border with the United States. For that reason, Canada's passenger rail system is strung out more or less through the middle of this population—covering an area roughly 4,000 miles long but just 200 miles wide.

Amtrak operates some 2,100 separate trains every week and offers sleeping-car service on a dozen overnight trains every day. VIA operates fewer trains because of the long, narrow area it serves and a much smaller population (about 500 trains a week, most running along sections of the 725-mile corridor between Windsor and Quebec City). Just four of those are overnight trains with sleeping-car accommodations. But don't let those comparisons give you the idea that VIA trains don't have something very special to offer. On the contrary, those trains will take you through some of the most varied and magnificent scenery anywhere in the world, most especially VIA Rail's transcontinental train, the Canadian, which takes passengers on a glorious trip that should be on everyone's list of top-ten train rides in the world.

The Canadian Rail Epic

The story of Canada's transcontinental railway has grown to something of epic proportions in that country, and with good reason. There are many obvious similarities with the United States's transcontinental railroad, but there is one very significant difference: In the United States, people settled the West and the railroad followed. In Canada, the train came first. The idea was to link settlements on the far-off Pacific Coast with the growing cities of the East and, by doing so, encourage people to settle in the vast areas in between. Actually, British Columbia forced the issue by refusing to join the Canadian Federation until 1872, when its leaders secured the promise that a transcontinental railroad would be built within ten years.

And so indeed it was. In 1881, the Canadian Pacific Railway began construction of the railroad, and it was finished just four years later, a tribute to the honest and able people who financed, designed, and built it. It passed through some extremely difficult terrain, in particular an area north of the Great Lakes known as the Canadian Shield, where engineers had to blast their way through hundreds of miles of some of the oldest and hardest rock on earth. Then it was across the prairies, through the Rockies, into the dense forests of the Pacific Northwest, and finally to the sea. In terms of the difficulties involved, the Canadian Pacific overcame natural barriers and weather conditions at least as formidable as those encountered by Americans 20 years earlier.

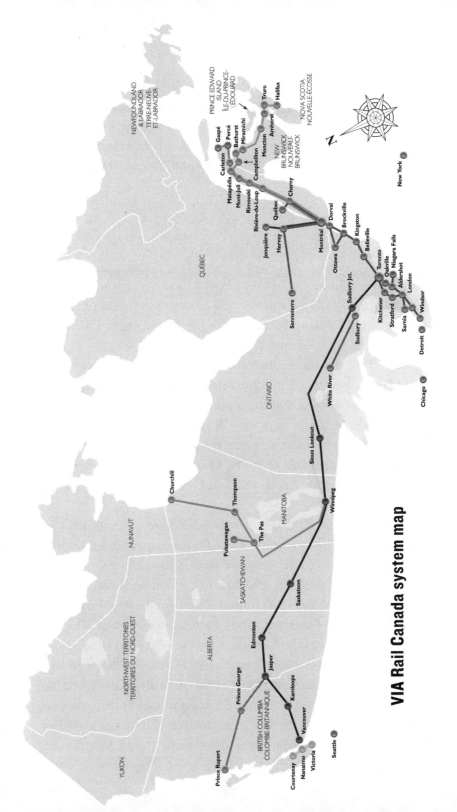

VIA Rail Canada system map

Two other railroads, the Great Northern and the Grand Trunk
Pacific, came a few years later. By the 1920s they had completed
another route farther to the north. The Grand Trunk struggled
financially for many years; for this and other reasons, the two
companies were eventually combined and became the Canadian
National (CN) Railway.

As had been expected, cities and towns sprang up along both
of the transcontinental routes. The Canadian Pacific (CP) in particular took a decidedly paternal approach to the communities it
had literally created. In fact, after deciding that the CP's western
terminus would be the town of Port Moody, a company official
evidently felt the name was uninspired and decreed that the community should instead be named for the British seaman who first
explored the area, George Vancouver. And so it was.

By 1924, the Canadian Pacific was claiming to have settled
55,000 families on 30 million acres of land between the Great
Lakes and the Pacific. While it's possible to argue those numbers,
it is considered a fact that the CP created some 800 cities and
towns in three provinces along its route. Farther to the north, the
Canadian National laid claim to 132 towns, although for many
of those dots on the map, the word "town" was probably an
exaggeration.

For many years, the CP and the CN competed vigorously for
passengers as well as freight. The CP took the additional step of
building along its route what are to this day some of the finest
hotels in the world. Each railroad ran its "name" trains, many
of which reached into the United States for business by terminating in major American cities such as New York, Chicago,
and Detroit. Two of the Canadian Pacific's best were the Moun-
taineer, which ran during warmer months from St. Paul, Minnesota, through the famous resort town of Banff in the Canadian
Rockies to Vancouver. Another CP train out of St. Paul was the
Soo-Dominion to Calgary. The Canadian National focused on
Chicago, with trains from there to Toronto, Montreal, and other

cities. Both railroads ran transcontinental trains within their own country.

Along Comes VIA Rail

Canadian railroads struggled against many of the same problems that beset American trains in the decades after World War II. In 1978 the Canadian Pacific and Canadian National merged their passenger operations. The result was VIA Rail Canada, a "Crown Corporation" wholly owned by the Canadian government. VIA Rail now provides passenger train service on a 9,000-mile system. It stretches coast-to-coast and extends more than a thousand miles north to the town of Churchill on the shores of Hudson Bay. A number of VIA Rail trains—the one to Churchill is a good example—provide the only link to the rest of Canada for hundreds of isolated communities across the northern part of the country. Although operating at a loss, those trains are mandated by the Canadian government. As is the case with Amtrak, VIA Rail owns almost no track of its own, mostly operating instead over tracks belonging to the CN.

Also like Amtrak, VIA has not had an easy existence, waging a constant battle against conservatives in the Canadian government who cannot or will not see the necessity, if not the wisdom, of a national rail transportation system. There have been periodic reductions in both personnel and service, but still the system remains more or less intact. Furthermore, you'll find the equipment to be modern, the service good, and the food really first-rate.

Things to Know About Canada's Passenger Trains

Basically, there really isn't a great deal of difference between VIA Rail's operation and Amtrak's, so there's no reason you can't include a trip on a Canadian train in a rail itinerary. In fact, I encourage it. I would suggest you try putting together your own schedule as much as possible and then turn everything over to a knowledgeable travel agent to double-check what you've done and to handle the actual ticketing. You can also go directly to VIA Rail, of course.

Most of the information contained elsewhere in this book will apply equally to either Amtrak or VIA Rail. There are a few things that deserve mention here, however, either because VIA does them a bit differently or because something bears repeating.

Reservations

Book as far in advance as possible, especially if your itinerary includes riding VIA's transcontinental train, the Canadian, during the summer months. For a number of weeks every year, the train to Churchill is often sold out too. The little town becomes a tourist attraction toward the end of each September and into October when polar bears, waiting for the ice to form on Hudson Bay, come wandering into the area. Whatever the train, if you choose to make reservations yourself, you can do it by visiting www.viarail .ca or by calling VIA Rail's toll-free number, 1-888-VIA-RAIL, or 1-888-842-7245. Schedules for all VIA trains are available online, or you can call the toll-free number for a free copy of their system timetable.

Discount Fares

There are quite a few opportunities to cash in on special low fares. In addition to the normal discounts, many special fares and discounts pop up periodically, so this is an area where a rail-savvy travel agent can be a big help. The VIA reservations agents are also very good about letting you know when a special fare is available. Generally speaking, regular fares are lower if you travel during off-peak times. That can mean certain periods of the year (such as during the winter months, except over the December holidays), on certain days of the week, or on travel to remote areas. There are other discounts, too: seniors 60 and over get 10 percent off, "youths" (ages 12 through 24) get a 25 percent discount on coach fares and 10 percent off in sleepers, and children (2 through 11) travel at half off in coach and get a 25 percent discount in sleepers. Infants under 2 travel free as long as they don't occupy a seat.

Discounted fares may also be available to members of the National Association of Railroad Passengers. NARP is a non-profit organization headquartered in Washington, DC, that advocates more, better, and faster passenger trains in the United States. As of this writing, VIA Rail very generously offers a 10 percent discount on both rail fares and sleeping-car supplements to NARP members.

Canrailpass

This is VIA Rail's equivalent to the now-famous Eurail Pass. Like that pass, it's a good deal as long as you plan to do a fair amount of travel. Basically, VIA Rail passes offer 7 days of economy-class travel within either a 10- or 21-day period. A good travel agent will know how to make sure the fare is computed to your best advantage, but (in my personal experience, anyway) so will a VIA reservations agent. If your itinerary includes travel during a peak season, there may be an additional charge. Even with the pass, you must have a ticket, however, so make your travel plans, get your pass, *then* buy your tickets. The pass is good for coach travel, but you can still upgrade to VIA 1 first class or into sleeping-car accommodations (provided space is available) by paying a supplement. Other benefits are added to the Canrailpass from time to time, so ask about those once your travel plans have taken shape.

Arrival Times

As with Amtrak, long-distance trains are more likely to run late than the short-haul trains. Whatever train you're taking, if you're planning to board at a stop other than its point of origin, your best bet for correct information is to call VIA's 800 number.

Parlez-vous Français?

No? Well, that's a pity, but don't worry about it. VIA employees (indeed, most of the people you'll meet, even in the French-speaking parts of Canada) are quite fluent in English.

Baggage

As in Europe, you'll find free baggage carts in many stations. The Montreal and Toronto stations are two exceptions. You may check heavy baggage on VIA trains if you wish, but be sure to find out in advance if that service is available at both ends of your trip.

Classes of Service

They're pretty much the same as Amtrak, but VIA gives different names to their various levels of service. *Sleeper class* refers to the private accommodations in sleeping cars on overnight trains, but there are some minor distinctions.

On the Canadian (Toronto–Vancouver) *sleeper class* comes in two sizes: Sleeper Plus Class, which includes accommodations ranging from upper and lower berths to cabins for one and two people, and the new Prestige Class, with oversized beds, en suite showers, a minibar, and even a flat screen TV. All dining car meals are included with both classes of service.

On the Ocean (Montreal–Halifax), VIA makes a distinction between Sleeper Class and Sleeper Plus Class. The choice of accommodations is the same for each, but the Sleeper Plus fare is offered only in the high season—from mid-June to mid-October—and includes all your dining-car meals. For the rest of the year, normal Sleeper Class fares apply and passengers pay for their meals.

Sleeping cars on the Winnipeg–Churchill train are not as luxurious as those used on the Canadian and Ocean trains, but they serve their purpose. There are several different accommodations for one and two passengers, including small one-passenger roomettes.

Within the Windsor–Quebec corridor, for a supplementary charge you can opt for business class in coaches on the shorter trips. If you board in Toronto, Montreal, or Ottawa, you'll get to wait for your train in a first-class lounge and board ahead of the regular coach passengers. The business-class cars are spiffy, and you'll get a good complimentary meal with drinks served to you at your seat. VIA's business class includes specific seat assignments, so you can reserve either a window or an aisle seat when you book. (I'm always disappointed if I can't sit by a window, so this one feature alone makes this class of service a very attractive option for me.) *Coach class*, as on Amtrak trains, means you'll be in a standard railcar with rows of two seats on each side of a center aisle.

Paying for Things

Cash or credit cards will be accepted either in railroad stations or onboard. You may also use your American dollars, but don't let that lull you into thinking you can get by without ever having to exchange your dollars for Canadian currency. Once off the train or away from major hotels, you'll need Canadian dollars.

What to Wear?

Comfortable clothing is the standard for both VIA Rail and Amtrak; however if you're traveling in Sleeper Plus Class on the Canadian, you might feel more at ease if you dress up just a bit for meals in the dining car, especially for dinner. The service and the ambiance in the dining cars on those trains are very nice, and a casual jacket over a sport shirt for men and a nice top and slacks for women just seem a bit more appropriate. Of course, you will not be tossed out into a passing snowbank if you show up in a polo shirt or a simple top. The truth? That's what most people will be wearing anyway.

Tipping

Basically, it's just about the same as Amtrak: not necessary in coach unless your attendant provides some special service for you; $10 (Canadian) per night, per person for car attendants in sleepers. Remember to tip the dining-car servers appropriately, even though your meals are included in your fare. Because only sleeping-car passengers take their meals in the VIA dining cars, there are no prices listed on the menus to help you calculate an appropriate tip. My suggestion: $2–3 for breakfast and lunch; $5–7 for dinner. That's Canadian currency, and it's per person. Remember too that if you're part of a package tour, tips are usually included in the cost of the tour. But do make sure.

Smoking Policy

There's a strict no-smoking policy on all VIA trains and in stations. On the long-distance trains, smokers will have occasional opportunities to step off at certain station stops for a smoke, but people who are caught smoking onboard, even in private sleeping-car accommodations, can be put off the train and fined.

Special Needs

There are provisions on all VIA Rail trains to accommodate passengers in wheelchairs or who may have some other special needs. VIA Rail's only requirement—and it's a reasonable one—is that a passenger who will need special care during the journey (feeding, bathing, medication, or anything else) must travel with an escort to perform these services. The good news is that VIA will permit the escort to travel at no charge—an enlightened policy, don't you agree?

What About Pets?

VIA is a bit more flexible than Amtrak, but only seeing-eye and other service dogs are permitted to actually ride with their owners. Other pets, limited to "cats, dogs, and small rodents," must ride in the baggage car and, of course, in an appropriate carrier. VIA baggage cars are heated, so your pet will be fine during colder months, but there is no air conditioning. For that reason, pets will not be accommodated in VIA baggage cars at any time during the months of June, July, and August. Be aware that you, not the VIA people, are responsible for looking after your pets. When that means a trip to the baggage car, a VIA employee will have to accompany you. You must inform VIA at least 24 hours in advance if a pet will be traveling with you, and you must be at the station with Fido at least an hour before departure.

Compliments and Complaints

If you run into problems and can't get things straightened out on the spot, by all means pursue the matter later with an e-mail or a letter. Be brief, be unemotional, and be polite. E-mail customer_relations@viarail.ca or write to Customer Relations, VIA Rail Canada Inc., P.O. Box 8116, Station A, Montreal, Quebec H3C 3N3. In a real emergency, you can call 1-800-681-2561 from either the United States or Canada. And if you get some excellent, genuinely friendly service along the way—as I rather suspect you will—send an attaboy e-mail to that same address, specifying the date, train number, and employee by name.

Rail Fans

Yes, Canada also has its proportionate share of folks who are fascinated by trains. As noted elsewhere, these people are referred to as *foamers* by professional railroaders in the United States, implying that they foam at the mouth upon catching sight of a train. That word is known north of the US border, but with a tact and gentility rather typical of the Canadians, the preferred term in that country seems to be "DRF" (for "demented rail fan").

Onboard Crews

Crew responsibilities are divided in almost exactly the same manner on VIA Rail trains as on Amtrak's. The only difference of note is that there is a service manager on all of VIA's long-distance trains who has overall responsibility for the quality of service provided by the onboard crew. He or she wears a prominent badge on the uniform with that designation.

Another point to note: Compared to Amtrak, you'll see fewer female conductors on VIA trains. In the late 1990s, the company made an effort to hire more women in nontraditional jobs. Mandatory cuts occur from time to time, and on those occasions the most recent hires are always the first to be let go. Unfortunately, that has usually meant the women.

Passenger Train Equipment

When it got started some 30-plus years ago, a lack of quality rolling stock was one of VIA's biggest problems. Like Amtrak, VIA Rail went through a make-do period with the older traditional railcars it inherited from both Canadian Pacific and Canadian National.

But also included in that collection of equipment were 200 classic stainless-steel cars originally built in the mid-1950s. Some saintly soul at VIA Rail decided these vintage cars were worth saving, and more than $200 million dollars was spent to rebuild the fleet completely from the wheels up. A number of structural and mechanical improvements were made in the cars, but the most important of these did away with the old steam heating systems in each individual car. Today these beauties are all heated with head-end power, meaning with electricity supplied by a powerful generator in one of the diesel locomotives pulling the train. It's a far more reliable system—if you're traveling across Canada in the winter, a reliable source of heat is a very good thing indeed!

The trains operating in the Windsor–Quebec corridor are designated as LRC (light, rapid, comfortable) equipment, and indeed they are. These trains are quite sophisticated. A computer system actually tilts both the locomotive and the cars as the train rounds curves, permitting higher average speeds and helping to neutralize the effects of centrifugal force on passengers.

Locomotives

All of VIA Rail's locomotives are diesel-electrics. The two types of engines that haul the LRC corridor trains are fast and power-ful—either 3,000 or 4,200 horsepower—and are capable of running at 95 and 100 mph respectively.

For their long-distance trains, VIA uses good old F-40s—the same locomotive that was the bulwark of Amtrak's fleet for years. They're tough, durable, and reliable. They'd better be, because—as you will one day hopefully see for yourself—all of those trains pass through long stretches of wilderness areas, which are not good places for breakdowns. (Don't worry, VIA uses two or even three locomotives on those trains, just in case.)

The Stainless-Steel Fleet

Even if you're not a true-blue train fan, the renovated and redec-orated interiors of these cars (especially the sleepers) will make you think you've died and gone to heaven. They're neat and clean and have a very attractive color scheme, without losing a feel for the 1950s when the cars were built. Both coaches and sleepers are now in use on the Canadian in the West. Here are some details on these wonderful cars.

VIA Rail's premier train, the Canadian, about to leave Jasper, Alberta, and continue westward on its journey through the Rocky Mountains. This consist includes four of the older but reliable F-40 locomotives. PHOTO COURTESY OF THE AUTHOR

Coaches

The layout is standard for most rail coaches: rows of two seats on each side of a center aisle. There are seats for 62 passengers plus room for a wheelchair. Chairs recline and include leg rests. There is a lavatory at each end of the car. There's space overhead for one or two small-to-medium-size bags, so plan to check anything more than that. Better yet, leave all that extra stuff at home.

Skyline Cafes

These cars serve coach passengers and include a food service area where a variety of sandwiches, hot meals, and drinks are available. Food may be taken back to your seat, or you can eat in a large lounge area with tables and chairs. There is a panoramic dome with 24 seats on the upper level. These cars are also available for sleeping-car passengers looking for a snack or a beverage when the dining car is closed.

Sleepers

There are two lavatories and a shower in each of these stainless-steel sleeping cars. There are three different types of accommodations, but all provide a call button, a reading light, and controls for heat and air conditioning in the cabins. *Sections* are two facing seats that convert into a lower berth at night; an upper berth folds down from the wall above the window. Heavy zippered curtains are pulled across each section for privacy. (Remember the sleeping-car scenes in *Some Like It Hot?* That's what a section looks like with the curtains pulled at night.) *Cabins for one* include a comfortable seat, a sink, a toilet, and a small closet where a few garments may be hung. At night, the bed folds down from the wall. It covers the toilet, however, so get some instruction from the car attendant on how to raise it in case you need to use those facilities during the night. There are six *cabins for two,* each including either a bench-type sofa or two chairs, a toilet, and a sink. The seating converts into two beds at night, a lower and an upper berth.

VIA Rail's stainless-steel fleet includes several of the classic bullet-shaped observation cars, each named for one of Canada's national parks. These beauties feature two passenger lounge areas and several deluxe sleeping compartments. Best of all, there is a glass-enclosed viewing dome on the upper level.

Here are some additional observations about the facilities in these sleepers that may prove helpful:

• Bedroom F is about a foot larger than the others, and on a three-night trip you'll appreciate the extra space. Try to get this particular room when you book.

- Bedrooms A, C, and E are configured so that your seats are facing toward the rear of the train. Some people don't care, but I much prefer to ride facing forward. (Just to complicate things, these sleepers come in two slightly different configurations. If these variables matter to you, double-check with the VIA Rail reservations agent when booking.)

- In my opinion the best arrangement for a family of four traveling together would be to reserve sections 1 and 2. They're located directly across from each other, so you'll be able to see out of both sides of the train. The downside might be having other passengers walking by your seats as they pass through the car, but you'll quickly get used to that. Also the reasonable cost of these accommodations should more than make up for it.

Park Cars

There are several of these cars; each is named for one of Canada's national parks. They're certainly easy to spot, always being the last car of each train and with the distinctive bullet-shaped end. Park cars are reserved for use by sleeping-car passengers only. There's a comfortable observation area at the end of the car, a lounge toward the middle where passengers can get coffee and other beverages, and a dome on an upper level with two dozen seats. These cars also include sleeping accommodations: one cabin for three and two bedrooms with two beds apiece. All of these rooms are quite a bit larger than the standard rooms in the other sleeping cars, but the cabins for two are priced the same which, to my mind, makes them my first choice. The three-person cabin is, of course, more expensive.

There are, however, two minor issues to consider when reserving one of the cabins in a Park car. First, there are en suite lavatories in each of the cabins but no shower facilities. For that, a trip to the adjoining car will be required. And second, quite understandably, these cars are a gathering place for many of the sleeping-car passengers. They come to ride in the dome and to gather for conversation in the lounge area at the rear of the car. For me, that's a very acceptable trade-off for a somewhat larger cabin in this wonderfully classic railcar.

The Renaissance Fleet

These cars were originally intended to carry passengers between England and France through the "Chunnel" but were acquired by VIA Rail in 2000 for service on the

The jewels of VIA's stainless-steel fleet are the Park cars with their distinctive rounded ends. This one at the platform in Toronto brings up the rear of train no. I, the Canadian, which is about to depart for Vancouver. The impressive 1,800-foot-high CN Tower is in the background. PHOTO COURTESY OF THE AUTHOR

Ocean, which runs between Halifax and Montreal. These railcars are also used on two express trains running daily between Montreal and Toronto. I rode the Ocean a few years back and must say I liked this equipment a great deal. The Ocean consists include coaches, sleeping cars with compartments accommodating either one or two people (all with toilets and some with both toilets and showers), a lounge car primarily serving coach passengers, and a full-on dining car for sleeping-car passengers. You can see interior photographs of these accommodations on VIA Rail's website, www.viarail.ca.

LRC Fleet

VIA's LRC ("light, rapid, comfortable") cars are found in the Windsor–Toronto–Ottawa–Montreal–Quebec corridor. Trains operating between these cities run quietly and smoothly at speeds of up to 100 miles per hour. The cars are well designed with large windows and are tastefully decorated. Two types of service are offered in this central corridor.

Coach

The standard LRC coach will accommodate 74 passengers in rows of two seats on each side of an aisle and includes room for a wheelchair. There are two lavatories at the rear end of the car. A small food-service area is located at the opposite end where passengers may purchase snacks and beverages.

Business-Class Cars

These newly renovated coaches have 20 fewer seats than the standard coach, which means more legroom. There are two lavatories at one end of the car and a fairly extensive food-service area at the opposite end where the complimentary meals are served. The food in business class is quite good, falling somewhere in between coach and first-class meals served by the airlines.

You Really Can't Go Wrong

Generally speaking, no matter which train you ride, you'll find VIA Rail's equipment to be modern, clean, and comfortable—which amounts to very pleasurable rail travel, especially in those stainless-steel beauties. If you want a taste of the golden age, ride the Canadian or the Ocean. You'll find a description of their routes, along with most of the other VIA trains, in chapter 17, "Pick a Train, Any Train," and on VIA's website, www.viarail.ca.

14

MEXICO'S COPPER CANYON TRAIN

In 1995, the Mexican government began privatizing the passenger rail service, and the results were predictable: trains are no longer a viable part of the public transportation system in that country. As veteran travelers know, Mexico has opted for an extensive system of buses instead. Most cities have large, modern bus terminals with the look and feel of many US airports and with half a dozen or more modern, air-conditioned buses ready to take you to a variety of destinations.

There is, however, one truly extraordinary train ride readily available for visitors to that interesting and colorful country. El Chepe (which is an affectionate nickname for the operating railroad, Chihuahua al Pacifico) runs daily in both directions over the Copper Canyon route from Chihuahua City in north-central Mexico through El Fuerte to Los Mochis on the Sea of Cortez. El Chepe is without doubt one of more spectacular train rides in the world, and I recommend it enthusiastically.

An American-Mexican Rail Link

In the 1860s, about the same time entrepreneurs were starting to push for transcontinental railways in the United States and Canada, an American named Albert K. Owen began looking for a way to link the American Midwest with a Pacific seaport by running a rail line through Mexico. An engineer by training, Owen tried to sell his idea to a number of US governors and to Congress without success.

Nevertheless, the idea had some serious economic potential, at least on paper, and other eager would-be railroaders followed Owen. In 1897, Foster Higgins, also an American, formed a company called the Rio Grande, Sierra Madre y Pacifico, which began building a rail line south from Cuidad Juárez for 160 miles to Corralitos. In that same year, a Mexican entrepreneur named Enrique Creel formed a rail company called the Chihuahua al Pacifico and started laying 125 miles of track between Chihuahua and Miñaca.

The first really serious effort to build a railroad to the Pacific through Mexico was driven by a visionary American businessman named Arthur Stilwell, who saw it as a way to open up trade between the eastern part of the United States and Asian markets. His plan called for a rail line to originate in Kansas City, head south through Texas and into Mexico, then swing southwest and terminate at one of North America's great natural deepwater harbors, Topolobampo, on the Sea of Cortez. Stilwell saw limitless potential in the future of trade between North America and the Far East and calculated that a rail line through Mexico would reduce the time it took to ship goods between Kansas City and the Pacific by four days—a major economic incentive. (By the way, Port Arthur, Texas, was named after Stilwell.)

Work on the rail line sputtered on and off over the next few decades, with several companies being formed to build various segments of the route. The Mexican Revolution was a major interruption, with Pancho Villa and his troops staging periodic attacks on railroad facilities and construction crews. Nevertheless, several different railway companies continued working during that period, and by 1914 Juárez on the Texas border was linked to Chihuahua. From Chihuahua the line had also been extended to the little logging town of Creel.

The Copper Canyon Route Is Completed

In 1940 the Mexican government took over several of the small railway companies and formed the Chihuahua al Pacifico, nicknamed El Chepe by the locals, which remains to this day as a private company owned by Ferrocarril Mexicano, the largest of Mexico's freight railroads. Most of the construction undertaken before then had been relatively easy. The really difficult terrain—some 160 miles across the Sierra Occidental range—had yet to be tackled. That work began in the early 1950s. By the time it was completed, the cost had run into many billions of pesos. And no wonder: the route goes through some of the most rugged country anywhere in North America.

It took almost 100 years to complete the rail line through the Copper Canyon. This photo, taken at least 50 years ago, shows Mexican workers constructing one of the 220 bridges along the route. PHOTO COURTESY OF CHIHUAHUA AL PACIFICO RAILROAD

The entire line was finally finished in 1961 and is truly an engineering marvel. In the 357 miles between Creel and Los Mochis, there are 88 tunnels. The longest is almost 6,000 feet, and all together their combined length is nearly 14 miles. One tunnel makes a 180-degree turn and descends 100 feet inside a mountain. Then there are the bridges, more than 220 of them. If joined together, their combined length would be more than five miles. One, the bridge in Chínipas, is 1,000 feet long and more than 300 feet high.

Privatization Comes to Mexican Trains

From its beginnings in the late 1940s, Mexico's national railway grew into a railroad of significant size and scope. Ferrocarriles Nacionales de México (FNM) hauled grain, coal, a variety of minerals, petroleum, fertilizers, automobiles, and auto parts in some 50,000 freight cars, many of which were owned by the companies that pumped the oil, dug the coal, built the cars, and so on.

By the mid-1990s, Mexico's struggle to stabilize its economy had taken a toll on a number of institutions, including the country's passenger rail service. FNM still ran passenger trains, but equipment was run-down and service was generally unreliable. Most of these problems were the result of budget cuts that led to "deferred maintenance," which, in turn, created a shortage of equipment. These problems were exacerbated by uncertainties coming in the wake of privatization. That was a shame too, because in the same tradition of railroads in the United States and Canada, the Mexican national railroad had a proud history and had offered some first-rate rail experiences to visitors over the years.

Privatization became official in 1997 when the Mexican government invited private companies to bid for the rights to operate both freight and passenger services throughout the country. There was a lot of interest, and consortiums were formed to bid on various routes. The following decade saw a succession of mergers, failures, and acquisitions. Today most of the freight is transported by two Class I railroads, Ferrocarril Mexicano (popularly known as Ferromex) and Kansas City Southern de México.

Just as it happened in the United States, privatization of passenger rail didn't work in Mexico. In 2013, Mexico's president, Enrique Peña Nieto, seemed to acknowledge that by announcing a multimillion dollar plan to improve the country's transportation infrastructure, including rail. Specifically, President Peña Nieto was said to favor restoring passenger service on routes linking Mexico City with the cities of Toluca and Queretaro as well as a key rail line on the Yucatan Peninsula.

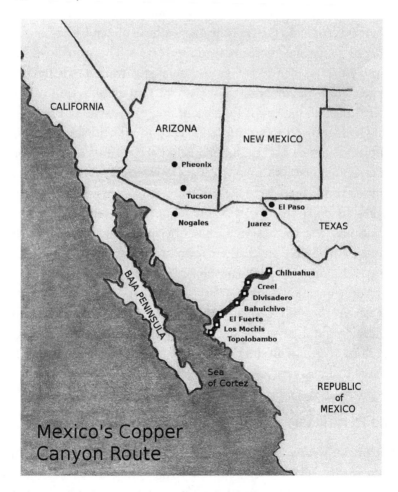

Be that as it may, today there are only two passenger trains running, both operated by Ferromex. One, the Tequila Express, is essentially a tourist train. The other, El Chepe, runs daily in both directions along the original route between Chihuahua and Los Mochis through the Copper Canyon.

The Spectacular Copper Canyon Train Ride

This is the only scenic rail route still operating for passengers in Mexico, but it's one of the truly great ones—and I mean in all the world. The real attraction of this rail journey is, of course, the terrain it traverses. As the train heads southwest from Chihuahua en route to the Pacific, there are fields and farms. They soon give way to pine forests; then for miles and miles, the train winds through gorges, hugs canyon walls, burrows into mountains, and crosses rivers (meandering or rushing, according to the time of year).

The locals call this route El Chepe, an affectionate abbreviation for the name of the Chihuahua al Pacifico Railroad that connects Chihuahua and Los Mochis. It's referred to as the Copper Canyon route, but it actually runs through a series of interlocking gorges, of which the Copper Canyon, or Las Barrancas del Cobre, is but one. Together, though, they offer an incredible experience. These canyons are more than four times larger and, in several areas, a full mile deeper than the Grand Canyon in Arizona.

You can take this trip pretty much year-round, but the best time is in the fall, with October being the prime month. The weather should be sunny but not too hot. Because it's just after the rainy season, you should see some spectacular waterfalls. The foliage will be at its best too.

Two Trains in One

For many years, the C&P ran two trains a day along this route—a first-class train, El Primero, and a second-class train, El Económico. Recently, the two trains have been combined three

El Primero, the Chihuahua al Pacifico Railroad's first-class train, rounds a curve along the spectacular Copper Canyon route. PHOTO COURTESY OF CHIHUAHUA AL PACIFICO RAILROAD

days a week in each direction. The combined train includes first-class cars, a dining car for the exclusive use of first-class passengers, and several second-class coaches. On Wednesdays, the train does not carry any second-class cars and it makes fewer stops. And—this can be confusing—even if you're discussing the combined train, they still talk about two separate trains: the front half of the train being El Primero and everything to the rear of the dining car referred to as El Económico.

Here's the new schedule:

On Monday, Thursday, and Saturday, the combined train leaves Chihuahua at 6:00 AM and gets to Los Mochis at around 9:30 that evening.

On Tuesday, Friday, and Sunday, the combined train leaves Los Mochis at 6:00 AM and arrives in Chihuahua at about 10:00 PM.

On Wednesday, an all-first-class westbound train leaves Chihuahua at 6:00 AM and arrives in Los Mochis at about 8:30 PM.

Meanwhile, also on Wednesday, the other all-first-class train departs from Los Mochis at 6:00 in the morning and, traveling west to east, arrives in Chihuahua at about 9:00 PM.

Fares change, of course, but according to my latest information, the one-way first-class fare for the entire journey is about $175. The fare in second class is around $110.

If it's most convenient for you to take the westbound train, you can fly direct to Chihuahua or get there by bus, which is a five-hour trip from Juárez just across the border from El Paso, Texas. (Don't let that deter you: the buses are big, new, and air-conditioned, and they even show movies en route.) If you opt for the eastbound train, I recommend catching it in El Fuerte rather than at its point of origin in Los Mochis. The reason is that boarding is at 6:00 AM in Los Mochis but not until 9:00 at El Fuerte, a much more convenient time. Whichever direction you choose, it will mean an overnight stay in Chihuahua or in either Los Mochis or El Fuerte.

El Primero is very comfortable and well maintained, with a decor that is appropriate to the great Southwest. In addition to coaches, the consist includes a dining car and a lounge car where drinks are served. Of course, all of the onboard staff speak excellent English.

Your next decision will be whether to go straight through—it's a 15-hour trip—or stop for a couple of nights along the way. For me, that was a no-brainer: I took the extra time and stopped for the night in Creel and again in Divisadero. There are plenty of interesting things to see in both places, either on your own or on a guided tour. At Divisadero, you'll be able to walk right up to the rim and gaze down into the canyon. (I did, and I couldn't get over seeing buzzards circling lazily in the air . . . more than a thousand feet below me.)

Also near Divisadero is the Copper Canyon Adventure Park. It features a cable car taking visitors across the canyon every 20 minutes from 9:30 AM to 4:30 PM. And of course there are zip lines—eight at last count—plus observation platforms, suspension bridges, repelling, and rock climbing. There are also playgrounds for children, a restaurant, and a picnic area. On my trip aboard

El Primero, I spent two very interesting days in Divisadero, and that was *before* the adventure park was opened, so do consider extending your visit there.

El Económico

You might also consider traveling in the second-class cars that are part of the train's consist six days a week. (See schedule above.) There is no dining car for passengers riding in these second-class cars, but sandwiches are for sale onboard. The fare is about 35 percent less than what you'll pay for the first-class section, and it will certainly provide an opportunity to be around and perhaps get to know some of the ordinary folks.

By the way, most locals refer to this train as El Segundo, obviously because it's a second-class train. It also has a very unofficial nickname, El Pollero, which, they will tell you with a good-natured smile, is translated as "the Chicken Train." Don't get the idea that this train is dilapidated and run-down or that every other passenger has a live chicken under his or her arm. Yes, it is indeed a second-class train, but the equipment being used is the same that comprised what was the first-class train a decade or so ago. It's just that some of the details you expect to be covered on a first-class tourist-oriented excursion may be considered unimportant for El Segundo passengers.

A Few More Details You Should Know

Many Americans become uneasy at the thought of travel to Mexico. Yes, if you don't speak any Spanish, you'll have to deal with that, but in my experience—in Mexico, France, Italy, Hungary, or China, for that matter—you'll find that a lot of people speak English, and some of your best memories will be from encounters with people who don't. As with any trip abroad, however, you can enhance your Mexican travel experience and minimize the possibility of any problems along the way with a bit of study and some commonsense preparation ahead of time.

Crossing the Border

Assuming you're going to Mexico as a visitor and will be staying less than six months, you'll need a passport and a tourist card. You must obtain the passport in advance, but you can get a tourist card when you cross the border or, if you're flying to Mexico, at the airline counter before you leave.

I've said this elsewhere, but it bears repeating here: Make photocopies of all your travel documents before you leave home. This includes your passport, tickets, and itinerary. Keep one set of copies with you when you travel and leave another set with someone back home.

¿Habla usted Español?

It's always great to be able to speak another language when traveling. But if you don't speak Spanish, don't let that deter you. Get a simple Spanish phrase book and work on the basics, and I mean the *real* basics. And don't worry: you'll find everyone friendly and more than willing to deal with you in rudimentary English or simple gestures. (The first phrase I learned was *"Lo siento, no habla Español,"* or "I'm sorry, I don't speak Spanish." The first time I used it was when I crossed the border from El Paso. The Mexican immigration officer looked at me and said in flawless English, "And why not, may I ask?" Then, with a big grin, he said, "But welcome to Mexico anyway, señor.")

Paying for Things

Change most of your cash into pesos before you cross the border and, when you do, make sure you get plenty of bills in small denominations. Large notes can be hard to change, even in some hotels. You won't be able to use your credit cards onboard the train—use either pesos or US dollars—but credit cards will be accepted in virtually all the hotels and in most (but not all) restaurants.

What to Wear

Dress comfortably by all means, but be prepared for real swings in temperature along the Copper Canyon route. After all, Chihuahua is situated in a desert environment—the highest point along the way is over 8,000 feet, and Los Mochis, at the other end of the route, is at sea level. The "layered look" is definitely the way to go.

Health and Safety

The best advice I can offer—and it applies wherever in the world you may be traveling—is to use common sense when it comes to where you go and what you do. I doubt you would venture alone into strange areas of New York or Los Angeles, so don't do it anywhere else.

When it comes to health issues, there are some basic precautions you should take—not so much because there's any kind of serious risk, but because they're simple and easy and could save you a great deal of discomfort and inconvenience.

- Pack all the medications you need, plus those you *might* need.

- It can be very hot at sea level, so take and wear a hat and use a strong sunscreen.

- It's unlikely that you'll have a problem, but there are some serious diseases lurking in some parts of the country, most of which are transmitted by mosquitoes. Do the logical and sensible thing: bring a good insect repellant. And use it!

- The local water is the most common cause of the ever-popular *la turista*, or travelers' diarrhea. I'm told that the tap water in Los Mochis is safe to drink because the city has a filtration system for the public water supply. But when in doubt, follow this one simple rule: *Do not drink the tap water.* There is plenty of bottled water available (just make sure the seal around the cap is unbroken). Drink it, brush your teeth with it, and wash your face with it. Shower with your mouth closed. Don't eat any raw vegetables that may have been washed. Fresh fruits and vegetables you peel yourself are fine. It's also a good idea to wash your hands with soap before you eat.

I know all this sounds ominous, but don't let what are really only routine and commonsense precautions put you off. The chances that you will get sick are small anyway, and you can reduce them to virtually nil with what amounts to a few very minor inconveniences. Makes sense, doesn't it?

The Tequila Express

The other train ride that should be mentioned here is the Tequila Express. As the name implies, the national Mexican drink is the theme of this excursion. The train is operated by Ferromex and runs cross-country out of Guadalajara to the town of Amatitán. Here passengers tour a hacienda that is home to one of the country's better-known distilleries, which produces the very excellent Herradura tequila. Yes, for some passengers this is a rolling party, but the world is full of folks who know and appreciate truly good tequila. For them, this excursion is a serious business, one that could be compared to the Napa Valley Wine Train, for instance.

The excursion includes the train ride, of course, plus lunch and live entertainment on the train and at the hacienda. After that is a tour of the distillery. Two classes of service are offered.

The last information I had was that the train runs on Saturdays and Sundays, with the possibility of a Friday-night tour to come. If you book through a tour operator, he or she will have all the current information. You can also go to the Tequila Express website, www.tequilaexpress.com.mx.

Booking Your Trip

I recommend going through a tour operator to book a trip through the Copper Canyon on El Primero. There are choices to be made, as I have noted earlier, and small but important details can and do change all the time. The tour operator gets paid to make recommendations, to handle those details, and to keep you informed, right up to the last minute.

You can work through one of the travel agencies specializing in rail travel listed on page 384, or you can directly contact one of the tour operators. There are several, but one I can suggest is S&S Tours, located in Arizona. This particular company has been introducing people to the Copper Canyon for more than 20 years, and because of personal relationships developed in Mexico over that time, they're frequently able to offer unexpected and unusual experiences, especially interaction with the local people. You can check them out at www.coppercanyon.com.

15

YOUR TOP TEN RAILROAD STATIONS

There are about 500 railroad stations in the United States and more than 150 in Canada. Some are architectural wonders built of granite and marble; others are flimsy shacks that could be hauled away to a landfill on a flatbed truck. But every one is a portal to the rest of the world for the community it serves. And so every single one is important. But if you're traveling around the United States or Canada by train, some stations are almost certainly going to be a lot more important than others.

They're all "stations" to most of us, but each one has a formal name, usually ending in "station" or "terminal" or sometimes "depot," and each of those terms has a specific meaning. Strictly speaking, if the railroad tracks end there, it's a *terminal*, whereas if the tracks continue on to other destinations, it's a *station*. If the station is called a *depot*, it means in addition to being a stop on a rail line, it also has—or once had—a significant repair and maintenance facility. Got it? Good. But now you need to know that there are lots of exceptions. Chicago Union Station is that facility's formal name, but technically it's both a station *and* a terminal. And all the tracks coming into Boston's South *Station* end there.

A great many stations, especially in bigger cities, have the word "union" as part of their formal name: Washington Union

Station, for example. Originally, that meant the tracks of more than one railroad met there and ran through that station together—a union of railroads, as it were. Today, however, there are "union" stations where the only tracks running through them belong to Amtrak. In some other stations, the trains are Amtrak's, but the tracks belong to one of the freight railroads.

Let me say here that, yes, my list is limited to just ten stations and, yes, a number of significant stations have been left out. However, as you will see, my choices were not made using the usual criteria, which invariably emphasize the station's architecture or the teeming numbers of passengers passing through every day.

Architectural significance and volume of ridership were considerations, of course, but I began the process by looking at stations where a single passenger—you, perhaps—might be between trains with several hours to kill. Rather than spend that time observing the passing humanity, as fascinating as that can be, you might like to know just a bit about the building you're in. When was it built? What's special about it?

But you may also want to know if there are any good restaurants in the station. And, if not, what are the culinary possibilities nearby? If you've got several hours before your next train departs, you might be interested about any points of interest close by. And if you end up spending the night, is there a decent hotel in the vicinity?

So that's how I arrived at my top-ten list. Besides, whether or not your train travels ever take you to any of these stations, there's something interesting or special about each of them.

I. Washington Union Station (WAS)

I travel to Washington, DC, at least once a year and, if possible, I try to arrange my schedule so that I have at least a couple of hours to kill in this magnificent building.

Many thousands of people flow through the Great Hall in Washington Union Station every day, but it's also a favorite gathering spot for lunch dates or an after-work rendezvous. And no wonder! PHOTO COURTESY OF KEITH STANLEY (WWW.KESTAN.COM)

First of all, it's perfect for Washington: a classic design, built in 1908 of white granite from Vermont. The main hall is breathtaking with a vaulted ceiling that's almost 100 feet high. Mounted high on the walls around the entire room are statues of Roman legionnaires, and there are also allegorical statues placed around the room, each weighing some 25 tons, representing electricity, fire, agriculture, and mechanics.

In the late 1980s, the station underwent a major renovation at a cost of $160 million. It was the most costly public/private restoration project ever undertaken in this country. And—you'll agree when you see it—worth every penny.

In addition to normal railroad station business with around 80,000 people coming and going every day, Union Station is often the venue for major civic events such as concerts, cultural performances, and even presidential inaugural balls.

Altogether, some 90 trains a day go in and out of Washington Union Station. In addition to the many trains operating up through the Northeast Corridor to New York and Boston, several of Amtrak's long-distance trains use this station. It's a terminus for the Capitol Limited, which operates daily between there and Chicago. And while they originate in New York, the Cardinal, the Crescent, and both the Silver Meteor and Silver Star all pass through Washington Union Station en route to their various destinations. Then there are all the commuter trains operated by Maryland Area Regional Commuter (MARC) and Virginia Railway Express (VRE). Union Station is also a stop for the Metro, Washington's transit system, so you can arrive on a train from Chicago or Miami or New Orleans, then seamlessly transfer to the Metro or one of the commuter lines. For that matter, you can also get off a train and switch here to a bus, either local or long-haul, grab a taxi, or pick up a rental car from one of the counters in the station.

Where to Eat?

There are several restaurants located in and just off of the Main Hall. I've tried most of them and they're all very good. If you're looking for something to grab and go, there are more than 30 establishments throughout the station, many of which are on the lower level in a large food court. These include the usual fast-food restaurants, plus a lot of places serving ethnic food, pastries, specialty coffees, gourmet ice cream—you name it.

There aren't any restaurants worth mentioning in the immediate vicinity of the station, but—trust me on this—whatever kind of food you're looking for, from inexpensive to pricey, you'll find it right there in Union Station. My advice is to pick a place where you can do some people watching as you dine.

Things to See and Do

If you have a spare hour or two between trains and want to do a little sightseeing, just walk through the Great Hall and out the front door. Voila! The Capitol building and, beyond it, office buildings for the members of Congress, both the House and the Senate, are all within walking distance. You can also connect with guided motor tours right there at Union Station: conventional tour buses, double-deckers, duck boats, and trolleys.

Washington is a wonderful city. If you're not just passing through, or if you can adjust your itinerary, spend at least a few days here. The truth is, it would be easy to spend a full week and spend all day, every day, just sightseeing. A few suggestions: the Smithsonian, especially the Air and Space Museum; the Holocaust Museum; the Capitol building; the White House; the FBI building; Ford's Theater; Mount Vernon, which is across the river in Virginia; the Lincoln, Jefferson, and Martin Luther King memorials; and the Vietnam Veterans Memorial Wall. Contact your local member of Congress to arrange Capitol and White House tours.

Overnight Accommodations

Of course Washington is loaded with hotels, and there is a wide variety of choices at rates that vary from surprising to shocking. No kidding, Washington is notorious for its high hotel rates. That said, I can still recommend two hotels, both quite close to Union Station. I have stayed at both.

Phoenix Park Hotel
520 North Capitol NW
1-202-638-6900
www.phoenixparkhotel.com

The location of this hotel is a big plus. You're right next door to the station. In fact, step out of the station's main entrance and there it is, just to your right. There's an Irish theme that runs throughout the Phoenix Park, and that includes the restaurant and a pub. And a lot of green carpeting.

Hotel George
15 E Street NW
1-202-347-4200
www.hotelgeorge.com

The George (as in General or President) has recently been reno-vated and it's quite interesting to see; for instance, entire walls are covered with huge blow-ups of one of Washington's letters. Post-modernism meets the eighteenth century, but somehow it works. The George is on a side street, so it should be reasonably quiet.

2. Chicago Union Station (CHI)

This is another of the great stations in the United States. It's an important one and it's big, too, taking up more than 10 city blocks.

Construction began on the station in 1913 and took 12 years to complete. Typical of railway stations from that era, Chica-go's Union Station features the Great Hall, where travelers wait for their trains on classic wooden benches and through which 120,000 people still pass every weekday, hurrying to or from their trains.

The Great Hall is as long as a football field and features a vaulted ceiling—skylights, actually—that are 115 feet above the polished marble floor. A number of major motion pictures have shot scenes in the Great Hall, and major civic events are regularly held here. No wonder; what a venue!

A majority of Amtrak's long-distance trains claim this sta-tion as a terminus: the Empire Builder, the California Zephyr, the Southwest Chief, the City of New Orleans, the Texas Eagle, the Capital Limited, the Lake Shore Limited, and the Cardinal, plus Amtrak service to St. Louis, southern Illinois, Indiana, Michigan, and Milwaukee. And by the way, there are local Metra trains car-rying commuters to and from a number of suburban areas every weekday.

There are Great Halls in most of the older big-city railroad stations around the country, but this one, in Chicago Union Station, is the one that makes you stop and gaze around and up . . . every time. PHOTO COURTESY OF FOTO GRAPHICS BY SHERYL E THOMAS

If you're a passenger on almost any one of Amtrak's long-distance trains, you'll be spending some time here. And the waiting is not unpleasant: there's a Metropolitan Lounge available if you're traveling in a sleeping car. There are comfortable chairs, complimentary soft drinks, a large-screen TV, Wi-Fi, and a checkroom where you can store your luggage.

Where to Eat?

I have spent a lot of time and had a lot of meals in and around this station. There's a food court on the upper level for sandwiches, pizzas, and Chinese and other ethnic foods, and a bar where you can sit and have a drink. But it's all essentially fast-food. There are, however, plenty of good restaurants nearby.

Let me suggest one in particular: Lou Mitchell's Restaurant. It's at 565 W. Jackson, just down the street from the station and about a two minute walk. This place has been there since 1923 and is a huge favorite. You'll see why as soon as you walk in the door. The place is hopping with an atmosphere that makes you feel like you're a regular patron from the moment you step inside. It's not fancy, but the food is terrific and—trust me on this—the breakfasts are memorable. They are not open for dinner. You can call 1-312-939-3111 for more information.

For lunches and dinners, there's also Dylan's Tavern at 118 S. Clinton (1-312-876-2008) or South Branch Bar & Grill at 100 S. Wacker (1-312-546-6177); both are very good, and both are within easy walking distance.

Things to See and Do

If you have some time between trains here in Chicago, you're in luck. There is a lot to see and do and much of it is right there in the vicinity of Union Station. Here are three quick suggestions:

See all of Chicago from the Skydeck at the top of the Willis Tower (formerly called the Sears Tower). It's impossible to miss, and a trip up to the 103rd floor is worth doing. Go to the entrance on Jackson Boulevard on the south side of the building. It's open until 10:00 PM in summer months. There is an admission charge.

It's a short taxi ride away, but a visit to the Shedd Aquarium is a wonderful way to spend a few hours between trains in Chicago, especially if you're traveling with children. There are nearly 1,500 different species from all over the world on display in this marvelous facility. There is an admission charge.

In June 1944, the US Navy captured a German submarine, the U-505, which had been attacking allied shipping in the Atlantic. It's now on display in the Museum of Science and Industry. It's a rare opportunity to see a piece of history up close and is, of course, of particular interest to older generations. It, too, is a taxi ride from the station and there is an admission fee.

Overnight Accommodations

Chicago is another city where hotel rates can take your breath away, but I do have a couple of recommendations:

The Congress Plaza Hotel
520 Michigan Avenue
1-312-427-3800
www.congressplazahotel.com

This is my kind of hotel. It's old and has seen better days, but it's a Chicago landmark and it still has class. And considering it has a stunning view of Grant Park and the lakefront, the rates are very good. It's not that far from Union Station, but you'll need a cab to get there.

The W Hotel
172 West Adams
1-312-332-1200
www.starwoodhotels.com/whotels

This hotel is at the opposite end of the atmosphere spectrum from the Congress Plaza. Everything is hip or chic or post modern, almost to an extreme. I found it unusual and rather interesting. Assuming decent weather, it's within walking distance from the station for some—maybe 10 to 15 minutes.

3. Los Angeles Union Station (LAX)

Next to Chicago's Union Station, I find myself passing through this station a lot because it's where most of my long-distance train trips begin. Los Angeles is the point of origin for three of Amtrak's long-distance trains: the Sunset Limited, the Southwest Chief, and the Coast Starlight. There are also Amtrak's Pacific Surfliner trains, almost 40 a day, that travel between L.A. and San Diego to the south, and up the coast as far north as San Luis

A steady stream of passengers passes through the Los Angeles station's lovely Art Deco waiting room, hurrying to catch trains to Chicago or Seattle or New Orleans . . . or just to an L.A. suburb. PHOTO COURTESY OF MICHAEL MINN

Obispo. The station is also served by Metrolink commuter trains and the Red, Purple, and Gold lines of the city's light rail system. At last count, about 1.7 million passengers a year come through this station.

You probably didn't know it at the time, but you've no doubt seen this station in any number of movies shot in and around the building. The station's original name was Los Angeles Union Passenger Terminal when it was first opened in 1939 right in the middle of the golden age of train travel. Somehow, even today, it wouldn't seem at all strange if Carol Lombard, Will Rogers, or Douglas Fairbanks suddenly appeared, hurrying to board the Super Chief, ready to depart for Chicago on Track 11.

Architecturally speaking, the station is described as a combination of Spanish Colonial, Mission Revival, and Art Deco, and it all works wonderfully. Top to bottom, inside and out, this building and the surrounding grounds say "Southern California."

The main waiting room is spacious and airy, with lots of big comfortable chairs where you can sit and relax, read a newspaper, or just watch the people coming and going. In fact, I'm willing to state that the waiting room in Los Angeles Union Station offers the best people watching *anywhere*. This is L.A., after all!

To stretch your legs, you can wander out through side doors into lovely enclosed courtyards and patios. And, for sleeping-car passengers, there is a delightful Metropolitan Lounge on the second floor, where you can relax in quiet and comfort. Complimentary coffee, soft drinks, and Wi-Fi are available.

There is, by the way, the FlyAway bus service connecting the station with Los Angeles International Airport, which means those of us who come by plane and go by train can avoid a $50–60 taxi ride.

Where to Eat?

There are sundry shops where you can purchase packaged snacks, and there is the Traxx Restaurant (1-213-625-1999), located right off the main waiting room. The food is quite good, and the atmosphere is beautifully compatible with the station. The restaurant is closed on Sundays.

Step out the main entrance of the station, and look across the access road and beyond North Alameda Street. That's Olivera Street—more detailed information below—and in amongst all the shops and kiosks you will find some great Mexican food being served from food carts and sit-down restaurants.

Then there's Mexicali Taco & Co. (1-213-613-0416) at 702 N. Figueroa, which has been rated one of the ten best restaurants in the downtown area. Trust me, you have *never* had a taco like any one of the creations you'll find there. And, in particular, try the *vampiro*, which is the most popular choice among the regulars. This restaurant is less than a mile from Union Station, but much of the walk is uphill. Take a cab. It'll be worth it.

Things to See and Do

Union Station is located right in downtown Los Angeles and, if you find yourself with a couple of hours to kill between trains, that means you're in luck. There's quite a lot worth seeing in the general area.

First—and it should be at the top of everyone's list—is Olivera Street, a Mexican marketplace that dates back to 1930 and offers a close-up look at traditions going a lot further back than that. It's almost literally across the street from the station. There are food booths, full-on restaurants, gift shops, and all kinds of vendors but, much more than all that, Olivera Street is a cultural experience, with pageants, displays of various arts and crafts, and a variety of activities on a year-round basis. And it's all free of charge—except, of course, for all the stuff that ends up in your shopping bag.

Elsewhere in the general area is the Museum of Contemporary Art, located at 250 South Grand Avenue. There is a truly notable permanent collection as well as special exhibitions. You can call 1-213-626-6222 to find out what's current.

Overnight Accommodations

I've stayed at several different hotels in the downtown area, and only one of them is within walking distance of the station, so you might think about that if you'll be arriving at night. That's not a knock on Los Angeles, by the way. I wouldn't recommend setting out on foot at night for a hotel, especially trundling luggage behind you, in any big city. At any rate, here are three hotels I can recommend from my own experience.

Metro Plaza Hotel
711 N. Main Street
1-213-680-0200
www.metroplazahoteldowntownla.com

This hotel is very close to the station and does the job for a quick in-and-out of the city. It's definitely not fancy, and the rates will reflect that. But it's clean and it's got all the basics, including a complimentary continental breakfast.

Doubletree by Hilton
120 Los Angeles Street
1-213-629-1200
www.doubletree.hilton.com

This hotel was originally owned and run by New Otani, the Japanese hotel chain, and is located on the edge of what's known in L.A. as Little Tokyo. It's gone through some renovations over the last few years, but there is still kind of an Asian feel to it. In particular, there is quite a beautiful rooftop garden on Level G, and it's worth spending some time relaxing there. The hotel is just half a mile from Union Station.

Millennium Biltmore
506 South Grand Avenue
1-213-624-1011
www.millenniumhotels.com

This is another old hotel, going back to the 1920s, and everything about it is reminiscent of those days: high ceilings, ornate décor, and quite a grand feeling everywhere. There's an indoor Roman-style swimming pool that's available to all guests. I suppose this hotel is not for everyone, but I feel quite special when

I'm a guest there. And the location is wonderful—in the heart of the cultural district. It's just a mile and a half from Union Station, but take a cab anyway.

4. New York Pennsylvania Station (NYP)

Penn Station in New York City is the busiest railway station in all of North America, with half a million people passing through every day. That includes both Amtrak passengers and commuters on trains operated by the Long Island Rail Road and New Jersey Transit. That's reason enough to include Penn Station on this top-ten list, but it's also here because it's emblematic of some of the short-sighted mistakes we've made in the past.

The station was built by the Pennsylvania Railroad and was greeted with rave reviews when it first opened for business in 1910. A prestigious architectural publication at the time acclaimed it as "a lasting monument to a great city" and, more than a century later, the original structure is still considered to have been a masterpiece of Beaux Arts architecture, inside and out. But, as the traveling public began driving cars and taking planes, the railroads fell on lean times and "The Pennsy," as it was known at that time, finally sold the air rights to developers. The building was demolished in 1963, and in its place arose Madison Square Garden—New York City's major sports arena—and an office building. Not a good exchange, especially since in late 2013 news stories appeared saying that Madison Square Garden had become outmoded and a new facility in a new location was needed.

The Penn Station of today is certainly not the first impression visitors to New York City should be getting. As for the rest of us . . . well, we deserve better, too. The waiting room is crowded, and the platforms, on additional levels below, are dark and dismal. Eventually New York will have a new station, already

This photo was taken within months of Penn Station's opening in 1910. COURTESY OF MICHAEL PERLMAN, REGO-FOREST PRESERVATION COUNCIL

named after the late Senator Daniel Patrick Moynihan. Phase I is well under construction and planning for Phase II is underway. It can't come soon enough!

Despite Penn Station's inadequacies, all of Amtrak's high-speed Northeast Corridor trains either terminate or stop here. It's also the terminus for overnight trains to Miami, New Orleans, and Chicago. Add to those a dozen or so other trains going to Pittsburgh, south to Charlotte and Savannah, north into Vermont, and to both Montreal and Toronto. Then there are all the commuter trains operated by New Jersey Transit and the Long Island Railroad. It's easy to see that Penn Station is a very, very busy place.

There is an oasis if you're traveling in first class on the high-speed Acela or in a sleeping car on any of the overnight long-distance trains: a Club Acela. It's located off the main concourse on the upper level at the 8th Avenue–end of the building.

Where to Eat?

New Yorkers eat on the run. There are a lot of places in Penn Station where you can grab a bite: Starbucks, KFC, Dunkin Donuts, Pizza Hut, Taco Bell—all the usual suspects. You'll have to leave the station if you want a serious meal, but you won't have to go very far. This is New York City, after all!

Directly across from the main entrance to the station, at 7th Avenue and 31st Street, is the Hotel Pennsylvania, and the Statler Grill is right off the hotel lobby. It's basically a steak house, and I can tell you from first-hand experience that the food is really excellent. The service is, too, but please note: *it has been their policy in the past to add an 18% tip to your check*, so don't just automatically add another 15% out of habit when the bill arrives. Call 1-212-736-3353 for more information.

Things to See and Do

There is no end to the sightseeing in New York City, of course, and since you're going to be starting from right around Penn Station, there's plenty to see that's within walking distance. You can stroll along Fifth Avenue, just two blocks over, and then head uptown to see Times Square and the Empire State Building, just a dozen blocks away. But don't be hesitant to take an actual guided tour, especially if it's your first time in New York and your stay is going to be limited. It's the best way to see a lot and to know what you're looking at. Just ask the concierge or someone at the front desk of the hotel. They'll know all the options and will be able to recommend something that fits your interests and your schedule.

Overnight Accommodations

As in Washington, DC, hotel rates in New York City can be shocking. For me, it depends on how long I'm going to need the room. On a recent trip into New York, I got to the hotel at about

10:00 PM and left early the next morning. I'm a lot less picky for a stay like that. Anyway, here are two hotels of acceptable quality, both a very short walk from Penn Station.

Hotel Pennsylvania
401 7th Avenue
1-212-736-5000
www.hotelpenn.com

I've already mentioned that the Hotel Pennsylvania is right across 7th Avenue from the station's main entrance. This was once a first-rate hotel, but it has seen better days. On my last visit, I was given a room that had recently been renovated. It was a decent size, it was clean, and everything worked. The time before that, the room was clean, but small and dingy. It looked (and was) old. And you can easily find horror stories on the web from people who say they found age-stained draperies, rusty pipes, and mold in the bathrooms. That said, there are two compelling reasons to stay here. First, it's literally 100 feet from Penn Station and, second, the rates are affordable compared to most of the other hotels in the city. That's exactly why I stay here when I'm overnighting in New York City. However, for anything more than just overnight, I would probably look for another hotel.

Affinia Manhattan
371 7th Avenue
1-212-563-1800
www.affinia.com

This is another modestly priced hotel that is also within easy walking distance from Penn Station. The Affinia has recently been renovated but, like the Hotel Pennsylvania, it's an older building with some of the same foibles and idiosyncrasies. Same pluses and minuses, too.

5. New Orleans Union Passenger Terminal (NOL)

I've included the New Orleans station on this list because three of Amtrak's long-distance trains terminate here and their schedules are such that you will almost certainly have to spend an overnight in order to make connections. Or two nights. Or three. (Please don't throw me in *that* briar patch!)

The Sunset Limited operates three days a week between here and Los Angeles; the Crescent runs every day through Atlanta and Washington, DC, all the way to New York; and the City of New Orleans is also a daily train with Chicago as the other terminus.

The station is actually an intermodal facility, also serving Greyhound buses.

The building itself was opened in 1954 and replaced no less than five other stations that were scattered around the city. The consolidation also helped reduce the number of grade-crossing accidents that had been plaguing the city. At the time, it had the distinction of being the only air-conditioned railway station in the entire country.

The waiting room in the New Orleans station is large, but pretty ordinary except for the murals depicting the history of Louisiana. They are really quite special. PHOTO COURTESY OF HENRY KISOR

In terms of architecture, there's nothing particularly special about the building, but there's a real treasure inside: four fresco murals by Conrad Albrizio, an art professor at Louisiana State University. They depict the ages of exploration, colonization, conflict, and the modern age. Altogether, they cover almost 2,200 square feet and they're quite wonderful.

The station is on high ground—a relative term in New Orleans—and that helped save it from sustaining any serious damage during Hurricane Katrina. In fact, the building was used as a temporary jail for some time after the storm. Amtrak was, by the way, the first public transportation out of the city in the aftermath of Katrina.

There is a separate lounge in the station for use by sleeping-car passengers, but it's not to be confused with one of the Metropolitan Lounges. Basically, this is just a separate room with more comfortable chairs, complimentary soft drinks, and a big-screen television.

Where to Eat?

There's not much in the station. There's a sundry/souvenir shop with a few packaged items and a fast-food counter, but this is New Orleans! If you've got some time to spare in *this* town, get yourself off to one of the multitude of outstanding restaurants and enjoy some of the seafood or Creole dishes for which New Orleans is justly famous. I have two suggestions for you.

The first is Irene's Cuisine on St. Phillip Street in the French Quarter. I've been known to stay an extra night in this town just to be sure I have at least one meal at Irene's. It's described as an Italian restaurant, and it is, but traditional ingredients from this area are incorporated wonderfully into the dishes. Call early for a reservation: 1-504-529-8811.

If you're into food, then you need to try La Petite Grocery at 4238 Magazine Street in the Garden District. The menu is contemporary French, but local ingredients are prominent, not to mention delicious. This is a very popular spot, so make sure you call for reservations: 1-504-891-3377.

And, just two blocks from the station, and on the same street, is the Whole Hog Café, which features—surprise!—ribs. They're located at 639 Loyola Avenue, and I guarantee you will not leave hungry. You can reach them by phone at 1-504-525-4044.

Things to See and Do

If there's one must-do here, it's a visit to Preservation Hall at 726 St. Peter Street to hear authentic New Orleans jazz. Of course most of the other tourists have the same idea, and the place only seats about 100 people, so go there close to noon when the box office opens and buy your tickets for one of the three evening performances. Preservation Hall is not a nightclub, so there is no food or drink available, but you are permitted to bring beverages into the performance as long as they're in plastic containers.

New Orleans is also the site of the National World War II Museum at 945 Magazine Street. This should also be on every visitor's must-do list, and you should allow several hours if you're going to do it justice.

Overnight Accommodations

There are a number of hotels closer to the railway station, but it seems to me that if you're going to be spending the night in New Orleans, it really ought to be in the French Quarter. And I have two suggestions for you, both places where I have stayed on my several visits to this city.

Hotel Provincial
1024 Chartres Street
1-504-581-4995
www.hotelprovincial.com

I've been a guest here three times and really enjoy it. First of all, it's a wonderful old building that's listed on the National Register of Historic Places. Most of the rooms are different and have different furnishings, and I always feel like I'm spending the night in the guest bedroom of a private home. There's another reason for overnighting here: just up the street on the corner is Irene's Cuisine (see above).

Maison Dupuy
10012 Toulouse Street
1-504-586-8000
www.maisondupuy.com

Here's another French Quarter hotel with more in the way of on-site amenities. There's a lovely courtyard with a heated swimming pool and an informal bistro and bar that's open for breakfast, lunch, and dinner. There's a really top-notch restaurant adjacent to the hotel, too.

6. King Street Station, Seattle (SEA)

This wonderful building was constructed of granite and brick by the Great Northern Railway and was completed in 1906. Its distinguishing feature is a clock tower that's been a landmark in downtown Seattle ever since. It was, in fact, the tallest structure in Seattle for years, although it's long since been dwarfed by all the high-rise office towers.

There have been minor improvements to the facility over the years, but in 2008 the City of Seattle bought the station from the Burlington Northern Santa Fe railroad for the token price of $10 and a major four-phase renovation was begun. (The first order of business was to get the clock in the tower working again.) Today, King Street Station has been refurbished, restored, and reinforced—Seattle is in an earthquake zone—and is once again a credit to the city.

It's a busy station, too. Two of Amtrak's most popular long-distance trains—the Empire Builder and the Coast

In 2013, the City of Seattle completed a multimillion-dollar renovation of the King Street Station with the renovating and repainting of the splendid waiting room. PHOTO COURTESY OF ZGF ARCHITECTS LLP

Starlight—arrive and depart every day. There are also a dozen or so Cascades trains: two a day in each direction between Seattle and Vancouver across the Canadian border and several more running southbound to Portland and Eugene in Oregon.

Where to Eat?

There are lots of excellent Italian restaurants in Seattle, one of which is Tulio at 1100 Fifth Avenue. It's not all that far from the station in terms of distance, but take a cab because the walk includes several blocks up a very steep hill. The food and the ambience are both great. Call them at 1-206-624-5500.

If you visit Pike's Market—and you should, it's great fun—try Pike Place Chowder (1-206-267-2537). It's very informal, and they're only open for lunch, but the food—a whole assortment of chowders and a seafood bisque—is terrific.

For a more formal setting and a really extensive seafood menu, there's The Crab Pot at Pier 57 (1-206-624-1890). They have all kinds of seafood but, as the name implies, they feature shellfish—varieties of crab, shrimp, prawns, clams, mussels, scallops . . . you name it.

And then there's Assaggio, another wonderful Italian restaurant located on 4th Avenue next to Hotel Andra (see below). The food is outstanding, and I felt at home from the moment I first walked in the door. Whenever I travel to Seattle, I try hard to adjust my schedule to allow for at least one meal here. Call 1-206-441-1399.

Things to See and Do

If you're in Seattle and have a few hours to kill, your first stop should probably be Pike Place Market, located at 1st Avenue and Pike Street. It's a farmers' market that's been here for over a century, and it's great fun just to wander around among all the vendor stalls. There's a great deal more than fruits and vegetables, too. In particular, check out the Fish Market. The guys who work there put on quite a show. (I won't spoil the experience by telling you anything more about it.)

There was a World's Fair in Seattle back in 1962 and, as a kind of symbol of that event and of the city itself, the Space Needle was constructed. It's a 600-foot-high observation tower from which you get a 360-degree look at the city, Puget Sound, and the Cascade Mountain Range in the background. It's fun and the view is astounding. The SkyCity restaurant is up there, too.

Near the Space Needle and just a couple of miles from King Street Station is the Olympic Sculpture Park. It's a nine-acre outdoor site with more than a dozen works of art, several of them extremely large. What with the impressive and imaginative works of art and the backdrop of Puget Sound and the Cascade Range beyond, this is a wonderful place to spend a few hours on a beautiful Seattle day.

Overnight Accommodations

There is really only one hotel within walking distance of King Street Station, and I would think twice about staying there if you'll be arriving after dark. Besides, taxis begin showing up just minutes after trains arrive, and traffic seems to move reasonably well in Seattle, so the fare will be under $10 to any of the downtown hotels.

Best Western Pioneer Square
77 Yesler Way
1-206-340-1234
www.bestwestern.com

I've stayed here frequently because it's only 7 or 8 blocks from King Street Station. The front desk folks are very accommodating, the rooms are fine, the rates are reasonable, and a very good breakfast buffet is included. In other words, it's fine for a quick overnight. But there really aren't any good restaurants nearby and, truthfully, it's not the best neighborhood. Look elsewhere for a longer stay. My personal choice is . . .

Hotel Andra
2000 4th Avenue
1-206-448-8600
www.hotelandra.com

I won't deny it: one reason I come to the Andra is because the restaurant, Assaggio, is right next door (see above). But I really like the hotel anyway. It's just a few minutes by cab from the railway station in a relatively quiet neighborhood just outside the central downtown area. It's got all the pluses: really good staff, nice accommodations, and a very welcoming atmosphere generally. The hotel's own restaurant, Lola, is quite nice and has an excellent breakfast menu.

7. Toronto Union Station

There are several iconic railway stations in Canada, but Toronto Union Station is arguably the one that's the most significant. It's certainly a busy one, with a quarter of a million people passing through every day.

Construction started on the building in 1914 but, because of a shortage of materials due to the First World War, the station wasn't completed and open for business until more than a dozen years later. Nevertheless, it was, and remains, typical of the great railway stations of that era: impressive, built in the Beaux Arts style, and in its own way a monument to the railroads that helped build the nation.

In 1975, Toronto Union Station was added to the list of National Historic Sites, assuring its preservation. In 2000, the building was acquired by the City of Toronto, and the last time I was there, a massive restoration project was underway. The plan calls for saving those elements that are part of the building's history and the railroad tradition, for modernizing to better handle

Toronto Union Station is another of those grand buildings that somehow makes every departure seem like an elegant adventure. COURTESY OF VAHAGN STEPANIAN, NORR LTD.

the additional traffic, and for turning the station itself into a destination, with shops and restaurants and community activities. And good news for those of us who travel in business class or in sleeping cars on VIA trains: there is a new Panorama Lounge on the upper level where we can relax in comfort before boarding our trains.

In keeping with the very sensible trend these days, Toronto Union Station is a multimodal facility. Every day, a total of 42 VIA Rail trains go in and out between there and London (Ontario), Niagara, Ottawa, and Montreal. This station is also the terminus for VIA's premier transcontinental train, the Canadian. Amtrak's daily Maple Leaf arrives from New York City in the early evening and heads back the next morning. In addition, the station handles commuter trains, the local subway system, and buses. There's even a secure bicycle parking facility for locals who come in from the suburbs, then pedal off to their jobs in Toronto's dynamic business center.

Where to Eat?

There are a few places in the station where you can grab a quick something, but there is no actual sit-down restaurant—at least not yet. But there are a lot of options within a stone's throw, including the omnipresent Tim Hortons (roughly the Canadian answer to Dunkin Donuts).

If you're looking for fine dining and very classy ambience, you can walk directly across the street and into the Royal York hotel where you will find the EPIC restaurant (1-416-860-6949). It's really excellent. Furthermore, there is a more casual lounge-bar with a simpler, more limited menu immediately adjacent to it.

Almost next door to the hotel, at 156 Front Street, is a good steak house, Canyon Creek Chophouse. You will probably need to call 1-416-596-2240 and make a reservation; this place is very popular.

Then there's Jack Astor's Bar & Grill (416-585-2121), very close by and also on Front Street. It's a Canadian chain offering sandwiches, salads, burgers, steaks, and such.

Things to See and Do

The first thing you see in this city is the CN Tower, which is *the* Toronto landmark, and no wonder: it's 1,815 feet high. At 1,168 feet up there's a revolving restaurant—aptly named 360 and serving very good food—and the EdgeWalk, a ledge five feet wide with no railing where they hook you to a harness and . . . . Never mind, I can't even write about it without getting queasy.

In the summertime, head for the Harbourfront where you can stroll on a boardwalk at lakeside. There's regular entertainment, lots of shops, and a number of restaurants. In colder weather, check out Toronto's PATH system. It's an underground mall with walkways that run below the streets. Everything is there, including the usual shops and restaurants, but also doctors, dentists, pharmacies, beauty salons, and much more. It's absolutely fascinating for those of us from warmer climates.

Also close by is AGO, the Art Gallery of Ontario at 317 Dundas Street. It's one of the truly distinguished museums in North America, with works from all over the world and including representations from some of the great masters.

And, if you're into sports, you're about a 15 minute walk to the Rogers Center, home to Toronto's professional sports teams: the baseball Blue Jays, the football Argonauts, and the Maple Leafs–one of pro-hockey's historic franchises.

Overnight Accommodations

I don't know what it is about Toronto, but it always seems as though I do a lot of walking there. That's a pleasure in the summertime, but in the winter you'd better revert to the underground city, or pick one of the hotels really close by.

The Fairmont Royal York
100 Front Street
1-416-368-2511
www.fairmont.com/royalyork

As would be expected, there are a number of hotels in the area around Union Station but none closer than the wonderful Royal York, which is directly across the street. Originally built by the Canadian Pacific railroad and opened in 1929, it still retains much of the elegance and style of those days. I really prefer these classy, older hotels, and this one has been my choice every time I've come to Toronto.

InterContinental Toronto
225 Front Street
1-416-597-1400
www.intercontinental.com

This would be a good second choice. It's about six blocks up the street from the station, still within walking distance and in the same general area. It's a modern hotel, and that's reflected in the ambience and the decor. It will probably be somewhat less expensive than the Royal York.

8. 30th Street Station, Philadelphia (PHL)

This is another icon among American railroad stations. Construction started in 1929, about the same time as many of the great ones, but there's much that was different about this edifice. For instance, the roof was reinforced to provide a landing area for small airplanes, and—I can't help wondering if the architects made the connection—a chapel, a hospital, and a mortuary were also incorporated into the building.

It's an imposing building, to be sure, both inside and out. Two sides of the exterior feature huge columns more than 70 feet high. Inside, the main concourse is almost as long as a football field and half as wide, and it's illuminated in part by eight large Art Deco chandeliers suspended from the ceiling 95 feet above the gleaming marble floors. No wonder that 30th Street Station has been on the National Register of Historic Places since 1978.

This station is a rarity in another way, too: trains arrive and depart from all four points on the compass, heading north to New York and Boston; east to Atlantic City; south to Washington, DC, and on to Florida, Atlanta, or New Orleans; and west to Pittsburgh or Chicago.

Originally built and owned by the Pennsylvania Railroad, 30th Street Station now belongs to Amtrak and has evolved into a center for many of the company's business activities. There was a $75 million renovation some 25 years ago, which has led to more development and civic improvements to the entire neighborhood.

It's a busy station, with an average of almost 120 trains a day passing through, including commuter trains operated by SEPTA.

Entering Philadelphia's 30th Street Station through the imposing porte cochere is certainly a good start to any rail journey. PHOTO COURTESY OF AMTRAK; CHUCK GOMEZ PHOTOGRAPHER

Amtrak trains making stops here include all the high-speed Ace-las and Northeast Regionals, plus no less than ten of the medium-and long-distance trains.

Where to Eat?

Within the station there is a food court with the usual fast-food options. Bridgewater's Pub (1-215-387-4787) has a good variety of reasonably priced entrees and a great selection of beers, including no less than 10 on tap.

Then, just a very short walk away, there's Bistro St. Tropez, an excellent French restaurant. Exit the station onto Market Street, turn left, and cross the Schuylkill River. The restaurant is on the 4th floor of the Marketplace Design Center at 2400 Market Street (1-215-569-9269). They're open every weekday for lunch, but only Wednesdays and Thursdays for dinner.

Failing that, there's a very good rib joint about six blocks in the opposite direction. Baby Blues BBQ is at 3402 Sansome Street and is a very popular spot. One look at the menu and you'll know why. The ribs come every way you can possibly imagine. They also have sandwiches and salads. Call them at 1-215-222-4444.

Things to See and Do

This is the city where the Continental Congress met in 1776 to deliberate the Declaration of Independence and where both that document and our Constitution were signed. When you step off the train at 30th Street Station, you're only a couple of miles from Independence Hall, and that's where it all happened. There is no admission fee, but access to the building is by guided tour only. The Liberty Bell and the Benjamin Franklin Museum are right there, too.

If you're traveling with kids aged seven and younger, the Children's Museum of Philadelphia in Fairmont Park is a must. For a long time it was called the Please Touch Museum, and that certainly tells you what you need to know about the enlightened approach they have taken. It's less than a ten-minute cab ride and will keep your little ones enthralled and occupied. They're open until 5:00 PM every day. Reach them by phone at 1-215-581-3181.

Overnight Accommodations

Sonesta Hotel
1800 Market Street
1-215-561-7500
www.sonesta.com/philadelphia

Depending on the weather and how much luggage you have, the Sonesta can be doable on foot from the station. Cross the river and stay on Market Street for about eight blocks, about a half mile in all. It's a nice hotel with a couple of good restaurants, and there's a good breakfast buffet that's included in the room rate. This is the only hotel I feel comfortable recommending from my own personal experience or from others whose judgment I trust.

9. Boston South Station (BOS)

When the very first train rolled out of South Station on New Year's Day 1899, it was departing from the biggest railway station in the world. It's five stories high, neoclassic in design, has a waiting room clad in marble that could easily accommodate as many as 1,500 people, and hosts hundreds of trains coming and going to destinations all over North America. In its day, South Station set the standard for railway stations, and it's been an active transportation hub ever since.

And that in itself is a miracle. In the 1960s, as passenger railroads began to struggle and fail, this majestic station fell into a state of neglect leading to disrepair. A fire caused serious damage to one entire floor, the homeless began haunting its recesses and, at one point, demolition was actually begun.

Thankfully, South Station was saved from the wrecking ball when a group of outraged citizens managed to have it placed

Here's a wonderful old photo taken in 1902 when South Station was one of the largest facilities of its kind in the world. That magnificent clock was saved when part of the original building was demolished.

on the National Register of Historic Places in 1975. Three years later, the property was sold to the Massachusetts Bay Transportation Authority (MBTA), and a project to restore what remained of the original building was begun with almost $200 million scrounged from a variety of government agencies and programs.

Looking at South Station today, you would never believe its age, let alone that history. The focus of activity—outside of the actual passenger train activity—is still in the Great Room and, while it is certainly large, it somehow manages to have a comfortable feel, too.

That's not to say this isn't a busy station. South Station serves Amtrak, of course, as the terminus for all of the Acela Express and Northeast Regional trains heading south to New York and Washington, DC. And this is also where the Boston section of the Lake Shore Limited originates on its daily run overnight to Chicago. MBTA commuter trains from Boston suburbs and the city's popular transit system, known simply as the T, provide the rest of the rail activity. That combination produces a grand total of about 1.5 million passenger comings and goings every year.

Where to Eat?

There are a dozen fast-food places scattered around the main waiting room, so you can certainly find something to eat more or less on the run. And the station is right on the edge of Chinatown, so that's another dining option. Other choices are a bit farther away, so a short taxi ride will probably be the way to go.

It's about a half mile from the station, but The Barking Crab has been a favorite for many years. It's at 88 Sleeper Street right on the water and is a very casual place—part of it is literally under a tent. Seafood is the specialty, but there are plenty of other choices, including vegetarian options.

Sebastians Café is just a couple of blocks away at 100 Summer Street. It's only open for breakfast and lunch, but they have an extensive menu and they're fanatic about using the freshest possible ingredients. It's a very popular spot, and you'll see why if you eat there.

If you're into Vietnamese food, one of the best spots in town, Pho Pasteur, is a 2- to 3-minute taxi ride away at 682 Washington Street.

Things to See and Do

Presuming to recommend just one or two stops of a historical or cultural nature in Boston is absurd; there is enough to keep you going for weeks. Understanding that, and our entire premise being that you're a rail traveler finding yourself in Boston for a few hours or perhaps a day between trains, let me suggest the following options and leave you to use the internet to look into the details.

Absolutely the best way to see and feel the history of the American Revolution is by walking the Freedom Trail—on your own or with a guide. Either way, you start at Boston Common at the visitor center. To get there from South Station, take the Red Line two stops to Park Street. Among other highlights, the Freedom Trail includes Paul Revere's home, Old North Church

("One if by land, two if by sea . . ."), Bunker Hill, and the USS *Constitution*, a wooden frigate built in 1795 and known as "Old Ironsides."

Boston's Museum of Fine Arts is a cultural must. From South Station, take the Red Line two stops to Park Street; change here to the Green Line and take one of the "E" cars to the Museum of Fine Arts (that's what the stop is called).

Overnight Accommodations

There's an almost limitless array of choices when it comes to spending a night or two in Boston. Most of them are pricey, but I'm going to recommend three, and each of them is special—to me, anyway. You'll need a cab to get to any of them.

The Parker House
60 School Street
1-617-227-8600
www.omnihotels.co/boston

If you're going to splurge on a hotel room, let it be for a room in a place like The Parker House. It's an elegant hotel dating all the way back to 1855 and located in the heart of downtown Boston. In fact, it's right on the Freedom Trail. You've heard of the Parker House roll? Well, this is where it originated.

Boston Park Plaza
50 Park Plaza at Arlington
1-617-426-2000
www.bostonparkplaza.com

This is another of the classy old hotels. It dates back to the 1920s and, while it may have lost a bit of its luster, it's still a pleasure to spend a few nights here. Furthermore, the location could hardly be better—very close to Boston Common and the jump-off point for the famous Freedom Trail. And there are lots of excellent restaurants close by.

Eliot Hotel
370 Commonwealth Avenue
1-617-267-1607
www.eliothotel.com

The Eliot is not a big hotel, but it's been a classy place to stay for years. It's in the upscale Back Bay area but close to the T, Boston's transit system that will quickly get you almost anywhere. The Eliot's intimate restaurant, Clio, is a real winner and has been named Best French Restaurant in Boston. (When a native Bostonian finds out where you're staying, they light up: "Oh, good! You're at *The Eliot!*")

10. Grand Central Terminal, New York (GCT)

Once a year, as a teenager, I would take the New Haven Railroad into New York City with my cousin to see a matinee performance of a Broadway show. Walking from the dingy platforms into Grand Central's magnificent Great Hall, with the sun streaming through skylights seemingly hundreds of feet above us and spilling across the gleaming marble floors, was a thrill every time.

When it first opened in 1913, Grand Central Terminal was more than just a magnificent Beaux Arts building; it was a transportation breakthrough with trains arriving and departing from underground electrified platforms.

While still an imposing edifice, Grand Central Terminal is no longer a significant part of our national passenger rail system. Not that long ago, trains departed from Grand Central heading west to Chicago or St. Louis, or north to Boston and Montreal. Today, however, all of Amtrak's eastern trains come and go from Penn Station, with Grand Central left to serve commuter trains only.

Amazingly, and even when it was one of the country's busiest stations, it appeared likely that Grand Central would meet the same fate as Penn Station. In the late 1960s, the Penn Central Railroad leased the station to a developer who had plans to

Grand Central has been a part of everyday life for generations of New Yorkers. Probably the most common meeting spot in all of Manhattan was "by the clock in Grand Central."
PHOTO COURTESY OF THE NEW YORK METROPOLITAN TRANSPORTATION AUTHORITY

demolish most of the building and construct a high-rise in its place. Fortunately, a number of influential people with a sense of civic pride and responsibility—not to mention outrage—rose up in opposition. It took ten years of battling in court, but in 1976 Grand Central Terminal was officially designated a national historic landmark. One of the leading proponents of that effort was Jacqueline Kennedy Onassis.

Unfortunately, for as long as the station's fate had been uncertain, repairs and maintenance kept being deferred, and by the late 1980s, Grand Central had a leaking roof, structural problems were developing, and huge, garish advertisements were defacing much of the Great Hall.

Metro-North, the commuter railroad serving large areas of both Connecticut and New York, had taken over operation of Grand Central in the mid-'80s. Railroad officials were painfully aware that their trains were bringing hundreds of thousands of commuters into the city every day and depositing them in crumbling not-so-grand Grand Central. And so, in 1990, Metro-North stepped up to the plate with a $450 million master plan to renovate and restore this extraordinary building to at least a reasonable representation of its former glory. The plan was adopted by the Metropolitan Transit Authority, and a first phase was launched with $160 million for upgrades and repairs.

Where to Eat?

In this case, you don't have to leave the building. Grand Central has some 25 different places to get a bite to eat on the lower level in the dining concourse. There are also several fine dining establishments.

But before you dine, visit The Campbell Apartment up on the balcony level overlooking the main concourse. Once the living quarters of a multimillionaire tycoon in the 1920s, it's now beautifully restored and serving as a cocktail lounge that's been described in the national media as one of the best bars in the country. Sit, relax, and enjoy an aperitif.

From there, you can go next door to Cipriani Dolci (1-212-973-0999), an outstanding Italian restaurant. Or, should you be in the mood for a superb steak, immediately adjacent to The Campbell Apartment and also on the balcony level is Michael Jordan's The Steak House (1-212-655-2300). And, finally, on the lower level in the dining concourse, is the famous Oyster Bar & Restaurant which, believe it or not, has been a fixture in Grand Central from day one in 1913. And it's still *the* place to go for a mind-boggling assortment of shellfish and seafood. Call them at 1-212-490-6650.

Things to See and Do

Step out of Grand Central Terminal and you are at East 42nd Street and Park Avenue, smack in the middle of Manhattan. Stroll down 42nd, cross Madison Avenue and Fifth Avenue, and you'll see the New York Public Library. Just beyond that is Bryant Park. Keep going a little more and you'll be in Times Square and right in the Theater District. Or you can exit Grand Central onto 42nd Street, turn right on Fifth Avenue, walk seven blocks—that's not a lot in New York City—and you'll be at Rockefeller Center. Almost across the street from there is St. Patrick's Cathedral. Or walk up Madison Avenue to 53rd Street, turn left, and one block later you'll see the word-class Museum of Modern Art. In New York City, finding something to see or do is definitely not a problem!

Overnight Accommodations

There are any number of hotels within walking distance of Grand Central. Here are three, all less than four blocks away, more or less comparable in terms of amenities, and all rated about the same—good to excellent. Of the three, room rates at the Seton will probably be a bit lower than the other two, but by all means check for yourself before making a choice.

Hotel Boutique
128 East 45th Street
1-212-297-0300
www.hotelboutiqueatgrandcentral.com

Roosevelt Hotel
45 East 45th Street
1-212-661-9600
www.theroosevelt| hotel.com

Seton Hotel
144 East 40th Street
1-212-889-5301
www.setonhotelny.com

Honorable Mentions

With literally hundreds of railway stations in the United States and Canada to consider, narrowing it down to just ten was difficult, and strong cases can be made for any number of stations that didn't make the cut. Most often, the axe fell because there just wasn't enough Amtrak activity and very little chance, therefore, that you or other Amtrak passengers would be stopping there, let alone spending hours or days in or around that station.

Cincinnati Union Terminal is a good example. It's a beautiful Art Deco building dating back to the early 1930s, and it's worth going out of your way to see, even if you are not traveling by train. But I didn't include it because the Cardinal is the only Amtrak train stopping at that station, and it only runs three days a week. Furthermore, the westbound Cardinal arrives at 1:13 AM and the eastbound doesn't show up until 3:27 AM.

I considered at least a dozen others: Portland (Oregon) Union Station, St. Paul Union Depot, Gare Centrale in Montreal, San Diego Union Station, and Union Station in Kansas City. All are interesting, wonderful, and unique in their own ways.

For a wealth of information about all of these stations, and almost any other station in whatever city or town you care to name, visit the website for Great American Stations (www. greatamericanstations.com). It's a wonderful project backed by Amtrak, and it provides photographs and information about literally hundreds of railway stations all across the country.

But in addition, it underscores a simple but powerful fact: when a railroad station is renovated and restored, and especially when its role is expanded to serve municipal transit, buses, and taxis as well as trains, the entire surrounding area experiences a redevelopment and an economic upturn. It's happened everywhere. I can't think of a single exception. For just two excellent examples, go to the Great American Stations website and check out the stations at Meridian, Mississippi, and Galesburg, Illinois. You will be astonished.

16

WILL THERE BE TRAINS IN OUR FUTURE?

Many Americans are still surprised to learn that people in other parts of the world are routinely riding trains comfortably and safely at speeds surpassing 200 miles per hour. What's really amazing is that most of it is being done with traditional technology: electric locomotives taking power from an overhead wire to pull cars with steel wheels along steel rails. That's the way railroads have been running their fastest trains for 100 years, and although exotic new technology is certainly out there, that's probably how we'll be doing it for a while. What mystifies people around the world is that, so far, the United States is not part of this transportation renaissance. After all, we've been a leader in the field that dates back 200 years to John Fitch's steamboat and includes the Wright brothers, Henry Ford, Neil Armstrong, and a thousand others in between.

Is Everyone Else Wrong?

The fact is that every other industrialized country in the world has seen the advantages of a rapid and efficient passenger rail system. Most countries have already built such systems and are now busy expanding and updating them. The rest are planning and building high-speed rail systems as fast as they can.

High-speed rail technology was developed in Japan where the *Shinkansen*, or "bullet train," began operating in 1964. The first trains ran at 125 miles per hour along a 320-mile route between Tokyo and Osaka. That original system has since been expanded to more than 1,500 miles and now carries passengers at speeds of up to 200 miles per hour. Since its inauguration more than 50 years ago, the Japanese high-speed system has carried almost 8 billion people in near-perfect safety. The single fatality was caused by a malfunctioning door that closed on a passenger. In 2003, some 160,000 individual *Shinkansen* trips were reviewed, and the average arrival time came within six seconds of the actual scheduled times. How's that for pretty good on-time performance!

The French have become the acknowledged leaders when it comes to high-speed rail. The famous TGV (*train à grande vitesse*, or "high-speed train") now routinely operates at speeds of 199 miles per hour, with trains running as close as ten minutes apart during busiest times. A year or so ago, a specially modified TGV was officially clocked at just more than 357 miles an hour. But even at "only" 199 miles an hour, a ride on the TGV is quite remarkable: smooth, quiet, and without any real sensation of traveling at such speed. On-time performance is 98 percent, so the French are pretty good at punctuality too. A few years ago, I had a TGV itinerary that included a *three-minute* connection in Dijon. When our inbound train came to a stop at the Dijon station, the connecting train was right there on the adjacent platform. We made our three-minute connection with two minutes to spare.

High-speed trains, long since proven safe, reliable, and immensely popular, are running everywhere in Europe, connecting most major cities. Russia now has a high-speed train linking Moscow and St. Petersburg. It's not as fast as the French TGV but has cut the travel time between these two cities from more than eight hours to less than four.

Russia's new high-speed train in the St. Petersburg station ready to depart for Moscow.
PHOTO COURTESY OF THE AUTHOR

Japan is adding to its Shinkansen network and has constructed an extensive test facility for even faster trains powered by magnetic levitation. (More about "maglev" later in this chapter.) In less than ten years, China has built a 7,500-mile high-speed rail network that already covers most of that huge country and which, according to most experts, has been a major factor in China's economic boom.

And what about the United States? Are we finally getting serious about high-speed trains in this country? Well . . . maybe.

On Election Day in the fall of 2008, California voters approved a $10 billion bond issue that was a green light for preliminary work to begin on a high-speed rail line linking Los Angeles and San Francisco. Governors and other public officials in several Midwestern states began talking about and planning for the possibility of high-speed rail routes. Decisive leadership came from Washington when, within months of first taking office, President Barack Obama announced his administration's support for high-speed rail lines that would link a number of major US cities along several population corridors. Congress followed the president's lead by passing the American Recovery and Reinvestment Act of 2009, which contained $8 billion intended to provide start-up funding for high-speed rail projects in several states.

Then came the 2010 midterm elections with Republicans gaining the majority in the US House of Representatives. Republican governors in Florida and Wisconsin announced they would refuse the federal dollars allocated for high-speed rail projects in their states. In California, anti-rail forces kept up a relentless attack in the media and the courts in an effort to stop that project. And by the end of 2013, it seemed as though much of the momentum behind high-speed rail had disappeared.

The Case for High-Speed Trains

Have you ever made that grueling four-plus-hour drive across the desert from Los Angeles to Las Vegas? A train like the TGV could get you there in two hours in air-conditioned comfort. And the trip from L.A. to San Francisco would take just over two-and-a-half hours. High-speed trains would bring about equally dramatic changes in the travel habits of people across the country—in the Northwest, Portland, Tacoma, Seattle, and Vancouver would be connected; in the East, Philadelphia would be linked with Harrisburg and Pittsburgh; in Florida, people could go from either Tampa or Miami to Disney World in Orlando. High-speed rail lines should be linking Chicago with any number of cities, including St. Louis, Milwaukee, Minneapolis, Cleveland, Cincinnati, and Detroit. In Canada, the corridor from Windsor through Ottawa and Montreal to Quebec is a textbook opportunity for high-speed rail.

Unfortunately, the future of *any* kind of a national passenger rail system has periodically been in doubt, because influential Republican voices in Congress have been quite willing to let

Amtrak wither and die. One of the budgets offered by former President George W. Bush actually recommended zero funding for Amtrak, which would have forced the railroad to shut down within 90 days. It's a position that's hard to understand, given the obvious popularity and success of rail travel in all these other countries. Why have we been so reluctant to learn from them? When hearing about innovations within his own field, a shrewd and successful banker friend of mine asks this question first: "What do they know that I don't know?" It's a sensible question, and it's a shame we have had to wait so long before our elected

VISION *for* HIGH-SPEED RAIL *in* AMERICA

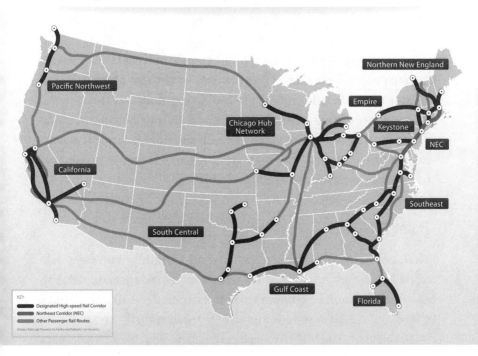

An important first step in the development of high-speed rail in the United States was the designation of a number of corridors around the country that would link major cities. Now it's a question of where the money will come from.

officials began asking that same question about passenger trains in general and high-speed rail in particular.

The High-Speed Advantage

Let's start with two safe assumptions: First, our population will continue to increase. Second, all those people will want the same kind of mobility the rest of us enjoy now. If those assumptions prove to be true—and they will, of course—it will invariably mean more cars on more highways. It will also mean more airplanes flying around in the same amount of sky. In other words, it means more congestion, more pollution, and more safety concerns.

But what if we didn't commit those megabillions to support and expand our car-plane transportation habit? What if, as a nation, we threw serious resources into building a nationwide passenger rail system instead, with high-speed trains operating in and around 15 or 20 of the major urban areas? The answer is that people would travel just as efficiently and quickly but in greater safety. Furthermore, we could stop and even reverse the degradation of our environment caused by our automobile and airplane addictions. The catch is that it can only be done if people can be convinced that the high-speed train is indeed a reasonable transportation alternative.

Trains Can Be as Fast as Planes

Well, all right, I'll concede that a train certainly won't get you from New York to California as fast as a passenger jet. But in most cases, it *will* be comparable for a trip under 400 miles (that's a two-and-a-half-hour run for a high-speed train).

Consider Amtrak's Acela service between New York City and Washington, DC. Those trains can take you from Washington's Union Station—just a few hundred yards from the Capitol itself—to midtown Manhattan in just over two hours and 45 minutes. You'd be hard-pressed to make it any quicker by air—you'd take a taxi from the Capitol to the airport, check in, go through security, wait to board, and wait again to take off. After the actual flight, it's another very long cab ride into Manhattan. No wonder some three quarters of the people traveling between New York and Washington are now doing so comfortably on the train. Furthermore, when you add the cost of those two cab rides to the airfare, the train is cheaper too.

The fact is, 300–400 miles is how far most of us travel most often. That's certainly the case at Chicago's O'Hare Airport, one of the busiest in the nation, where 30 to 40 percent of the arriving flights are from destinations 400 miles away or less. O'Hare is not unique: A large number of flights in and out of most of the major hub cities—Dallas–Forth Worth, New York City, Los Angeles, San Francisco, and Atlanta, for example—are to and from cities less than 400 miles away.

Chicago has been a major railroad center since day one. Proponents of high-speed rail have long argued that trains could carry people between there and other nearby cities in the Midwest—Milwaukee, St. Louis, Indianapolis, Fort Wayne, Toledo, Detroit, Cincinnati, and a host of smaller towns—faster, cheaper, and safer than planes. They're already doing it in Europe, after all. Alas, despite crowded skies around Chicago from air traffic at O'Hare and Midway airports, there is still some talk about a *third* major airport south of that city. The costs—billions and billions of dollars, thousands of acres of land, the displacement of homes and businesses, and the inevitable impact on the environment—would be staggering.

Long-Term High-Speed Rail Is Cheaper

Depending on the terrain, it costs anywhere from $3 million to $9 million per lane-mile to build a typical interstate highway through rural areas. But once highway construction moves into urban areas, the cost soars to anywhere from $18 million to as much as $75 million per lane-mile. In other words, a six-lane freeway can cost—let's round off the numbers and be conservative—$40 million per mile in the country and $400 million per mile when it goes through urban areas. And there is a huge hidden cost to highway construction: all those new roads require vast quantities of land that will stop generating billions of dollars in property taxes once the roads are built—revenue for cities and towns that will be lost forever.

New modern airports are currently costing many billions of dollars each. Depending on which expert you talk to, this country supposedly "needs" anywhere from 10 to 20 new ones. You and I will be paying for those airports, of course, with our tax dollars and higher fares the airlines must charge to cover the increased landing fees they'll be forced to pay.

The cost for building a high-speed rail system? Depending on the terrain, the cost of land acquisition, and other variables, it's somewhere between $40 and $80 million a mile. But far less land is used for the train's right-of-way, and the fuel saved by passengers taking the train instead of driving or flying will be in the billions and will keep adding up indefinitely.

Trains Are Better for the Environment

This one is a slam dunk. New highways and airports gobble up thousands of acres of land. Pollution from automobiles and jet planes fills the air in most of our major cities, where it's measured and calculated by the ton. Then there's the whole issue of noise pollution.

Electric high-speed trains, on the other hand, have no exhaust and therefore emit no pollution. The amount of land used by two parallel tracks is obviously a great deal less than the amount used by a six-lane interstate highway. In many instances, the rail line would be built along the existing highway's right-of-way, which would mean little or even no cost for land acquisition. As far as noise is concerned, a high-speed train is roughly as loud as a stream of traffic—the difference is that noise from automobiles is continuous, while a train passes very quickly.

Trains Are More Energy Efficient

Calculated on a per-passenger-mile basis, a high-speed train uses less than two-thirds the energy consumed by an automobile and only about one-fifth the amount consumed by a jet plane. Actually, those figures give the family car a big break, since they assume it's carrying four people. We can really begin to see the potential benefits by comparing energy consumption in the United States with areas in Europe where high-speed rail is a viable alternative to the private automobile. On a per-capita basis, a typical American uses about 400 gallons of gasoline a year, while a resident of a typical European city uses just more than 100 gallons.

Trains Are Safer, Too

Most of us are painfully aware of the carnage that occurs year after year on our highways: between 35,000 and 40,000 people are killed annually, and many times that number are injured. Statistically, planes are many times safer than automobiles, but there are real concerns about our ability to maintain that high standard. The airlines of the world are now using about 20,000 planes to carry their passengers, and many of those planes are flying around in American skies. There has been concern for some time that our current air-traffic-control system is operating at or near capacity. That has raised demands for an improved system that would allow more planes in the air at the same time and permit them to fly even closer together.

OK, how safe are trains . . . really? If done right, a high-speed rail system is perfectly safe. Certainly in the case of the French and Japanese high-speed systems, we can take that statement literally—they have *perfect* safety records. Here at home, it's quite true that Amtrak has been less than perfect, although I know of no serious accident involving a passenger train where responsibility has been laid at Amtrak's doorstep. In the worst incident, some 40 people were killed when a barge collided with a bridge while traveling through a dense fog. The barge knocked the tracks out of alignment moments before the train started across. Amtrak has compiled an excellent safety record, and the fact remains that you're many times safer on a cross-country train ride than you are driving your own car to the local convenience store for a bottle of aspirin.

Ideally (by that I mean the way they do it in Japan and France) passenger trains should operate on their own exclusive rights-of-way. Except for most of the Northeast Corridor, Amtrak is forced to share tracks with freight trains, which results in increased rail traffic operating at different speeds. It's a safe arrangement, but it's one that often requires slower speeds or delays for Amtrak trains. Furthermore, all railroading, whether freight or passenger, will be made even safer once the Positive Train Control system has been implemented. (There's more information about PTC in chapter 12, "Safety is Priority Number One.")

Small Towns Need Trains

Often overlooked in the plane-car-train argument are the thousands of US and Canadian communities for which the train is the only public transportation link to the rest of the country. Canada's VIA Rail runs a twice-weekly train that passes through more than 80 tiny communities on its thousand-mile journey from

Winnipeg to Hudson Bay. Amtrak also serves countless towns all over America, towns that have no airport and are bypassed even by buses. When complicated diagnoses or highly specialized medical care is needed, small hospitals and individual physicians in rural areas frequently send their patients to facilities in major cities—the Mayo Clinic, for example. Very often, the train is the most comfortable—or even the *only* way—for these people to get to the medical attention they need. High-speed trains will never be a realistic option for most of these communities, but the people in these small towns will be more than glad if they can simply keep their existing rail service.

Will People Accept High-Speed Trains?

Absolutely. They have almost everywhere else in the world. The Japanese have had it figured out for decades. With their TGV trains, the French are the acknowledged leaders. The Spanish have turned to high-speed rail in a big way, pouring billions of dollars into their AVE (Alta Velocidad Española) system that now links their major cities at speeds nearing 200 mph. There are high-speed trains running all over Europe; as soon as a new route opens, passengers flock to use it.

Let's not forget the Chinese: In 2011, I rode what was then their brand-new high-speed line connecting Beijing and Shanghai. The train routinely ran at speeds well in excess of 200 mph, and we completed the 800-plus-mile journey in just about five hours. That's an average speed of more than 165 mph, and this same equipment has been run on a test track at more than 300 mph.

Why do people all over the rest of the world choose to ride high-speed trains? Because they can take you from one city center to another 400 miles away in less time, for less money, and far more comfortably than if you made the trip by plane.

What About Maglev?

Just when we're beginning to grasp the idea of traveling up to 200 mph on land, along comes yet another new transportation technology: *magnetic levitation* (maglev). Do you think it's some kind of exotic, pie-in-the-sky, science-fiction idea? Nope, maglev is already here, and it really works.

As with so many great ideas, the basic concept is quite simple. We've all held a magnet in each hand and, by turning them one way or another, felt them either attract or repel each other. That's how maglev works. Large, electric-powered magnets are built into both the train and the guideway. By using the magnets' pushing and pulling forces, the train can be lifted free of its track and moved forward.

This is not futuristic stuff. A maglev train is operating today in China, carrying passengers between downtown Shanghai and its airport, the Pudong International Airport. The train covers a distance of 18.6 miles in just over 7 minutes, averaging approximately 150 mph and boasting a top speed of 268 mph.

Other maglev vehicles are currently being run on test tracks in several parts of the world. One in Japan reached 361 mph. Engineers there say that there is really no reason why a speed of 500–600 mph can't be achieved. (Perhaps "passenger terror" would become a factor at those speeds. There must come a point when, no matter how smooth the ride might be, extreme speeds at ground level become fearful for anyone without the psyche of a test pilot.)

Because a maglev train has literally no contact with the guideway, proponents claim there is no friction and virtually no sound. Witnesses at a maglev test track in Germany reported being able to hear a pair of crows cawing while the train was racing by. Maybe so, but I had a somewhat different experience. Having often heard the descriptive phrase about maglev—"riding on a cushion of air"—I fully expected a smooth, quiet trip when I took the short maglev ride out to Shanghai's Pudong Airport. It was neither. It was, in fact, a very rough ride and quite noisy inside the train.

Although potentially able to travel much faster than today's bullet trains and the TGV, a maglev system offers virtually the same benefits: it's energy efficient, pollution free, and safe. Furthermore, once all testing and certification has been completed, maglev trains can be ordered up "off the shelf," with manufacturers offering standardized vehicles to systems around the world. Some estimates say that the cost of building a maglev system will be about the same as building a high-speed rail. Even if you have just a casual interest in this futuristic stuff, stay tuned—we haven't seen anything yet!

But First, Baby Steps

Maglev is all well and good, and it's exciting to see interest in high-speed rail. The more immediate problem, however, is to make sure our conventional rail system stays up and running. We turned an important corner with the presidential election of Barack Obama, who has been an outspoken advocate of rail transportation. Then the Democratic Congress followed by increasing financial support of rail by the federal government. That was encouraging, but—whoops!—Republicans, many of them espousing the Tea Party philosophy, took back control of the House in 2012, and the bashing of both high-speed rail and Amtrak resumed. When and if some degree of stability has been achieved, the problem becomes finding additional money to expand the Amtrak system with new equipment and greater frequencies. In the near term, the federal government can encourage the freight railroads to improve track conditions and insist that they give priority to Amtrak passenger trains. If that happens—

and if Positive Train Control is fully implemented—Amtrak trains will be able to travel at higher speeds, which will mean reduced running times. That in turn will make train travel an attractive option for more and more people.

The problem, as always, is money. *Subsidy* is still considered a dirty word in some circles. Strangely, most of those people see nothing wrong with government support of municipal bus systems, for example, but they stubbornly continue to oppose subsidies for Amtrak. Yet it's a simple fact that, in one way or another, government subsidizes *every* form of public transportation. The government builds highways for cars and buses, airports for planes, and even bike paths for cyclists and sidewalks for people on foot.

But wait, you say, the government doesn't subsidize American Airlines, Delta, or United, so why should the taxpayers assist Amtrak? But the government *does* subsidize the airlines. There are lots of examples, but the most obvious is our nationwide air-traffic-control system that is run by the Federal Aviation Administration (FAA), an agency of the federal government. Railroads have traffic control systems too, but they pay all the costs themselves. Cities and states float bonds to build and expand airports, and I'll bet dollars to donuts that as you read this, there's construction underway at whatever airport you use. Remember too that you and I pay a special tax on every airline ticket we buy. That money goes into a separate trust fund and is spent to advance the aviation industry. But there's no subsidy for highways, claim the anti-subsidy folks; that's what the gasoline tax is for. Nope, sorry. The federal tax on gasoline only covers about half the cost of highway construction and maintenance. The rest comes right out of the general fund, and that, folks, is a direct subsidy.

The frustrating aspect to this whole argument is that on one hand there are planners and engineers and government officials who are looking for ways to make sure as many Americans as possible have mobility, meaning access to public transportation that enables them to travel for all the reasons that other Americans travel. When it comes to rail, they're being opposed not by other planners and engineers with different solutions but by ideologues against *any* solution.

There is not one national passenger rail system in the world intended for the general public's use that isn't subsidized by government. So why do some politicians continue to insist that Amtrak should be able to provide a nationwide rail transportation system without assistance from our government? That's especially puzzling when it's so clear to many of us that for some very important reasons—environmental, economic, and societal—rail is the one means of transportation government should *encourage*, not discourage.

The Pendulum Is Swinging Back to Rail

There are those in this country—people who know a great deal about trains and the transportation industry—who are fighting hard for the future of rail travel in North America. It's important that they continue to do that—after all, the Reagan and both Bush administrations tried persistently to do away with any subsidy for Amtrak. Now, at a time when budget cutting is on everyone's mind, there are still anti-rail people left in Congress. Thankfully, they are in a minority. With the constant threat of higher gasoline costs, continuing chaos in the airline industry, and ever-worsening traffic congestion on our roads and highways, public officials and community leaders at the local and state levels have begun to organize and beat the drums for passenger rail. They want more frequencies. They're asking that existing routes be extended to their cities and towns. They're pushing for the restoration of rail service that had been discontinued. They want trains like the

Cardinal and the Sunset Limited to run daily instead of just three days a week.

In the meantime, the American public has made it abundantly clear that they like trains. Long-distance trains in particular run full much of the year, particularly in the sleeping cars. Even Amtrak critics agree that for six to eight months a year, the company could double the number of trains and still fill up most of them.

In spite of the many obstacles in its path, Amtrak continues to make incremental improvements in its operation and finances. In fact, Amtrak can actually lay claim to being the most cost-efficient national rail system in the world by one very important yardstick: the company's revenue covers almost 90 percent of its operating costs. No other national passenger rail system anywhere comes close to that. (In the previous edition of this book, published in 2011, that authenticated number was 80 percent.)

Make no mistake, however: Amtrak will always need support from federal and state governments. Today, whether they like it or not, individual states are more involved than ever. In 2008, Congress passed the Passenger Rail Investment and Improvement Act that contained a provision requiring states to share in the cost of Amtrak trains if a route passing across their borders totaled less than 750 miles. (Good idea in theory but with the potential for real problems: What, for instance, would happen to a train passing through four states if one state would not agree on the amount of subsidy it was asked to pay?)

The fact is, a number of states were already heavily subsidizing passenger trains within their borders because they understand those trains are providing essential transportation links for their citizens. California is at the top of this list, with heavy financial support of Pacific Surfliner trains, which operate between San Luis Obispo and San Diego through Los Angeles; the Capitol Corridor trains, which run throughout the Bay Area; and the

San Joachin trains, which operate through the central part of the state.

Washington and Oregon chip in to support the Cascade service. These trains operate between Eugene, Oregon; Portland, Oregon; and Seattle, Washington. There is additional service into Vancouver, British Columbia.

Maine and Massachusetts subsidize the Downeaster, which runs between Portland and Boston. The State of Illinois helps to fund trains running between Chicago and Quincy, between Chicago and Carbondale, and also from Chicago to St. Louis, Missouri. Then there's Michigan, which supports trains between Detroit, Pontiac, and Grand Rapids. There are others, too, but the point is that all of these states have recognized the importance of a rail system to their citizens—that is, to their taxpayers.

What Amtrak really needs—in fact, all Amtrak has *ever* needed—is a stable source of adequate funding. The key words are *stable* and *adequate*. How can Amtrak be expected to plan for the orderly replacement of worn-out equipment, for example, if they have no idea from one year to the next how much money will be coming from the government? With stable and adequate funding, however, Amtrak could add new equipment and replace the old on a systematic basis. That would provide more trains on its popular routes, run them at more convenient times, improve on-time performance, and—OK, so this is my own personal addition to the list—wash every window on every train every day. Sounds like a good program, doesn't it?

What You Can Do

Write Letters

We all get to vote for or against one member of Congress, two US senators, and the president. Let me tell you: nothing has more effect on an elected official than a real letter from a constituent. Keep each letter short and to the point. Tell them you think America should have a decent passenger rail system and that you want them to support trains in general and Amtrak in particular.

Join the Club

There are many nonprofit organizations around the country that actively promote rail transportation at the state and local levels. I've included a list in the back of this book. The National Association of Railroad Passengers is a nonprofit, nonpartisan organization that advocates more, better, and faster trains on behalf of the rail passengers of this country. I would certainly encourage you to join this organization. I have been a member for years and have served on NARP's national board of directors. Dues are very reasonable, and Amtrak gives NARP members a 10 percent discount on all rail fares. In addition, the NARP membership entitles you to discounts on other rail- and travel-related products and services. For more information, go to www.narprail.org.

Take a Train Ride

Amtrak needs the money. For that matter, VIA Rail does too. Besides, now that you've read this book, you'll certainly know how to get the most possible enjoyment from the trip.

So . . . *all aboard!*

17

PICK A TRAIN, ANY TRAIN

This chapter contains information about the long-distance trains operated by Amtrak in the United States and VIA Rail in Canada. There's also information about trains operated by Alaska Railroad. Some of the shorter routes are also mentioned, because of either high ridership or noteworthy scenery. (Information about the Copper Canyon train in Mexico may be found in chapter 14.)

I have not provided specific information about individual Amtrak trains running within the Northeast Corridor. For one thing, there are a lot of them—some run between Washington, DC, and New York; others extend up to Boston; and still others swing northwest at New Haven, Connecticut, to go up through Hartford to Springfield, Massachusetts. Some make more stops than others and thus take longer to complete their routes. Some of the trains are the high-speed Acelas, while the rest are Amfleet cars and locomotives. In other words, there are simply too many variables. I do have information for trains that pass through the Northeast Corridor between New York and many points farther south and west—the Cardinal and the Crescent, for example— and for the Florida trains too.

I've provided both the name and number for each train—odd numbers are for trains headed south and west, and even numbers are for those headed north or east. A third number given to a train usually means it operates at a different time on weekends. I've given a few of the major stops along the route, but not all; you can go online at www.amtrak.com and click on "Routes" for maps and more detailed information about specific trains.

You can also access current timetables on the Amtrak website. They will provide the mileage from each train's point of origin to each of the stops along the way. You may notice that some trains seem to take longer to travel in one direction than they do on their return trip, even though they're covering exactly the same route. There can be several reasons for that apparent discrepancy: a long grade that takes more time on the uphill run, more freight traffic encountered on the trip because it operates at a different time of day, or padding in the schedule. And don't forget that many of these trains pass through different time zones, gaining and losing hours (and confusing passengers) as they go.

I've also tried to tell you something about each trip's scenery and anything else that may make the trip different or interesting. In some cases, I'll tell you whether you'll see more or better scenery when traveling in one direction on a certain route as opposed to the other. This can indeed be the case: since a train may pass through a particularly scenic area during daylight hours when traveling in one direction, it may pass through that same stretch at night on its return trip. Occasionally I'll note from which side of the train you can best see special points of interest or particularly scenic areas. Between New York City and Albany, for instance, the westbound Lake Shore Limited travels for more than two hours along the east bank of the Hudson River. But if you're in a roomette on the right side of the train, you might never realize it. Of course, if you're traveling in the opposite direction—that is, eastbound toward New York City—the river will be on the right side. If you're riding in coach, you'll be able to see out of both sides of the train, but you'll still probably prefer to grab a seat on the side where the great scenery will be.

Please remember that both Amtrak and VIA issue new timetables regularly. There are always changes, and they are not necessarily minor details. Case in point: for years VIA Rail's westbound transcontinental train, the Canadian, left Toronto at 9:00 in the morning. The schedule was changed several years ago; the Canadian now leaves Toronto at 10:00 in the evening! Use the following information to help you plan a wonderful, scenic rail journey, but check everything with an Amtrak or VIA Rail reservations agent or a knowledgeable travel agent before your plans are set in concrete.

Amtrak
Northeast Corridor Trains
Springfield, MA–Washington, DC

Stops:	Hartford, New Haven, New York, Philadelphia, Baltimore
Frequency:	Several times a day in each direction (some connect in New Haven)
Duration:	7 hours
Equipment:	Amfleet coaches, business class, quiet car (some trains), cafe car

This is a busy route with trains operating fairly often during the day. Going southbound, the train crosses the Connecticut River after leaving Springfield and runs through some very attractive areas of rural Connecticut. In the summertime you'll see entire fields of tobacco covered by some humidity-raising material that looks like white cheesecloth. The tobacco is a special variety used for cigar wrappers. Hartford's railroad station has had a facelift and now looks much the way it did around the turn of the century. The gold-domed State Capitol is on the left just as you leave the station. The track from Springfield to New Haven has not yet been electrified, so southbound trains change their diesel-electric locomotives for all-electric ones there. New Haven is also the home of Yale University. From here to New York you're sometimes within sight of the ocean—actually, it's Long Island Sound. Once you reach Bridgeport, you'll be passing through communities where lots of people commute to work in New York City. You'll cross the Hell Gate Bridge onto Manhattan Island, then dip underground and below the streets. These trains used to end up in wonderful old Grand Central Terminal (the commuter trains still do), but Amtrak now uses a bypass and goes straight to Pennsylvania Station. Some of these trains continue on to Washington.

Boston–New York

Stops:	Providence, New Haven, New London
Frequency:	10 to 12 times a day in each direction
Duration:	3½ hours for Acela trains; 4 hours for Northeast Regional service
Equipment:	Acela trains: First class, business class, quiet car, cafe car; Northeast Regional trains: Amfleet coaches, business class, quiet car, cafe car

This is really a nice ride. After leaving Boston, the southbound train passes through some typically New England areas. Soon after Providence, Rhode Island, the ocean is frequently visible on the left. Also look for submarines as you cross the Thames River at New London. I'm not kidding—that's where they're built by the Electric Boat division of General Dynamics. The Merchant Marine Academy is also here. Along the Connecticut shore you'll see some wonderful old homes built early in the century and pleasure boats by the hundreds. Approaching New York City, you'll get a good view of the classic city skyline. Wi-Fi is now available in trains on this run. (Note: All of these trains continue south to Washington, with a few continuing on to Newport News, Virginia.)

New York City–Washington

Stops:	Trenton, Philadelphia, Wilmington, Baltimore
Frequency:	Multiple times a day in each direction
Duration:	2¾ hours for Acela trains, 3¼ hours for Northeast Regional service
Equipment:	Acela trains: First class, business class, quiet car, cafe car; Northeast Regional trains: Amfleet coaches, business class, quiet car, cafe car

This is Amtrak's high-speed run, with the Acela trains reaching speeds of 150 miles per hour in some stretches and the Northeast Regional trains running at more than 100 miles per hour. Leaving New York City, the trains pass beneath the Hudson River and emerge in New Jersey. There's occasional farmland, and you'll cross a number of rivers, including the Delaware, but much of this trip is through industrial areas, apartment buildings, and tenements. For me, there's nothing very scenic about it, but on one of my trips I happened to sit next to a young man from Nebraska who was absolutely fascinated by it all. You just never know, do you? As on the run north to Boston, Amtrak is now providing free Wi-Fi on these trains.

Eastern Trains
Adirondack (68, 69)

Stops:	New York City, Poughkeepsie, Albany, Ticonderoga, Lake Placid, Montreal
Frequency:	Daily
Distance:	381 miles
Duration:	11 hours
Equipment:	Amfleet coaches, lounge car

This is one of the more scenic trips in the eastern part of the United States, and when the fall colors are at their best, it would get my vote for being one of the top three or four in the entire Amtrak system. The Adirondack operates during daylight hours in both directions. Leaving New York City, you'll travel along the eastern bank of the Hudson River for almost the entire run up to Albany. Along that stretch, you'll pass right by the walls of Sing Sing prison and have a good view of the US Military Academy at West Point on the opposite shore. After leaving Albany, the train continues due north with several stops at picturesque towns, including Saratoga Springs and Ticonderoga, and through lovely rural areas with small farms and lots of woodlands.

Downeaster (680–699)

Stops:	Boston, Woburn, Exeter, Dover, Old Orchard Beach, Portland
Frequency:	Five times a day in each direction
Distance:	102 miles
Duration:	2½ hours
Equipment:	Amfleet coaches, business class, cafe car

There's an interesting story behind this train. In fact, it's an inspiring story. Back in the late '80s, people from a number of communuities in Massachusetts, New Hampshire, and Maine got together with the singular goal of getting Amtrak to extend rail service north of Boston to Portland, Maine. They organized as TrainRiders/Northeast, met with Amtrak and with public officials, and launched a campaign to inform and include the general public. It took more than 10 years and help from the federal, state, and local governments, but in 2001 the first Downeaster rolled out of Portland station headed for Boston. Since then, the popularity of the Downeaster has climbed steadily—it has even posted double-digit increases in ridership for several years. In the summer of 2010, with both federal and state funds, workers began laying new track to permit the Downeaster to extend service beyond Portland to Brunswick, Maine. That service was launched at the end of 2012. Here's an idea: If you're in Boston and can manage a few extra days, take the Downeaster through some quaint New England towns and up to Old Orchard Beach on the Maine coast. Visit some historical sites and check out the shops, then pick a nice restaurant and order a lobster dinner. You'll be a happy camper when the Downeaster takes you back to Boston the next day. (Note: This train departs and arrives from Boston's North Station. All other Amtrak trains, whether heading south to New York City or west toward Albany, use South Station.)

Ethan Allen Express (290, 291, 292, 293, 296)

Stops:	New York City, Poughkeepsie, Albany, Saratoga Springs, Rutland
Frequency:	Daily
Distance:	241 miles
Duration:	5½ hours
Equipment:	Amfleet coaches, business class, cafe car

Another very scenic ride, especially in the fall. If you're aboard the northbound train, be sure to grab a window seat on the left side of the train for the two-and-a-half-hour run up the Hudson River to Albany. From there, you'll see farms and small towns in what's known as upstate New York. There will also be a stop at timeless Saratoga Springs. Get off and spend a few days there, especially if it's horse-racing season. From here, the Ethan Allen heads northeast for Rutland. It's Vermont's second largest city, but the population is less than 25,000. My idea of a great way to see New England in the fall? Take this train to Rutland, rent a car, and leisurely drive around the area for a few days. Stop at some of the delightful bed-and-breakfast places all through that area, then drop the car in Montpelier (Vermont's capital) or White River Junction, and take the Vermonter back down to New York.

Maple Leaf (63, 64)

Stops:	New York City, Poughkeepsie, Albany, Buffalo, Niagara Falls, Toronto
Frequency:	Daily
Distance:	544 miles
Duration:	Northbound: 12½ hours; southbound: 13 hours
Equipment:	Amfleet coaches, business class, cafe car

This train also runs along the east bank of the Hudson River between New York City and Albany, but be aware that the southbound train passes through that stretch after dark, except during the longest days of the summer months. If you have never seen Niagara Falls, take my advice and stop off for a day to experience it. As with the Adirondak, the fall colors will be spectacular if your timing is right.

By the way, many Americans still think they can enter Canada with a wave of the hand. Nope. You'll need a valid passport. If there's anything out of the ordinary about your status, check carefully ahead of time to be sure you have the documentation you need.

Vermonter (54, 55, 56, 57)

Stops:	Washington, New York, New Haven, Hartford, Amherst, Claremont, White River Junction, Stowe, St. Albans
Frequency:	Daily
Distance:	611 miles
Duration:	14 hours
Equipment:	Amfleet coaches, business class, cafe car

I love this trip! Talk about contrasts: you start out in Washington, DC, run up the industrialized East Coast to New York City, and travel along the scenic Connecticut shoreline to New Haven. There the Vermonter swings inland through the middle of Connecticut and western Massachusetts before entering Vermont. The train follows the Connecticut River much of the way, crossing into New Hampshire, then back again into Vermont. It ends the all-day journey at St. Albans, which is just a stone's throw from the Canadian border. From New Haven north, you'll pass by hundreds of little New England towns. It's a great way to view the spectacular fall colors, and maybe even a moose. I love this trip—but I already said that, didn't I!

Lake Shore Limited (48, 49)

Stops:	Chicago, Cleveland, Albany, Buffalo, New York City or Boston
Frequency:	Daily
Distance:	Chicago to Boston: 1,017 miles; Chicago to NYC: 959 miles
Duration:	Chicago to Boston: 23 hours; Chicago to NYC: 20 hours
Equipment:	Amfleet coaches, Viewliner sleepers, dining car, lounge car

The Lake Shore follows the same route as the New York Central's famous 20th Century Limited, skirting two of the Great Lakes—Michigan and Erie. The scenery will be quite different, however, depending on which direction you travel. The westbound train runs in daylight roughly from Toledo to Chicago; while the eastbound Lake Shore travels in daylight from about Erie, Pennsylvania, to either of its final destinations, Boston or New York. In my opinion, the eastbound train is the more scenic trip. Off and on between Buffalo and Schenectady, you'll be following the old Erie Canal, and a number of the canal locks can be seen from the right side of the train. When it was finished in 1825, the canal connected Buffalo on Lake Erie with the Hudson River at Albany, allowing people and goods to travel by water all the way from the Great Lakes to the Atlantic Ocean. The eastbound Lake Shore splits into two trains at Albany. The New York section runs due south for several hours, with the Hudson River on the right, before reaching New York City. After leaving Albany, the other section heads east to Pittsfield in the middle of the Berkshire Mountains, which is one of the choice skiing areas in the entire East. From there through Springfield and Worcester, you'll pass through many charming little New England towns before reaching Boston.

Capitol Limited (29, 30)

Stops:	Chicago, Toledo, Cleveland, Pittsburgh, Harpers Ferry, Washington
Frequency:	Daily
Distance:	780 miles
Duration:	17½ hours
Equipment:	Superliner coaches, sleepers, dining car, lounge car

The eastbound trip is, I think, the more scenic of the two. The train leaves Chicago in the early evening and reaches Pittsburgh by dawn. You'll have daylight from there all the way into Washington. It's a very pretty run—you travel across the Allegheny Mountains in West Virginia, make a stop at Harpers Ferry, pass through Maryland farm country, and finally arrive in Washington by early afternoon. The westbound trip is very nice too; it's just that you'll be passing through that stretch around Pittsburgh in darkness. The Capitol Limited is one of the few eastern trains to have Superliner equipment.

Pennsylvanian (42, 43)

Stops:	New York City, Philadelphia, Harrisburg, Pittsburgh
Frequency:	Daily
Distance:	444 miles
Duration:	9¼ hours
Equipment:	Amfleet coaches, business class coach, cafe car

This is really one of the more scenic trips among the eastern trains. The Pennsylvanian passes through the some beautiful countryside, including Pennsylvania Dutch farmlands, and does so during daylight hours in both directions. A highlight of this trip, especially for rail fans, is the famous horseshoe curve near Altoona, Pennsylvania. For the best look at it, be on the left side of the train if you're heading west and have your camera ready.

Cardinal (50, 51)

Stops:	New York, Philadelphia, Washington, White Sulphur Springs, Cincinnati, Indianapolis, Chicago
Frequency:	Departs from New York Sunday, Wednesday, Friday; departs from Chicago Tuesday, Thursday, Saturday
Distance:	1,147 miles
Duration:	27¾ hours
Equipment:	Amfleet coaches, Viewliner sleepers, diner/lounge car

The Cardinal is one of my favorite trips in either direction, but personally I'd give an edge to the eastbound trip. It will be dark or close to it when you leave Chicago, but the real scenery happens the next day almost from the moment you wake up and lasts all the way into Washington. Probably the best part of the trip occurs as the train winds its way through the New River Gorge in West Virginia. About 25 minutes after leaving Montgomery, West Virginia, you'll pass under the New River Gorge Bridge. It's 1,700 feet long and almost 900 feet above the river. The Cardinal crosses the river more than once, but most of the time it will be on the right side. This is a lovely ride any time of the year, especially crossing the Blue Ridge Mountains, but it's really something if you can manage to have your trip coincide with the fall colors.

Florida Trains
Silver Meteor (97, 98)

Stops:	New York City, Philadelphia, Washington, Richmond, Raleigh, Charleston, Savannah, Jacksonville, Orlando, Miami
Frequency:	Daily
Distance:	1,389 miles
Duration:	27½ hours
Equipment:	Amfleet coaches, Viewliner sleepers, cafe or lounge car, dining car

You pretty much see it all on this trip: big cities and small towns, industry and agriculture, temperate and tropical. The first part of the southbound trip covers Amtrak's Northeast Corridor and is the high-speed part of the run. Because they're so long, none of the three Florida trains can reach the 125-mph speed of one of the regional service trains, but you'll still be moving more than 100 mph en route to Washington. You'll see some important rivers here. Actually, you go under the Hudson right after leaving New York City, then over the Delaware, the Schuylkill, and the Susquehanna. In between the industrialized areas, there are some very pretty communities, particularly around Philadelphia, Wilmington, Baltimore, and Washington. If you're breaking your trip here—and I'd certainly recommend it—be sure to spend some time right there in Union Station. It's been restored to its original grandeur and then some.

After leaving Washington the train crosses the Potomac River, and the countryside gets very pretty indeed. You'll encounter lots of familiar Civil War names through here. Unfortunately, unless you're traveling in the long days of summer, this part of the southbound trip will be after dark. You'll miss the Carolinas too. Early risers will be up in time to see Savannah, however, and it really is one of the South's most charming cities. By the time you've finished a leisurely breakfast, you'll be in Jacksonville. From here, the Meteor takes you through Orlando and Kissimmee (both stops for Disney World), then on down the East Coast to Miami.

Silver Star (91, 92)

Stops:	New York City, Philadelphia, Washington, Richmond, Columbia, Savannah, Jacksonville, Tampa, Miami
Frequency:	Daily
Distance:	New York City to Tampa: 1,223 miles; New York City to Miami: 1,522 miles
Duration:	New York City to Tampa: 25¾ hours; New York City to Miami: 31 hours
Equipment:	Amfleet coaches, Viewliner sleepers, cafe or lounge car, dining car

This train covers mostly the same route as the Silver Meteor, but it cuts across Florida to Tampa before heading back to Miami. I think it provides more in the way of scenery in either direction than the Meteor, too. Its midmorning departure from New York means that you'll still have some daylight left for the very pretty countryside south of Washington. At Rocky Mount, North Carolina, the Silver Star heads inland for a stop in the wee hours at Columbia, South Carolina's capital. After passing through Orlando and Kissimmee, the train turns west and crosses the state, passing through orange groves and some of Florida's horse country en route to Tampa on the Gulf Coast. From there it's back east and down the coast to Miami.

Auto Train (52, 53)

Stops:	Lorton and Sanford (no intermediate stops)
Frequency:	Daily
Distance:	855 miles
Duration:	17½ hours
Equipment:	Superliner coaches, sleepers, dining car, lounge car, bi-level cars for transporting automobiles

The Auto Train's northern terminus, Lorton, Virginia, is a suburb of Washington, DC. At the other end, Sanford, Florida, is just a few miles from Orlando and Disney World. This is really a classic case of finding a need and filling it. Maybe you want to have your personal automobile with you in Florida and don't want to make the long drive south. Or maybe you'll be spending enough time in Florida to make renting a car an expensive proposition. Either way, the Auto Train is the perfect answer: your car will be on the train with you. Note that there are no intermediate stops—you board in Lofton and end up in Sanford or vice versa, because special facilities are required to load and unload the cars (which is a fascinating operation to watch, by the way).

Automobiles are carried in specially designed bi-level railcars while their owners ride up front in either coach or sleeping-car accommodations. Only passengers with cars can ride the Auto Train. (If you're heading for Florida without a car, the other Florida trains will be faster and more convenient anyway.)

This is by far the longest train Amtrak operates, frequently consisting of as many as 44 cars. Because about half of those are basically freight cars, operationally that's the way this train performs—as a freight train. That only means you'll be traveling at somewhat slower speeds. Almost by definition, people who ride the Auto Train take it in both directions. For what it's worth, the southbound trip will be the most scenic—through Virginia and much of the Carolinas during daylight hours.

Southern Trains
Carolinian (79, 80)

Stops:	New York City, Philadelphia, Washington, Richmond, Raleigh, Charlotte
Frequency:	Daily
Distance:	704 miles
Duration:	13¼ hours
Equipment:	Amfleet coaches, business class, cafe car

For some years, the Carolinian's southern terminus was at Raleigh, North Carolina, but the route has since been extended to Charlotte, which added 175 miles and 3½ hours to the schedule. The Carolinian follows some of the same routes as the Florida trains, but it travels at a somewhat more leisurely pace, makes some additional stops, and, because of an early morning departure, passes through all that pretty countryside south of Washington in daylight hours.

Palmetto (89, 90)

Stops:	New York City, Washington, Richmond, Rocky Mount, Fayetteville, Southern Pines, Savannah
Frequency:	Daily
Distance:	829 miles
Duration:	Southbound: 14¾ hours; northbound: 15½ hours
Equipment:	Amfleet coaches, business class, cafe car

The Palmetto follows the same route as the Silver Meteor between New York and Savannah, traveling mostly during daylight hours but making a few more stops.

City of New Orleans (58, 59)

Stops:	Chicago, Champaign-Urbana, Carbondale, Memphis, Jackson, New Orleans
Frequency:	Daily
Distance:	926 miles
Duration:	19¼ hours
Equipment:	Superliner coaches and sleepers, Cross Country Café car

I really like this train too. Given a choice, I prefer the southbound trip because it offers a bit more daylight—although, come to think of it, maybe it's because that's the direction Willie Nelson was headed. (If you don't get that reference, go and buy his recording of "The City of New Orleans," which is very possibly the best railroad song ever recorded.) Anyway, it's dark or very close to it when the train leaves Chicago, so you won't see much of all that Illinois farmland as you head south to Cairo. That's where you'll cross the Ohio River into Kentucky in the early morning hours. At about dawn, and just before you stop in Memphis, you'll see the 32-story Great American Pyramid. It's on the right—believe me, you can't miss it. Then it's on through the Mississippi Delta to the capital city of Jackson. By now, the river itself is well to the west. Another 80 miles or so, after passing through the town of Magnolia, Mississippi, the train crosses into Louisiana. This is swamp country. You can almost see the alligators and snakes out there, but it's interesting and very picturesque nevertheless. After a stop in Hammond, the train skirts around Lake Pontchartrain along the longest continuous railway curve in the world and into New Orleans. Let the fun begin!

Crescent (19, 20)

Stops:	New York City, Philadelphia, Washington, Greensboro, Charlotte, Atlanta, Birmingham, New Orleans
Frequency:	Daily
Distance:	1,377 miles
Duration:	Westbound: 30½ hours; eastbound: 30 hours
Equipment:	Amfleet coaches, Viewliner sleepers, dining car, lounge car

This train was the pride of Southern Railway for years. Southbound, it still follows the same route through all the major cities along Amtrak's Northeast Corridor to Washington, then it swings down through Virginia farm country before running along the edge of the Blue Ridge Mountains for several hours. Stay alert for the 210-foot-high Wells Viaduct after you leave Toccoa, Georgia (depending on the time of year, you may cross it after dark on the northbound trip). After Atlanta you'll travel west through impressive pine forests along the southern end of the Appalachian Mountains on the way to Birmingham. From there, the Crescent crosses into Mississippi, then turns and runs straight south. Just a few minutes after a stop at Slidell, Louisiana, you'll cross Lake Pontchartrain on a six-mile-long causeway. It's just a single track and none of the structure can be seen from either side of the train, which creates the sensation that you're rolling right along on the water itself. From there you're just a half hour or so from arriving in New Orleans. If the Crescent's on schedule, you'll be there in plenty of time to enjoy a fabulous meal (try a place called Irene's Cuisine) and maybe catch a set by the jazz band at Preservation Hall. What a town!

Western Trains
California Zephyr (5, 6)

Stops:	Chicago, Omaha, Denver, Salt Lake City, Reno, Sacramento, Emeryville
Frequency:	Daily
Distance:	2,438 miles
Duration:	53 hours
Equipment:	Superliner coaches, sleepers, dining car, lounge car

This is arguably Amtrak's most scenic trip; it's spectacular in either direction. But if the eastbound train is running more than an hour or so late, you could miss some of the more impressive views coming out of the Rockies and descending into the Denver area.

Westbound out of Chicago, it's vast fields of corn and soybeans, then a dinnertime crossing of the Mississippi River at Burlington, Iowa. Omaha comes at about midnight; when you wake up you are in cattle country just east of Denver. Things start getting spectacular after you leave Denver as the Zephyr begins its climb into the Rockies, with best viewing from the right side of the train. In the next two hours, you'll pass through 27 tunnels, the last of which is the six-mile-long Moffat Tunnel. Before it was completed in 1928, trains had to go over Rollins Pass, which added five hours to the trip. For the rest of the day you'll follow the Colorado River through a series of canyons. The train crosses the river several times, but the best viewing will be from the left side. You should see lots of rafters, although the waters are not the real white-water stuff. (You'll also see a lot of at least a few of the rafters, since mooning the Zephyr has become a kind of tradition.)

You'll cross Utah and enter Nevada during the night, getting to Winnemucca just before sunrise. Butch Cassidy once robbed a bank here. Following a stop in Reno, the Zephyr starts its climb into the foothills of the Sierra Nevadas. After you leave Truckee, California, find a seat on the right side of the train for the ride along mountain ridges and past Donner Lake. It was named for

The California Zephyr's route takes it across both the Rocky Mountains and, as shown here, the Sierra Nevada range. It's a spectacular journey at any time of year. PHOTO COURTESY OF AMTRAK

87 settlers led by George Donner who were trapped by snow in the winter of 1846–47. Next comes the American River Canyon on the left side. The California Gold Rush took place in the 1850s and '60s all throughout this area. After leaving the mountains and stopping at Roseville, you'll pass McClellan Air Force Base and enter Sacramento Valley, which is known for producing almonds and rice. Next stop is Sacramento, the capital of California and the home of the very-much-worth-seeing California State Railroad Museum. Sacramento is followed by Davis, then Travis Air Force Base on the left. Next come the vineyards of Napa Valley and the Navy's "mothball" fleet of decommissioned ships in Suisan Bay on your left. After Martinez and Richmond, the Zephyr reaches its final stop, Emeryville, California. An Amtrak bus will be right there to take passengers across the bay to San Francisco.

Texas Eagle (21, 22, 521, 522)

Stops:	Chicago, St. Louis, Little Rock, Dallas, Austin, San Antonio (with a Los Angeles connection)
Frequency:	Daily
Distance:	1,305 miles
Duration:	Southbound: 32¾ hours; northbound: 31 hours
Equipment:	Superliner coaches, sleepers, Cross Country Café car

Southbound out of Chicago, you'll cross quite a number of rivers. There's the Chicago River first, followed by the Des Plaines and the Kankakee. You'll cross the Vermillion River just before a stop at Pontiac, Illinois (which was named for the same Native American chief as the city in Michigan). Before arriving in St. Louis, you'll cross the Mississippi River about 20 minutes after leaving Alton, Illinois. There's a great view of the city skyline on the left. Several minutes later, the Gateway Arch will be on the right.

Little Rock, Arkansas, comes and goes in the middle of the night. You'll wake up right around the time you cross into Texas at Texarkana. The Arkansas-Texas state line runs right through the town. In fact, it runs right through the railroad station. Depending on whether you're sitting toward the front or rear of the train, you'll either be in Texas or still in Arkansas.

By the time the train reaches Longview, you're in the middle of oil country. Then, as you follow the Sabine River, you'll see cattle and horses. Dallas comes right at lunchtime, with Fort Worth an hour and a half later. The route from there to San Antonio is a nice one. You'll probably be having dinner when the train stops in Austin, the state capital. Underway again, the Eagle will cross the Colorado River and complete the run to San Antonio around 10:30 PM. This is where the westbound train connects with the Sunset Limited for the trip on through to Los Angeles. You'll get a restful night's sleep here, because the train will be sitting in the station all night before the early morning departure.

If your trip began in Los Angeles, your car will be detached from the Sunset Limited here in San Antonio and become part of the northbound Texas Eagle. Once again you'll be arriving late at night and departing early the next morning, affording everyone a night onboard with no rocking and rolling. (Please note that while the Texas Eagle operates daily, the Sunset Limited runs only three days a week. That means this overnight connection only works on those three days.)

Sunset Limited (I, 2)

Stops:	Los Angeles, Phoenix, El Paso, San Antonio, Houston, New Orleans
Frequency:	Departs from Los Angeles Sunday, Wednesday, Friday; departs from New Orleans Monday, Wednesday, Friday
Distance:	1,995 miles
Duration:	47½ hours
Equipment:	Superliner coaches, sleepers, dining car, lounge car

At its inception, the Sunset Limited was a very ambitious undertaking for Amtrak. It was, in fact, the first true transcontinental train in the nation's history, since other cross-country trips always required either the passenger or the railcar to change trains somewhere along the way, usually in Chicago. When the Sunset service was inaugurated, it ran from Miami north to Jacksonville and then turned west, running through the Florida panhandle to New Orleans. From there it continued due west all the way to Los Angeles, completing an odyssey of nearly 3,100 miles. Some time later, the Miami–Jacksonville portion was cut, with the train either originating or terminating at Orlando.

The Sunset's Florida service came to an abrupt end in August 2005 when Hurricane Katrina slammed into New Orleans. Miles of track were undermined or washed away entirely. Although the track has long since been rebuilt, Amtrak has not yet restored the Florida segment, and the train still terminates in New Orleans.

Just after leaving New Orleans, the westbound Sunset passes the Superdome and crosses the Mississippi River on the Huey P. Long Bridge. This bridge is four-and-a-half miles long and 280 feet above the river at its highest point, and it must be seen to

Just as you're becoming accustomed to the flat, harsh west Texas landscape, the Sunset Limited crosses a long bridge high above the Pecos River. PHOTO COURTESY OF THE AUTHOR

be believed. For the next several hours the train rolls through bayou country. The ground is pretty soggy through most of these wetlands; as a result, much of the track was built on pilings. As a matter of fact, you'll notice that the cemeteries here are all above ground, because the water table is so high.

You'll be in San Antonio very early the next morning, and that's where the Texas Eagle consist will be added to this train. You'll be in Del Rio just after breakfast, and about 45 minutes after leaving there, you'll cross the Pecos River on a very high bridge—it's 320 feet down to the river. This is pretty dry country, and lots of cacti and mesquite can be seen. About 20 minutes farther on, the Sunset rolls through the town of Langtry, once the home of the legendary Roy Bean. He wasn't really a judge, but that didn't deter him from proclaiming himself the "only law west of the Pecos" and dispensing his own unique version of justice here for a number of years. Somewhere along the way,

Ol' Roy became infatuated with Lily Langtry, a famous British actress, and he named the town for her—a dubious honor at best.

The Sunset heads a bit more to the north now, climbing into the Del Norte Mountains. Just after a stop in Alpine, Texas, you'll cross Paisano Pass, which is over 5,000 feet in elevation and the highest point of the entire trip. It's just past lunch when you reach El Paso, located on the Rio Grande and surrounded by the Franklin Mountains. As you depart El Paso, the Mexican city of Juárez is just there on the other side of the Rio Grande. You'll cross the river and enter the state of New Mexico just a few minutes after leaving El Paso. It's here that the Sunset passes literally within a few feet of the Mexican border, which is marked by a low chain-link fence and a white post just to the left of the train.

You'll cross the Continental Divide shortly after leaving Deming, New Mexico, and you'll reach the Arizona border a couple of hours later. Mining of gold, silver, and copper is big in these parts.

During your second night aboard, the Sunset Limited crosses the Arizona-California border. If it's on time, you'll arrive in Los Angeles early in the morning. *Very* early. In fact, the schedule in effect as I write this calls for a 5:30 AM arrival. However, if your car attendant is following the normal procedure, you'll not be asked to relinquish your comfortable berths for another hour. My advice: get that detail straight earlier in the trip. I was on the Sunset in 2012 and the attendant woke us all at 4:30 so she could collect the bed linens and, presumably, leave the train that much earlier in L.A. Sorry, that's a no-no, and it cost her a tip from several passengers and a formal complaint to Amtrak from me.

Important note: Before planning any itinerary involving the Sunset Limited, see the note at the end of the route description for the Texas Eagle (page 333).

Southwest Chief (3, 4)

Stops:	Chicago, Kansas City, Dodge City, Trinidad, Lamy (Santa Fe), Albuquerque, Flagstaff, San Bernardino, Los Angeles
Frequency:	Daily
Distance:	2,256 miles
Duration:	Westbound: 43 hours; eastbound: 42½ hours
Equipment:	Superliner coaches, sleepers, dining car, lounge car

This is another of my favorite trips because it passes through some truly beautiful parts of the country. After a midafternoon departure from Chicago, you'll head west across Illinois farmland for several hours and then around 7:00 PM finally cross the Mississippi River into Fort Madison, Iowa. The Chief stops in Kansas City an hour before midnight. By the time you wake up the next morning, you'll be just about in Dodge City. Boot Hill is a bit up the street from the old brick train station.

The country will stay fairly flat for a short while, but by midmorning the Chief crosses into Colorado and climbs up toward Raton Pass and the New Mexico border. You've been following the original route of the Santa Fe Trail for quite a while by now; off and on through here it's still plainly visible from the right side of the train. Once you're through the pass, the third stop is Lamy, New Mexico, which is the station serving Santa Fe. It's a very old town and worth a visit of a few days. This was the final destination on the old Santa Fe Trail, but the Chief still has almost a thousand miles to go.

Next comes Albuquerque. If the Chief is on time, it will stop here for almost an hour for servicing, so you'll have time to get off and look at some of the jewelry being sold by Native

En route from Los Angeles to Chicago, Amtrak's train 4, the Southwest Chief, climbs through a narrow canyon toward Raton Pass, which is where it will cross the Continental Divide and head into Colorado. PHOTO COURTESY OF AMTRAK

Americans on the platform. During much of the year, someone from the New Mexico Historical Society boards the train here and in the lounge car provides commentary about the history and geology of the area all the way to Gallup. (Volunteers do the same thing on the eastbound train.) The Chief gets to Flagstaff around 10:00 PM. If you're making a side trip to the Grand Canyon, this is where you'll transfer to a connecting bus. You can also stay aboard for another half hour and get off at Williams Junction, where the next morning you can catch the Grand Canyon Railway to the South Rim. Otherwise, you'll probably sleep through all of Arizona, waking up in time for an arrival into Los Angeles around breakfast time.

Empire Builder (7, 8, 27, 28)

Stops:	Seattle or Portland, Spokane, Glacier Park, Fargo, Minneapolis–St. Paul, Milwaukee, Chicago
Frequency:	Daily
Distance:	Chicago to Seattle: 2,206 miles; Chicago to Portland: 2,275 miles
Duration:	Eastbound: 45¼ hours; westbound, 46 hours
Equipment:	Superliner coaches, sleepers, dining car, lounge car

I've taken the Empire Builder eight or nine times in both directions, and it is another of my favorite trains. I think I prefer the westbound trip because the scenery keeps getting better as you go, but it's really a toss-up.

Leaving Chicago, the Builder heads north into the heart of the Wisconsin dairy land, running along the Mississippi River and stopping in Minneapolis–St. Paul late in the evening. You'll be crossing the plains of North Dakota when you wake up the next morning, and by lunchtime you'll be in the Big Sky country of Montana. It will take all day to cross the state, but don't let anyone tell you this is a boring ride. It's a rolling terrain with vast fields of grain, grazing cattle, and oil wells here and there. When the Builder reaches the town of Havre in the midafternoon, you'll have time to get off and walk around a bit because there's a crew change here. There's also a magnificent steam locomotive on display right next to the station. About three hours later, after you leave the little community of Cut Bank, you should start seeing the Rocky Mountains up ahead.

The train's first stop in the Rockies is East Glacier. From the train you'll be able to see the venerable old Glacier Park Lodge, which was originally built to accommodate passengers of the Great Northern Railroad. Leaving East Glacier, the train will begin running along the southern edge of Glacier National Park, and about an hour later you'll go through the little community of Essex. It's a flag stop, so chances are you'll just go right on by, but watch for the Izaak Walton Inn on the right side of the train. This little hotel sits right on the Burlington Northern Santa Fe's busy main line and is a favorite train-watching spot for rail fans. At least two or three of them will be out in front of the hotel taking your picture as you roll by, so get up close to the window and wave as you pass.

In the wee hours while you're asleep, the Builder stops for about an hour in Spokane. This is where a sleeper, a coach, and the lounge car split off and, with a new locomotive, head southwest into Oregon. That train arrives in Portland around midmorning.

If you're staying on the Seattle section, wake up early the next morning; your journey is now taking you through the incredible Cascade Range, with towering evergreen trees in thick woodlands that are crisscrossed by rushing streams. When you stop at Wenatchee, Washington, you'll be smack in the middle of a huge apple-producing valley. In fact, this town is called the Apple Capital of the World.

About an hour before the stop at Everett, the train passes through the Cascade Tunnel. It's almost eight miles in length, accommodates only a single track, and is the longest railroad tunnel in the United States. Everett, by the way, is where Boeing builds most of its jet aircraft.

Edmonds is the Builder's last stop before its arrival in Seattle, but most of the last 90 minutes of the ride is along the shore of Puget Sound, literally within 50 or 60 feet of the water. Seattle is the Empire Builder's western terminus, and you'll end your rail journey in this wonderful city at just about the same time the other section reaches Portland, 200 miles to the south.

Coast Starlight (11, 14)

Stops:	Los Angeles, Santa Barbara, San Jose, Oakland, Sacramento, Klamath Falls, Eugene, Portland, Olympia, Seattle
Frequency:	Daily
Distance:	1,389 miles
Duration:	35 hours
Equipment:	Superliner coaches, sleepers, dining car, lounge car, parlor car

You really get to see a bit of everything on this train, especially on the northbound run, which provides a bit more daylight for some of the scenic highlights. Heading north out of Los Angeles, most of the interesting scenery will be on the left, since the train will be running along the shoreline for some of the way. After the stop at Oxnard, California, you should be able to see the Channel Islands about 20 miles offshore, as well as big platforms for the offshore oil wells too.

Just after lunch, the Starlight stops at the old mission town of San Luis Obispo, then begins climbing up toward Cuesta Pass. Below and on the left, you'll see the huge California Men's Colony, a state penitentiary. Then, if you move to a window on the right side, you'll see the entire train as it goes through two horseshoe curves. Later in the afternoon, you'll be in the Salinas Valley, where all kinds of fresh produce grow on many thousands of acres. It's very appropriately called America's Salad Bowl. At the northern end of the valley you'll pass through Castroville. Take note if you like artichokes, because most of them come from right here. By the time the sun goes down, you'll have a good idea as to how important agriculture is to California.

About 15 minutes after a stop in Oakland, the Starlight reaches Emeryville. If your destination is San Francisco, Amtrak

Amtrak's southbound Coast Starlight descends more than 1,000 feet and winds through
a sweeping horseshoe curve minutes before arriving in San Luis Obispo, California.
PHOTO COURTESY OF THE AUTHOR

will have a bus waiting to take you there when the train pulls in
at the Emeryville station.

If you're a very early riser and if you're traveling in the sum-
mer with extra hours of daylight, you may get a stunning view of
Mount Shasta from the left side of the train soon after you leave
Dunsmuir, California.

North of Klamath Falls is a big logging area, and you'll travel
though forests of Douglas fir. After the stop at Chemult, be on
the right side of the Starlight as it climbs to the Cascade Summit.
You'll see Odell Lake down there and Maiden Peak beyond. On
a single track, the train runs along the western side of Willamette
Pass and Salt Creek Canyon, giving you a constantly changing
vista for many miles. Building this railroad was quite a project—
you'll pass through 22 tunnels between here and Eugene. After a
stop in Salem, Oregon's capital, the train heads through the Willamette Valley toward Portland.

Hope for a clear day, because as you get closer to Portland,
Mount Hood and Mount St. Helens will also be on your right.

You'll be able to tell which of the two is Mount St. Helens—a violent eruption in 1980 blew away a large part of the peak. It's quite obvious, even from this distance. Leaving Portland, the "City of Roses," the train crosses the Columbia River and stops again in Vancouver, Washington. Switch to the left side of the train as it follows the Columbia River from here on and then runs along the edge of Puget Sound through Tacoma and right past the King Dome into Seattle. It is, as you will find, a wonderful city. Note, please, that this is the only Amtrak train that includes a Pacific Parlour Car, a wonderful, comfortable lounge car that is available only for sleeping-car passengers.

San Joaquin

Stops:	Oakland, Davis, Sacramento, Stockton, Merced, Fresno, Bakersfield
Frequency:	Four times a day each way; two other trains originate in Sacramento
Distance:	315 miles
Duration:	6 hours
Equipment:	Bi-level coaches similar to Superliners, cafe car

These trains run up and down the middle of California. Since three of the six daily San Joaquins make their runs during the day, viewing opportunities will be the same in either direction. The trains stick pretty much to the huge San Joaquin Valley, which produces a lion's share of California's agriculture—grapes, pistachios, almonds, citrus, and vegetables of all kinds. The terrain is pretty flat, but you can see the Sierra Nevadas off to the left on the southbound trip. Amtrak provides connections at stops along the rail route, with buses heading in a number of directions. By the way, most of the funding that supports these trains comes from the State of California.

Pacific Surfliner

Stops:	Santa Barbara or Los Angeles, Fullerton, Anaheim, San Juan Capistrano, San Clemente, Del Mar, San Diego
Frequency:	Seven or eight times a day
Distance:	Santa Barbara to San Diego: 231 miles; Los Angeles to San Diego: 128 miles
Duration:	Santa Barbara to San Diego: 5¾ hours; Los Angeles to San Diego: 3 hours
Equipment:	Bi-level coaches, business class, cafe car

The Pacific Surfliners run right along the coast for most of the way between Los Angeles and San Diego, and on most days you'll see lots of swimmers and surfers. You can pick from among several trains that run during daylight hours to enjoy the great scenery in either direction. Just try to get a seat on the right side of the train if you're heading southbound—that's where the ocean will be. This is a very pleasant ride, and the large bi-level cars are quite comfortable.

There is a business-class car on these trains. The surcharge is about 50 percent more than the regular coach fare, and for that you get an AC electrical outlet at your seat, free coffee and pastries in the business-class car, and complimentary soft drinks in the cafe car on some trips. Personally I wouldn't bother with upgrading, but if you think that's worth an extra 14 or 15 bucks, go for it.

Trains in Alaska

I haven't kept precise records, but I've logged close to 200,000 miles on passenger trains in North America between Amtrak in the United States and VIA Rail in Canada. What I've missed out on are trains in Alaska. So far, my only experience has been a relatively short ride from Anchorage to Prince William Sound.

All of Alaska's passenger trains are operated by Alaska Railroad, which was privately owned from the time it began in the 1920s until 1985 when the railroad was bought by the State of Alaska.

These days, railroads either haul freight or carry passengers—one or the other, but never both. Alaska Railroad is the only exception, hauling more than 6 million tons of freight a year and almost half a million passengers over 467 miles of track on a system that's laid out between Seward in the south and Fairbanks in the north. Several scheduled passenger trains originate in Anchorage and offer two classes of service.

The Coastal Classic runs between Anchorage and Seward and is about a four-and-a-half-hour journey. The Denali Star connects Anchorage and Fairbanks, and that ride takes about 12 hours. Both of these trains have bi-level dome cars for great viewing. The company also operates a train between Anchorage and Whittier called the Glacier Discovery, but it runs only a few days each year.

To find out more about these and other trains, and to make reservations, you can contact Alaska Railroad directly at 1-907-265-2494 or book online at www.alaskarailroad.com.

An alternative would be to contact Alaska Tour & Travel, a travel firm specializing in Alaska travel. They can book these same trains, but they also handle hotels and all the other details. Their toll-free number is 1-800-208-0200. They, too, are available online at www.alaskatravel.com

VIA Rail Canada
Windsor–Quebec Corridor

VIA Rail's heaviest traffic occurs in the busy 725-mile central corridor between Windsor (just across Lake Erie from Detroit) and Quebec. On much of this track, VIA trains run at speeds of more than 100 miles per hour. LRC (light, rapid, comfortable) equipment is used on all of these routes, and both stan-

A visit to the Old Town in Quebec City is a step back in time more
than 400 years and should be included in any VIA Rail itinerary.
PHOTO COURTESY OF THE AUTHOR

dard and business-class services are available on all trains. For
all corridor trains, I've provided a listing of routes and travel
times to help in planning an itinerary. For specific train numbers,
along with departure and arrival times, refer to a VIA timetable
online at www.viarail.ca or call VIA Rail at 1-888-VIA-RAIL, or
1-888-842-7245.

Trains Between	Distance	Duration
Montreal and Quebec	170 miles	3¼ hours
Montreal and Ottawa	116 miles	2 hours
Montreal and Toronto (via Kingston)	335 miles	5¼ hours
Ottawa and Toronto	277 miles	4½ hours
Toronto and Windsor (via London)	233 miles	4¼ hours

Eastern Trains
Ocean (14, 15)

Stops:	Montreal, Charny, Mont-Joli, Matapédia, Campbellton, Moncton, Halifax
Frequency:	Daily except Tuesdays
Distance:	836 miles
Duration:	20¾ hours
Equipment:	Renaissance equipment, classic stainless-steel cars

The Ocean leaves Montreal in the early evening, immediately crossing the Saint Lawrence, a major waterway, and then swinging due east along the river's southern banks. It will be on the left side of the train for nearly eight hours and, by the time the train turns south at Mont-Joli, will be nearly 30 miles wide. Unfortunately, because of the train's schedule, it will be dark through most of this area. About the time you wake up you'll be crossing into the province of New Brunswick. After making a stop at Campbellton, the train runs south along the coast of the Gulf of Saint Lawrence, which is on the left side. The famous Bay of Fundy is much farther south, but this entire region is known for its extraordinary tides, which rise and fall twice a day as much as 50 feet. At Bathurst, the Ocean turns inland, passing through forests and farm country. After leaving Newcastle, the train crosses the upper part of Miramichi Bay, a mecca for fishers looking for Atlantic salmon, then continues south to Moncton and into the province of Nova Scotia. The Ocean's final destination, the city of Halifax, was the jumping-off point for many World War II convoys headed across the Atlantic for England and Russia, and it's still a busy seaport. If you're into seafood, you've come to the right area.

Montreal–Gaspé (16, 17)

Stops:	Montreal, Lévis, Mont-Joli, Matapédia, Gaspé
Frequency:	Departs from Montreal Wednesday, Friday, Sunday; departs from Gaspé Tuesday, Friday, Sunday
Distance:	651 miles
Duration:	18 hours
Equipment:	Stainless-steel coaches, sleeping cars, Skyline car

After leaving Montreal around dinnertime, this train starts out following the Saint Lawrence River on the same route as the Ocean. During summer months, whales are often seen in the river, which is very wide here. In the wee hours after a stop at Mont-Joli, the train turns south, swings east at Matapédia, and heads along the southern shore of the Gaspé Peninsula. That big body of water you'll see off to the right when you wake up will be Chaleur Bay. (*Chaleur* means "warm" in French—a more accurate translation would be "not quite freezing.") At any rate, by the time you get to Chandler around midmorning, Chaleur Bay has broadened and become the Gulf of Saint Lawrence. This area is heavily forested, has many lakes and rivers, and is very popular for hiking, camping, hunting, and fishing. Just in time for lunch, the train reaches the centuries-old town of Gaspé. There are several wilderness parks in the area that offer tours. This is a great place to hole up and write a novel.

Western Trains
Winnipeg–Churchill

Stops:	Winnipeg, Dauphin, The Pas, Wekusko, Wabowden, Thompson, Gillam, Churchill
Frequency:	Departs from Winnipeg Sunday, Tuesday; departs from Churchill Monday, Saturday
Distance:	1,063 miles
Duration:	43 hours
Equipment:	Stainless-steel coaches, sleepers, dining car

Winnipeg, this train's southern terminus, is the biggest city in Manitoba with almost 700,000 people. At the far end of the train's route and the opposite end of the population spectrum is Churchill, a community of less than a thousand souls. It's located on the shores of Hudson Bay and just 600 or so air miles below the Arctic Circle. Between Winnipeg and Churchill, the train passes from prairie into dense forests and finally into tundra before reaching Hudson Bay. Along the way, it makes 26 scheduled stops, although the timetable lists another 54 flag stops where the train will only stop if someone wants to get on or off.

Every year in mid-October, the train runs full for six to eight weeks. That's when polar bears appear in and around Churchill as they wait for the bay to freeze over so they can go out onto the ice and hunt ringed seals, essentially their only food. People come from all over the world to see these bears, and I can tell you that it is a thrilling experience. Dog-sled rides are also available for visitors, though now—because of climate change—there is less snow and dog carts are sometimes substituted for sleds. Still, it's another extraordinary experience. Later in the winter, visitors take the train to Churchill for optimum viewing of aurora borealis, also known as the northern lights.

Because no roads link these very small communities in northern Manitoba with any major cities, VIA Rail is mandated to operate this train by the Canadian government. If you're looking for a unique rail experience, this would be it!

The Canadian (1, 2)

Stops:	Toronto, Sudbury, Sioux Lookout, Winnipeg, Saskatoon, Edmonton, Jasper, Vancouver
Frequency:	Departs Toronto (winter-spring) Tuesday, Saturday; (summer-fall) Tuesday, Thursday, Saturday. Departs Vancouver (winter-spring) Tuesday, Friday; (summer-fall) Tuesday, Friday, Sunday
Distance:	2,775 miles
Duration:	84 hours
Equipment:	Stainless-steel coaches, sleepers, dining car, dome/cafe/lounge car, observation car

This is VIA's premier train, and deservedly so. In my opinion, the westbound trip is the one to take—the scenery keeps getting more spectacular as you go. The Canadian travels north from the rich farmland around Toronto before turning west to cross just above Lake Superior through a lake-dotted wilderness. Then it travels across the vast plains—cattle and wheat country—and through the Canadian Rockies to Jasper before reaching Vancouver and the Pacific.

It's a sensational trip that the train itself enhances. The stainless-steel cars have been completely refurbished, and the dome cars—depending on the passenger load, there can be as many as three on each train—are the best possible way to enjoy the scenic beauty. During the very busy times of year, meaning roughly May through September, more cars, including a second diner, are added to accommodate the additional sleeping-car passengers. Meals for coach passengers are served in the glass-domed Skyline lounge cars that are part of the consist.

Some time ago, VIA changed the Canadian's schedule; it began to depart from each originating city at the end of the day and run at a more leisurely pace, which effectively turned the trip from three nights aboard into four. Part of the rationale was to have the train stop at some of the larger cities, such as Saskatoon, Edmonton, and Kamloops, at times that would encourage more passengers from those cities to take the train. Earlier schedules, for example, had the Canadian stopping at Saskatoon at 3:00 AM.

The new schedule has benefits for through passengers, too, because there are more daylight hours as the Canadian crosses the Rocky Mountains. This is a glorious experience and without doubt one of the best rail journeys in the world.

Jasper–Prince Rupert (5, 6)

Stops:	Jasper, Prince George, Smithers, Prince Rupert
Frequency:	Departs Wednesday, Friday, Sunday
Distance:	721 miles
Duration:	20½ hours
Equipment:	Stainless-steel coaches, dome/cafe/ lounge car, Park car, Panorama car in high season

While the cross-country Canadian passes through the resort town of Jasper in the Rocky Mountains, this train originates there on its westbound trip to Prince Rupert on the Pacific Coast. I've used the word *spectacular* in describing a number of these train rides, but the word certainly applies to the area surrounding Jasper. It's well worth stopping here for a few days. From Jasper, the train heads

northwest through the mountains, crossing into British Columbia and stopping for the night at Prince George, which is about
halfway through the train's journey. There are no sleeping cars
on this train, so passengers spend the night here in one of several
hotels. There's more marvelous scenery the next morning when
the train is underway again and meets the Skeena River, which
it follows all the way to the Pacific Ocean and Prince Rupert, its
final destination. In the busy time of year, from mid-May to late
September, VIA adds additional cars to the train's consist: a Park
car and a Panorama car, which has glass windows for the sides
and the roof of the car. There's no better way to take in all that
breathtaking scenery. There's also a "touring class" option during
those months, which includes the cost of meals in the fare.

18

SUGGESTED ITINERARIES

Here are some examples of long-distance train trips that will provide plenty of great scenery and opportunities for sightseeing. You won't need many suggestions from me before you begin plotting you own trip. It will help if you refer to Amtrak and VIA Rail system maps on pages 42 and 225. You can begin most of these trips from any of the principal cities included in the itinerary. For instance, in the Big City Tour listed below, you can start your trip from New York just as easily as you can from Chicago. For more detailed information about specific trains mentioned here, refer to chapter 17, "Pick a Train, Any Train."

I really think that one key to a great train trip is to travel with a reason. My train trips always seem more successful and fun if there's a specific purpose for them. Think about putting together a rail itinerary based on a special interest: the Old West, the Civil War, baseball, rail museums, and so forth. Maybe you are looking at prospective colleges for your 16-year-old son or daughter, or maybe you want to visit old friends. As you can see, the possibilities are almost endless.

Finally, there are several companies that specialize in preplanned rail tours. You can plug in to one of their tours or use their itineraries as inspiration for your own ideas. They all have free brochures outlining their various offerings. Three such firms are Amtrak Vacations, accessible online at www.amtrakvacations. com or by calling 1-800-268-7252; Vacations By Rail, found at www.vacationsbyrail.com or 1-877-929-7245; and Rail Travel Adventures, www.railtraveladventures.com or 1-800-639-3706.

Big City Tour: Chicago–Washington, DC–New York–Boston–Chicago

Take the Cardinal from Chicago to Washington—it's the most scenic train between those two cities. Plan to spend at least several days in Washington, then head up to New York City. Take an Acela so you can experience a 125-mile-per-hour train ride. New York is worth several days, too—museums, Broadway shows, and great restaurants abound. Pick a mid- to late-morning departure from Penn Station for the trip up to Boston. You've already experienced the Acela, so take one of the regional service trains for this leg. It'll be slower because it stops more, but it's a nice scenic run along the Connecticut shoreline and you'll conveniently arrive by midafternoon. Boston's got it all—Italian food in the North End, the Red Sox at Fenway Park, and colonial history all over town. From here, it's the Lake Shore Limited across New York State, along two of the Great Lakes, and back into Chicago.

Glaciers to Glitz: San Francisco–Seattle–Chicago–San Francisco

If you want variety, this itinerary certainly has it. From San Francisco (the train actually departs from Emeryville, which is across the Bay), hop on the northbound Coast Starlight for one of the more scenic rides in the Amtrak system. First, you'll pass through the Cascade Mountains on the way up to Seattle. From there, board the Empire Builder and, after cruising through more of the Cascades, get off at either Essex or Glacier Park in Montana. Catch the same train a few days later and head east to Chicago.

See the sights in the Windy City, then head west on the California Zephyr through the Rockies and across the desert to Truckee, a wonderful little town in the Sierra Nevadas. After a day or so, catch the Zephyr once again and continue on into the Bay Area. (An Amtrak bus will take you from Emeryville to San Francisco.)

A Western Triangle: Los Angeles–San Francisco–Portland–Chicago–Santa Fe–Los Angeles

Start in Los Angeles and take the Coast Starlight to San Francisco for a few days of fine dining and sightseeing. Then catch the Starlight again and continue up the coast to Portland. Take a few days in the City of Roses and be sure to make use of the wonderful trolley system running throughout the downtown area. Catch the Portland section of the Empire Builder; it will take you on a two-night trip through Spokane, the Rockies, and Montana and all the way to Chicago. Spend at least two days there, because there's a lot to see and do in the downtown area. There's the marvelous Shedd Aquarium on Lake Shore Drive, and don't miss the Museum of Science and Industry, which is also nearby. You can tour a captured German World War II submarine, the U-505, among many other exhibits. Next, catch the Southwest Chief and head through Illinois farmland, across the Mississippi River, through Dodge City, to Lamy, New Mexico, which is where you get off for a visit to Santa Fe and maybe the art colony in nearby Taos. Catch the Chief again a couple of days later for the overnight ride back to Los Angeles.

Big Mountains, Little Towns: Los Angeles–Santa Fe–Galesburg–Granby–Davis–Los Angeles

Still haven't had enough of the great American West? This trip starts with the Southwest Chief, which takes you from Los Angeles to Santa Fe, New Mexico. After a few days there, get right back aboard the Chief. It runs right alongside the original Santa Fe Trail for miles, crosses the Rockies by way of Raton Pass in Colorado, and then heads across the plains and through farmlands to Galesburg, Illinois. For a long weekend in June, this small town hosts an annual event called Railroad Days, which is worth seeing. You can catch the California Zephyr right there in Galesburg and head back westward, hopping off in the little town of Granby, Colorado, for a few days of fishing, riding, or just gazing at the mountains. Then it's back aboard the Zephyr, which follows the Colorado River through 130 miles of canyons to Glenwood Springs. The next day, you'll cross the Sierras by way of Donner Pass to the college town of Davis, California. Spend the night there at the Hallmark Inn—it's a two-minute walk from the station and has a terrific restaurant. The next morning, hop on the Coast Starlight for the scenic run back down the coast to Los Angeles.

Oh, Canada! New York–Toronto–Vancouver–Seattle or San Francisco

Let's plug VIA Rail into this itinerary, specifically to take advantage of that famous ride through the Canadian Rockies. Start out from New York City on the Maple Leaf. It's an all-day ride that will take you up the Hudson River to Albany, then across New York State to Niagara Falls, where you'll cross into Canada and arrive in Toronto before 8:00 PM. Take a day or two for this extraordinary, cosmopolitan city. Stay at the classic Royal York Hotel, which is right across the street from the train station. Next comes one of the truly great train rides anywhere in the world: the 3,000-mile journey across Canada to Vancouver aboard VIA Rail's premier train, the Canadian. Trust me, you'll have great sleeping-car accommodations in a traditional stainless-steel railcar, great views from the classic dome cars, and great food in the dining car. What's not to love about that? From Vancouver, you'll take one of the Amtrak Cascades back across the US border to Seattle, where you can spend a few days before flying back to New York. You can also take the Coast Starlight down through the Cascade Range to San Francisco and fly home from there. (Note that you can also begin this trip in Chicago, but the rail itinerary from there to Toronto is longer at close to 24 hours. The trip involves a night on the Lake Shore Limited from Chicago to Buffalo, then a connection with the Maple Leaf. Of course, that would be perfectly fine with me: the more trains, the better.)

The Santa Fe Trail: Chicago–Dodge City–Santa Fe–Grand Canyon–Los Angeles–Chicago

Here's another one that's one way by train, the other way by air. There's only one train in this itinerary, the Southwest Chief, but what a trip it is! You'll leave Chicago in the late afternoon, crossing the Mississippi just about dark. Are you a Western history buff? Get off the next morning at Dodge City, Kansas, and visit Boot Hill Museum. Then get back aboard the Chief the next day and travel on to Santa Fe, where you'll be dazzled by the silver jewelry made by Native American craftspeople. Two or three days here is a must, and your stop should include a side trip to the famous art colony of Taos. Back on the Chief again, and next you get off at Williams, Arizona. It's bedtime when the Chief arrives in Williams, so spend the night in one of several hotels there, then catch the Grand Canyon Railway for a wonderfully scenic two-plus-hour ride to the South Rim of the Grand Canyon. (NARP members get a 10 percent discount on the fare.) After at least a couple of days there, take the same scenic train back to Williams where you'll have time for a nice leisurely dinner before reboarding the Chief. Your car attendant will have your berth all made up, so get a good night's sleep and be ready for an early morning arrival into Los Angeles. Take your time seeing the sights in L.A., then fly back to Chicago. If you live on the West Coast, you can take this trip in reverse. The one thing you can't do, of course, is begin this itinerary somewhere in the middle.

The Ultimate Round Trip: New York–Washington, DC– New Orleans–Los Angeles–San Francisco–Seattle– Chicago–Boston–New York

Complete this itinerary and you can say you traveled around the country and mean it literally. Furthermore, you can begin anywhere along the way. I did it a couple of years ago, starting and ending in Los Angeles, but here we'll begin with the high-speed Acela from New York to Washington, DC, where you should spend several days. (Call your member of Congress and ask him or her to arrange a tour of the Capitol and the White House. They're happy to do it.) Next, you'll be on the Crescent for an overnight trip to New Orleans. I have three suggestions for you there: a visit to the National World War II Museum, a fabulous dinner at Irene's Cuisine, and traditional New Orleans–style jazz at Preservation Hall. From here, you'll get aboard the Sunset Limited for the two-night trip to the West Coast. You'll be crossing two bridges of note: the Huey P. Long Bridge over the Mississippi minutes after departing New Orleans, and the high bridge over the Pecos River in West Texas. Leaving El Paso, you'll pass within a few feet of the Mexican border. It will take all afternoon to cross New Mexico, and you'll be drifting off to sleep on your second night aboard about the time the Sunset gets to Maricopa, Arizona, the station serving Phoenix. The Pacific Ocean will be off to your left as the Coast Starlight travels north out of Los Angeles. You'll roll through the magnificent Cascade Range of Washington State after you leave Seattle on the Empire Builder, which takes you within 25 miles of Canada as you cross Montana the next day. You'll see two of the Great Lakes and travel alongside the Erie Canal while you're aboard the Lake Shore Limited en route to Boston, and Long Island Sound will be off to your left on one of the regional service trains taking you back to New York. When you stop and think about it, that's really quite a remarkable odyssey, especially when you consider the variety of people, cultures, and activities you'll encounter along the way.

Semigrand Tour: Seattle-Chicago-New Orleans-Los Angeles-San Francisco-Seattle

For this abbreviated version of the 'round-the-country trip, just lop off the eastern portion of the previous itinerary. Start in Seattle and head east on the Empire Builder to Chicago. From there, take the City of New Orleans due south to the train's namesake city. After several days of great food and music, take the Sunset Limited to Los Angeles. Connect with the Coast Starlight for the run up the coast to San Francisco, Portland, and back to Seattle. It's not "the ultimate," but it's still a great trip.

Fall Colors I: Philadelphia-Pittsburgh-Chicago-Washington, DC-Philadelphia

Time your trip so you hit the peak of the fall colors, and it will be sensational. Take the Pennsylvanian from Philadelphia to Pittsburgh, because the entire ride is done mostly during daylight hours. Just about dinnertime, you'll go through the famous Horseshoe Curve at Altoona. Stay in Pittsburgh for a day or so if you wish, or have a nice dinner while waiting for the Capitol Limited, which comes through later in the evening for the overnight ride to Chicago. From there, take the Cardinal south through the New River Gorge and over the Blue Ridge mountains back to Washington, DC. It's a glorious trip at any time of the year but really something special in the fall. After a few days in Washington, zip back to Philadelphia on an Acela.

Fall Colors II: New York City-Saratoga Springs-Ticonderoga-Montreal-New York City

Wait until the foliage is at its peak, then do this trip on a weekend with just a shoulder bag. Take the Adirondack north out of New York City, up the Hudson River to Albany, across upstate New York, and into Canada. Spend the night in Montreal at the Queen Elizabeth, an excellent hotel that's actually part of the train station complex. Take the same train back to New York the next day.

Take the Adirondack during the summertime if you have a week or ten days, and it becomes quite a different trip. First stop is Saratoga Springs, which is quite the spot during horse-racing season. Next, soak up some history in the museum at Fort Ticonderoga and spend a day or two in the Lake George area (Lake Placid is just a few miles away too). Then meet up with the Adirondack again and head up to Montreal. While there, visit Quebec City too. It's just three-and-a-half hours away by VIA Rail. The old part of this city dates back 400 years and will keep you fascinated for at least two or three days. You'll also dine on incredible French cuisine. Then it's back to Montreal to catch the Adirondack to New York.

Southern Comfort: Washington, DC-Richmond-Williamsburg-Charleston-Savannah-Jacksonville-Orlando

In many ways, Washington, DC, is very much a southern city—therefore it is an appropriate point of origin for this itinerary. Take a short trip on the Carolinian down to Richmond, Virginia, which was the capital of the Confederacy during the Civil War. Next, catch one of the two daily regional-service trains for the one-hour ride to Williamsburg, Virginia. This beautifully restored colonial town is a great experience for the whole family and worth at least one night's stay.

Then it's back to Richmond to catch the Silver Meteor, which leaves there after dinner and will deliver you to Savannah, Georgia, bright and early the next morning. Two days here will give you a good taste of the Deep South. Back aboard the Meteor, you'll ride two hours to Jacksonville, where you'll rent a car and drive 30 miles to St. Augustine, Florida, one of the older cities in North America. Ponce de León first visited the area in 1513; the city itself dates back to 1565 when it was founded by Don Pedro Menendez. There are several days' worth of historical sights to visit, not to mention the famous Marineland aquarium. From here you can take the Meteor back north to Charleston, South Carolina. The Civil War began here, and the city is full of historical sites and antebellum homes, many of which are open for tours. After a few days here, take the Silver Meteor overnight to Washington. I promise you will love this one.

A Princely Triangle Tour: Vancouver–Jasper–Prince George–Prince Rupert–Victoria

This trip was on my to-do list for several years, and I finally crossed it off during the summer of 2012. It begins in Vancouver, British Columbia, with the overnight ride on VIA Rail's Canadian through the Rockies to Jasper. After a day or so seeing this magnificent area—there's wonderful fly-fishing in the summer months, by the way—leave just after lunch and head back to the Northwest on VIA's train 5, the Skeena, to Prince George, a small city situated in the middle of an almost-endless forest of spruce trees. Prince George's 75,000 people enjoy frequent festivals and community events that are of interest to visitors, too. There are no sleeping cars on this train, so passengers spend the night in one of the hotels here. Back aboard the train the next morning, it's an all-day ride to Prince Rupert on British Columbia's North Coast where, according to the locals, "eagles, bears, and whales outnumber people." It's quite true that the wildlife viewing is unsurpassed; because of this, Prince Rupert is worth a stay of several days. From here, catch one of the BC Ferries for an all-day cruise down through the inland waterway to Port Hardy on Vancouver Island. It's a late arrival, so spend the night there, then rent a car the next day for the drive to Courtenay. It's about 175 miles to the south, but the route takes you inland for a while, then along the coastline, so there's plenty to see. The next day, continue the ride down to Victoria. It's only about 130 miles, but take your time and stop along the way. We did—at a wild bird sanctuary and a blueberry farm, after which we gobbled handfuls of the most delicious blueberries all the way into Victoria. By all means spend a night or two in Victoria. It's the capital of British Columbia and is a charming city with a very English feel to it. From here, you can take another ferry back to Vancouver. This is a wonderful trip, and I would do it again in a heartbeat!

RAILROAD TERMS AND SLANG

Compiling this list of railroad terms was one of the more interesting exercises involved in writing this book. I'm sure that sounds strange, but researching gave me a much better understanding of basic railroad operations. Furthermore, since the book first appeared, a number of people said they read straight through this list—from *air brake* to *yellow eye*—and found it to be as interesting as any other chapter. (I thought that over and decided to take it as a compliment.)

Railroad Terms

air brake: The standard braking system used on both passenger and freight cars. Compressed air is used to hold the brake shoe away from the cars' wheels. When air pressure is reduced, the brakes are applied. This concept has an important impact on safety: should anything go wrong with the system, the brakes are automatically applied. Every car on the train, including the locomotive, has its own brakes. The braking system for the whole train is controlled by the engineer in the locomotive. Sometimes—when a train is backing into a station, for example—the brakes can be applied by the conductor operating a special valve in the vestibule of the last car.

air signal: A separate air line runs the entire length of a passenger train. When activated by a valve in each car, it beeps in the locomotive cab. The conductor can use this means to signal the engineer but seldom does, since normal communication is carried out by handheld radios.

alerter (also deadman control): This device automatically applies the brakes and stops the train if the engineer should suddenly become incapacitated. If one of the controls in the locomotive (throttle, brake, or whistle) isn't touched in a specific length of time (usually 20 to 30 seconds), a horn will sound and a bright light will flash inside the locomotive cab. The engineer then has five seconds to respond before the brakes are automatically applied.

articulated car: Two or more railcars joined together to function as one unit. Passengers can pass from one car to another without opening and closing doors. The cars flex at each connection as the train rounds curves.

A-unit (also called the lead unit): There can be three or four locomotives pulling a long passenger or freight train. This term refers to the first locomotive at the head of the train, usually the only one with an engineer.

automatic-train-stop system (usually referred to as ATS): If a train passes a signal calling for reduced speed and the engineer doesn't electronically acknowledge it, this system will stop the train automatically. See also **positive train control**.

axle: The steel shaft on which the wheels of a railcar are mounted. Unlike most other wheeled vehicles, the railcar wheels are fixed to the axle, which then revolves with the wheels. This is an extra safeguard to prevent the wheels from slipping off the rails. It also transfers the weight of the car to the journal bearings.

axle generator: A small generator, run by the revolving axle, that provides electrical power to the specific car—a refrigerated car, for example.

ballast: Coarse gravel or crushed rock used to form the roadbed on which tracks are laid.

blue flag: When this signal (a flag or a solid blue signboard during the day and a light after dark) is displayed in front of and behind railcars, it means that people are working on or under that equipment. As a safety measure, a blue flag can only be removed by the person who put it there.

bogie: The European term for a railcar's wheel assembly, which is called a **truck** on this side of the Atlantic.

boxcar: This is what most of us call a "freight car"—a completely enclosed, box-shaped car with sliding access doors on each side. It's used for any kind of general cargo that can't be exposed to the weather.

cab: A compartment in the locomotive where the crew sits and operates the train.

caboose: This distinctive-looking car was located at the end of freight trains. Most of us thought crew members used the caboose for rest or sleep, but its primary function was as a post from which the train was observed and potential problems spotted—an overheated journal bearing, or **hot box**, for example. Cabooses have been replaced by trackside automatic detectors that are located every few miles and alert crews to such problems.

cab ride: A ride in the head end of a locomotive given to a "civilian." Since 9/11, a ride up front in a locomotive cab has been virtually impossible to arrange, but it's always been a rare privilege. For one thing, the railroad has to incur the cost of an additional employee—usually a road foreman or someone in a supervisory capacity—to interact with the visitor in order to avoid distracting the engineer. And, truthfully, most railroaders just generally don't like having to watch out for extra people underfoot while they're working.

cafe car: This is sort of halfway between a lounge car and a dining car, with a seating area and an attendant serving packaged foods and beverages from behind a counter in the middle of the car. Generally, these cars are used on small or short-haul trains.

catenary: The overhead system of wires and supports from which electric engines draw the power to operate.

coach: A railcar for carrying passengers. The normal configuration is rows of seats separated by a center aisle, with two seats on each side of the aisle.

coal car: An open-topped hopper or gondola car used for transporting coal. Many of us incorrectly use this term for a **tender,** the car placed immediately behind a steam locomotive from which coal was shoveled into the engine's firebox.

conductor: The onboard crew member ultimately responsible for the operation of the train and for overseeing the rest of the crew.

consist (pronounced CON-sist): The total number of cars, including the locomotives, making up the entire train. It could be as few as one or as many as one hundred.

container: The boxlike intermodal containers that are filled with various commodities and then loaded onto flatcars, swung aboard ships by giant cranes, or hauled to their destinations by truck.

continuous welded rail: These are steel rails that are welded together in quarter-mile-long sections. For passengers, welded rail means a much smoother, quieter ride, although a few travelers still claim to prefer the clickety-clack sound of rails that are bolted together. (Not me!)

coupler: The device at each end of every railcar used to hook cars together. The standard coupler works automatically when cars are shoved together, but for safety reasons, the uncoupling process must be done manually. (Once cars are coupled together, a yard worker does have to connect cables and hoses for electrical power and brakes.)

crossbuck: The traditional warning at railroad grade crossings, with flashing red lights and the crossed signs forming a flattened "X" shape, usually reading RAILROAD CROSSING.

crossover: A track arrangement that permits a train to transfer from one track to another (usually on parallel tracks).

cross tie: The wood or concrete structure to which the rails are fastened. These are called *sleepers* in other parts of the world.

cupola (pronounced CUE-po-luh): The small observation dome on top of a caboose.

cut: The passageway carved through earth or rock through which the train passes. **Cut of cars** refers to several railcars coupled together, which are moved from one train to another as a unit.

derailment: When the wheels of a car or locomotive come off the rail. While derailments are usually accidental, they are sometimes deliberately caused for safety reasons. Watch for a small, usually yellow sign in a rail yard that reads DERAIL. Near it you will see a device attached to the rail that will derail—in other words, stop—an unattended car that may be rolling toward a main track where a collision could occur.

diaphragm: The ribbed fabric shield stretched between passenger cars, protecting you from the weather as you pass from one car to another.

diesel-electric locomotive: This is the most common kind of locomotive and the one most of us mistakenly refer to as a "diesel" engine. The locomotive does indeed have a diesel motor—a very powerful one—but it doesn't actually move the train in the same way, for instance, that a diesel motor moves a bus. Instead, the diesel motor powers a generator, which, in turn, produces electricity that powers traction motors on each axle.

dispatcher: The person who works in a central location and directs and is responsible for the movements of all trains within a specific area. The aviation equivalent is an air traffic controller.

dome: The round, raised object that covers the opening on the top of a tanker car through which the car is filled. The dome also provides an area for the liquid in the tanker car to expand if it heats up.

dome car: A passenger car with a glass-enclosed upper-level viewing area. None is left in the Amtrak system, but these cars are still found in VIA Rail consists and on many of the private excursion trains.

driving wheel: Any of the locomotive's wheels that is turned by power from diesel or electric motors to move the train.

dynamic braking: This is another kind of braking, which uses the locomotive's traction motors to produce rather than consume electricity. If the locomotive is a pure electric, this power is fed back into the system through the overhead wire; if it's a diesel-electric, it's converted to heat and blown out through the vents in the top of the locomotive. Either way, the process slows the loco-motive. Dynamic braking will only slow a train gradually and therefore is used in much the same way a driver downshifts a car to control the speed when heading down a hill. See also **air brake**.

electric locomotive: Any locomotive that is powered by electricity and gets that power directly from an outside source—that is, from an overhead wire (the **catenary**) or from an electrified third rail.

engine: Technically, this refers to the machinery that produces energy. But in the context of this book, *engine* is frequently used as a synonym for *locomotive*.

engineer: The person who actually gets paid for sitting in the cab of a locomotive and driving it—something many of us would do for free. (In Europe and elsewhere around the world, this person is called the driver.)

equipment (also called rolling stock): Engines and railcars of all kinds—that is, anything that rolls along the tracks.

express train: A passenger train that operates with minimum delays, usually meaning it makes only a few stops—or none at all—between its point of origin and its ultimate destination. An **express freight** operates in the same fashion.

extra train: Any train that does not appear on the published time-table. The airline equivalent is called an **extra section**.

fireman: Except for special excursion trains powered by restored steam locomotives, firemen are—alas—part of an earlier time. In the days of steam, firemen were primarily responsible for keeping the firebox adequately fed with wood or coal. The second person in the locomotive cab is sometimes still referred to as the fireman, but on Amtrak trains, both are **engineers**. The freight railroads are now using either **assistant engineers** or **coengineers**.

first class: This term isn't used much in North America anymore, but it has always meant sleeping-car accommodations. Both Amtrak (on its Acela trains) and VIA Rail offer variations of upgraded coach class that are referred to as first class.

flag stop: A station or location, usually (but not always) included in the timetable, at which the train will stop only in response to a signal.

flange: The one-inch ridge on the inner rim of every railcar wheel that keeps the car on the track.

flatcar: A railroad freight car without top or sides used for hauling machinery or other bulky items that can be exposed to the weather.

flat spot: As the term implies, this is a spot on a wheel that has somehow been flattened, usually from the wheel that locks and slides along the rail. It's very uncommon on passenger equipment, but if there's such a spot on your car, you'll probably be able to hear and feel it (one more reason for securing space near the center of a car). This is not just a matter of comfort, however. Freight cars with flat spots on some of the wheels mean more fuel will be used and, if left unattended for too long, can turn into safety problems. Once spotted, the cars are promptly taken out of service for repairs.

foamer: This is railroad slang for a **rail fan**; that is, someone so hooked on trains that he or she supposedly foams at the mouth when one appears. It is not really a derogatory term, but it's not a compliment either.

FRED: Mounted on the rear of all trains, this is the part of the automatic detector system that electronically alerts the crew to any mechanical problems. It's an acronym for "flashing rear-end device." Though they get the job done, FREDs have replaced the traditional cabooses on freight trains, which are still missed by many railroad workers. That helps explain why they often translate the acronym as "f—— rear-end device."

freight car: Any railway car used to transport manufactured goods, fruits and vegetables, grain, coal and other minerals, machinery, and so forth. The term does not apply to tanker cars, which contain liquids.

frog: A special configuration of rails that permits trains to cross another track (as opposed to transferring from one track to a parallel track). You can tell when you go over a frog from the clattering noise the wheels make.

fusee: These are flares, basically the same kind police use warning cars to slow down for a highway accident. They are dropped off the rear of slow-moving trains to warn faster trains coming up from behind.

gandy dancer: Old-time railroad slang for anyone working on the tracks. The term comes from the brand name stamped on the specialized hand tools—picks, shovels, and sledge hammers—made by the Gandy Manufacturing Company more than 100 years ago.

gauge (or gage): In the railroad context, this refers to the distance between the rails, which has been standardized throughout

North America at 56½ inches. Any gauge less than that standard is referred to as **narrow gauge**, although 36 inches is the most common. Narrow-gauge track is usually found where the terrain requires curves in the track that are too sharp for the longer, standard-gauge railroad cars.

gondola car: A railcar with low sides and an open top for carrying anything that does not need protection from the weather. They're called "gonnies" by train crews.

grade: A change in elevation over a section of track. For example, a 2-percent grade means that the track goes up or down a total of 2 feet over a distance of 100 feet.

grade crossing: A place where a road or highway crosses the train tracks at the same level (on the same grade).

green eye: Railroad slang for a green or "clear" signal, meaning the train may proceed at normal speed.

gross weight (GW): The total allowable weight of a freight car plus its contents. You'll see this term or abbreviation stenciled on the side of most freight cars, along with the appropriate numbers.

handcar: A small four-wheeled vehicle usually powered by a gasoline engine that carries workers and inspectors along the tracks. Today these people more commonly ride in ordinary cars and trucks fitted with flanged steel wheels that keep them on the rails while being propelled by normal rubber-tired wheels.

head-end power (HEP): This refers to electricity being provided to the entire train by a special generator located either in the locomotive or in an additional unit immediately behind it.

helper: An additional locomotive, usually unstaffed and controlled remotely from the lead unit. Helpers provide extra power for long trains or for those going over steep grades.

highball: A signal or verbal instruction that authorizes the train to proceed at the maximum legal speed. For example, if Amtrak's train 5, the California Zephyr, is loaded and ready to leave Grand Junction, Colorado, the conductor may call the engineer on the two-way radio and say, "Highball Grand Junction, number five." The term originated from the old practice of hoisting a colored ball to the top of a signal pole to indicate a clear track ahead.

hopper car: These differ from gondola cars by having sloped sides and ends, permitting the contents to be dumped out of trap doors in the car's bottom. Hopper cars carry bulk cargo such as grain (in which case they're covered) or coal (in which case they're not).

hot box: An overheated journal bearing. If it's undetected for long, a hot box can mean serious problems, up to and including failure of the wheel, axle, or both.

hot-box detector: These are the devices, simply referred to as "detectors," that put the cabooses out of business. They're sensitive to heat and are placed at various intervals along the main tracks. When a detector senses an overheated bearing (a **hot box**), it broadcasts a recorded warning by radio to the train crew.

hump yard: When individual railcars are assigned to different trains, a switch engine pushes them, singly or in small "cuts," over a hump—literally a high spot in the rail yard. Once past the hump, a yard worker separates the cars from the engine, allowing them to roll slowly forward by themselves, carried along by gravity down the long, slight incline. In this manner, they are switched onto different tracks as they go, ultimately joining up with the proper train.

journal bearing: If there is one critical part common to all railcars, the journal bearing is it. There are two of these box-shaped bearings on each axle, and essentially they bear the weight of the car and help to distribute its weight over the axle. When a journal bearing fails, it overheats and is referred to as a **hot box.** If undetected, it can cause a serious breakdown.

lading: An industry term for whatever a freight car is carrying.

load limit: The maximum weight a given car is permitted to carry. It's computed by subtracting the weight of the empty car from its maximum allowable gross weight. The load limit is stenciled on the side of every car.

locomotive: Also referred to as "the engine," this is the self-propelled machine that hauls the train. If there is more than one locomotive in the consist, the first is called the "A" or "lead" unit. An additional locomotive is referred to as a "B" unit.

main line: A long stretch of track that receives regular, heavy use.

main track: The track that carries most of the scheduled train traffic. It is commonly referred to as "the main."

milepost (also mile marker): Small signs usually located trackside that indicate the number of miles to or from a specific point, most often a major city. Railroads use mileposts to confirm the location of a train or to let a train crew know where track repairs are going on.

observation car: A passenger car specially designed to be the last car in a passenger train, often featuring extralarge windows or a rounded end, or even an open-air platform at the end of the car. VIA Rail has several of these beauties, called **Park cars** because each is named for one of Canada's national parks. They elegantly bring up the rear on several of VIA's long-distance trains.

pantograph: This is the device that extends upward from the roof of an all-electric locomotive and presses against the overhead wire (the **catenary**), collecting the electricity that powers the train.

parlor car: Back in the golden age of train travel, these were the first-class coach cars used for short-haul daytime travel, with large, overstuffed swivel chairs and other features not found in ordinary coaches. There was an additional fare for all that comfort and luxury, of course. Amtrak has added a Pacific Parlour Car to the Coast Starlight's consist, in which folks traveling in sleeping cars can relax, chat with fellow passengers, and enjoy meals or beverages. Wine tastings are held each afternoon in this car as the train travels through the wine-producing areas along its route. There's even a small theater on the lower level where movies are shown on a huge flat-screen TV.

piggyback cars: Railroad flatcars designed for hauling semitrailers.

positive train control (PTC): A highly sophisticated system using global positioning technology that is designed to control train movement. Mandated by the federal government in 2008, PTC will not only improve rail safety, preventing collisions and derailments, but it will also allow trains to run closer together and at higher speeds. PTC requires special equipment in every locomotive cab, as well as in multiple locations along every route. All of the country's railroads are required to have PTC in place and functioning by the end of 2015.

quiet car: A single car on many of Amtrak's short-haul trains in which cell phones and loud conversations are not permitted.

rail: Made of rolled steel, the traditional rails are 39 feet long (to fit on 40-foot flatcars) but are being replaced today by great quarter-mile-long rails laid by machinery. The cross section of a rail can best be described as looking like an upside-down capital T. All rails look pretty much the same, but larger and heavier rails are used where high-speed or very heavy trains operate. Smaller, lightweight rails are used in rail yards and on sidings where traffic is less frequent and slower.

rapid transit: Any rail system operating on an exclusive right-of-way and used for moving people in and out of urban areas.

red eye: Railroad slang for a red (stop) signal.

refrigerator car: An insulated, closed car with cooling equipment designed to keep its contents at a specific low temperature. Many of these cars are also equipped with heaters to keep fresh produce from freezing during winter weather. Refrigerator cars are called "reefers" in railroad slang.

rerailer: A device used to guide a railcar's wheels back onto the track following a derailment.

right-of-way: The strip of land on which a railroad track is laid.

rim: The outer circumference of the wheel on a railroad car or locomotive; that is, the part of the wheel that comes into contact with the rail.

rock and roll: Railroad slang for excessive side-to-side movement of railcars caused by poor track conditions.

sander: A device operated from the locomotive cab that applies sand to the rail just in front of the driving wheels to prevent them from slipping. It is used going up steep grades or where ice or snow has covered the tracks.

siding: A track located parallel or adjacent to a single main track onto which one train is diverted to allow another train to pass.

signal: A mechanical or electronic device that communicates instructions to the train crew relating to the train's speed, usually in connection with other rail traffic or track conditions.

slide fence: These wire fences can be seen along the track where it runs along steep cliffs or slopes with loose rocks. If the wire is broken by falling rocks, a signal is automatically triggered and approaching trains are warned of possible obstructions on the track.

snow fence: You'll see a lot of these along the tracks in the open prairies of the West. They disrupt wind patterns and, if placed properly, help to keep snow from drifting over the tracks.

spur: Unlike a siding, which is relatively short and is usually parallel to a main track, a spur can be of any length and runs off in another direction. Often spurs are what freight trains use to provide irregular service to small towns or manufacturing businesses in the vicinity.

stock car: Railcars used for carrying livestock. They are usually the same size and shape as standard boxcars, but they have slats on the sides for much-needed ventilation.

stopping distance: How far the train travels from the time brakes are applied until it comes to a stop. A 100-car freight train traveling 30 miles per hour could require over a mile to come to a stop. An Amtrak passenger train traveling at 80 miles per hour has a stopping distance of about 4,000 feet, or just over three-quarters of a mile.

Superliners: The bi-level railcars—sleepers, coaches, diners, and lounge cars—used by Amtrak on its long-distance western trains and a few eastern ones too.

switch: A moving section of track usually operated by remote control and used to transfer a train from one track to another.

switching locomotive (also called a switcher): A locomotive used for moving individual railcars or sections of a train from one track to another in a station or rail yard.

tank car: A railroad car used for transporting liquids.

terminal (also terminus): More than just a station, this is by definition an important rail facility where both passengers and freight are handled, where passenger trains originate, and where many other railroad activities are carried out.

third rail: An additional rail, installed parallel to and within a foot or two of the regular track, through which electric power is supplied to the locomotive. The electricity is collected through a metal "shoe" that slides along the third rail.

throttle: The knob or handle in the locomotive cab that is used to increase or decrease the amount of fuel or electricity going to the engine and having a corresponding effect on the train's speed.

timetable: A published schedule detailing the movements of trains, both passenger and freight.

track: The entire structure seated on the roadbed and on which trains operate, including the rails, cross ties, and various fastenings that hold it all together.

traction motor: Electricity, either taken from an overhead wire or generated by an onboard diesel motor, goes to the traction motors that power one pair of the locomotive's wheels. There are several traction motors in every locomotive.

traffic control system. See positive train control.

train: One or more locomotives pulling one or more cars.

trainman: This term was used for an onboard railroad employee who assisted the conductor. Today, on passenger trains, these people are more appropriately called **assistant conductors.**

trainset: A train that functions as a complete unit over a long period of time. Typically, it has a fixed number of cars with a locomotive (or "power unit") at each end, making it unnecessary to "turn the train" at the end of each run.

trolley: The overhead wire that provides electric power for railroads and transit systems. This term is commonly used when speaking of light rail systems such as urban trolley cars, while the term **catenary** is used in connection with intercity trains.

truck: The entire wheel assembly at each end of a railcar: wheels, axles, bearings, brakes, suspension, and frame.

trunk line: Much more than a **spur,** this refers to a rail line that can extend over many miles.

turntable: This is literally a lazy Susan for trains. Turntables are used to swivel locomotives in any number of directions and route them down different tracks.

unit train: A freight train that carries only one commodity—coal or grain, for example.

vestibule: The drafty, noisy enclosed area you pass through when moving from one passenger car to another.

Viewliner: Amtrak sleeping cars used on most of the overnight trains in the eastern part of the country. Viewliners are easily spotted because they have a second tier of windows designed to provide more light in the bedrooms and nighttime viewing for passengers in upper berths.

weigh bridge: This is the railroad equivalent of weigh stations along an interstate highway where officials check for overweight trucks.

wheelbase: The distance between the first and last axles on a railcar or locomotive.

wide gauge: (1) a section of track that has spread wider than the standard 56½ inches, creating the potential for a derailment; and (2) tracks built to gauges wider than the North American standard, as they are in Russia, for instance.

work train: A train that transports workers to a place where track is being repaired. These trains do not generate revenue for the railroad.

yard: A rail center where, within a specific area, train consists are made up, railcars are moved about, and general railroad activity is carried out.

yard engine: A locomotive that is assigned to a yard and functions only within the yard area. The term is almost always synonymous with **switching locomotive**.

yardmaster: The person in charge of all operations carried out within the yard. The nautical equivalent would be the harbormaster.

yard speed: The speed that will permit a locomotive to stop within a distance equal to half the range of vision.

yellow eye: Railroad slang for a yellow (or caution) signal.

The Railroad in Everyday Language

Some are obvious while others are obscure, but many expressions we all use in our daily lives have origins that can be traced to the railroad. These are but a few.

blocked: Today it means to prevent something from moving forward, but originally the word described a train prevented from entering a stretch of track, which is called a "block."

blow off steam: To relieve boiler pressure when it reaches dangerous limits.

blow one's stack: If worse comes to worst, the boiler explodes, which is usually fatal to the head-end crew.

cut and run: When a steam locomotive ran low on water, it had to uncouple from the rest of the train and head for the next watering point.

doubleheader: Originally, two locomotives coupled together to pull a long, heavy train.

flag someone down: This refers to the railroad practice of signaling to a train with colored flags. Radios are now used to signal the engineer to stop for passengers at remote stations, but they're still called "flag stops."

full head of steam: This expression originally referred to a steam engine with maximum pressure in its boiler.

Hell on Wheels: This expression was a reference to the gamblers and prostitutes who followed railroad crews in their own railcars (on wheels) while the transcontinental railway was being built.

highballing down the road: Early signals were given to a moving train by hoisting colored balls onto a pole; a ball at the top of the pole meant "all clear."

light at the end of the tunnel: The consensus is that this common expression originated with the railroad.

making the grade: The expression is a reference to trains successfully overcoming inclines with out losing traction. The steepest railroad grades increase less than three feet of elevation for 100 feet of distance.

on track, off track: A railroad track is the obvious origin of these expressions.

over the hump: When freight cars are pushed over the hump, or high point, in a rail yard, they roll easily by themselves to a siding.

sidetracked: A reference to diverting a train onto a siding until another can pass.

HOW TO FIND A RAIL-SAVVY TRAVEL AGENT

As I have said elsewhere in this book, you should consider using a travel agent if the train trip you have in mind is at all complicated. By that, I mean if you'll be changing trains along the way, if you want to stop en route for side trips, or if there are any special requirements you might have, such as if you need wheelchair accessibility or if you travel with a service dog.

In my experience, however, many travel agents can sell you a plane ticket and reserve a hotel room, but they don't know a lot about booking train travel. The Amtrak and VIA Rail reservations people are very good; you will get good service working directly with them if you choose to go that way. But if you opt to use a travel agent, here are a couple of questions you can ask: Does the roomette in a Superliner sleeping car include a lavatory? (Answer: No.) Is there a window for the upper berth in a Viewliner sleeping car? (Answer: Yes.) How the agent responds will tell you in a flash how much he or she knows about train travel.

If you can't find a rail-savvy travel agent on your own, contact one of the agencies on the following page. They all have rail-travel experts on staff. (I'm quite sure there are many other agencies with train-smart people on staff, but these firms I've either used myself or have had recommended to me by people whose judgment I trust.

Advantage Travel
Albany, NY
1-888-444-4240
www.advantagetravelinc.com

Gateway Travel
Brattleboro, VT
1-800-639-3706
www.gatewaytrav.com

Holiday Vacations
Eau Claire, WI
1-800-826-2266
www.holidayvacations.net

RMA Travel & Tours
Denver, CO
1-800-841-9800
www.rmatours.com

Train Travel Consulting
Klamath Falls, OR
1-800-347-0645
www.accentontravelusa.com

Vacations By Rail
Chicago, IL
1-877-929-7245
www.vacationsbyrail.com

APPENDIX C

PRIVATE RAIL EXCURSIONS

If you've always dreamed about traveling around the country in the luxury of a private railcar, there really are ways to make that happen. A number of firms offer exclusive rail tours, either in their own private cars or in equipment they lease from the owners: vintage sleeping cars, dome cars, railcars with open observation platforms—a wide variety, but all offering a unique experience and providing a glimpse back in time to the golden age of train travel.

Tours being offered come in an equally wide variety, from those lasting just a few hours to extensive itineraries lasting for a week or more. Some are posh, with just a few passengers and several crew members to prepare meals and look after every need. Others are quite informal. Of course, the cost varies, too.

I can suggest three companies that offer these kinds of private charters:

Altiplano Rail offers longer tours lasting up to 14 days and which, in my experience, are quite affordable.

adam.auxier@altiplanorail.com
1-612-910-5154
www.altiplanorail.com

Tours offered by **The Cincinnati Railway Company** are more luxurious and can even come with a personal chef.

info@cincinnatirailway.com
1-513-791-7245
www.cincinnatirailway.com

Finally, there's **LA Rail** which specializes in shorter trips mostly on the West Coast.

pacificsands@larail.com
1-877-452-7245
www.larail.com

APPENDIX D

PASSENGER RAIL ADVOCATES

All over the country, ordinary people have recognized the critical importance of rail transportation. These individuals have mobilized to take action by joining nonprofit organizations that advocate more and better passenger trains.

The one organization with a national overview is the National Association of Railroad Passengers. NARP has a full-time paid staff and an office in Washington, DC, which makes a lot of sense because that's where most of the power and the money are.

There are also many other organizations around the country that focus on local and regional transportation issues. These organizations, representing many thousands of voters, are taking the passenger rail message directly and forcefully to elected officials at all levels of government. *Nothing* is more effective.

You can help by joining NARP and adding your voice to the chorus. (Go to www.narprail.org and click "Join NARP.") Since Amtrak and VIA Rail give NARP members a 10 percent discount on most rail fares, the savings on just a few trips can more than pay for the cost of your membership. (Note: The Amtrak discount does not apply to sleeping-car fares; the discount from VIA Rail does—and that's a big deal!) A NARP membership also entitles you to discounts on a number of other travel-related products and services. You could also consider membership in one of the regional organizations. For an up-to-date listing, go to www.on -track-on-line.com and click on "ARP List."

EXCURSION TRAINS AND RAILROAD MUSEUMS

As interest in trains and train travel continues to grow, so too do the opportunities to take interesting and unusual rides on a wide variety of excursion trains. In fact, there are excursion trains and/or railroad museums in all 50 states (yes, even in Hawaii) and in every Canadian province. Whether you're planning a long-distance train trip or taking a more conventional vacation, consider connecting with one of the excursion trains or visiting a railroad-themed museum.

Excursion Trains

The Internet is the best, most immediate source of information. Go to www.traintraveling.com or www.touristrailways.com for excellent lists. The most comprehensive printed source, which lists both excursion trains and railroad museums, is the *Tourist Trains Guidebook*, published by the people who put out *Trains* magazine.

Railroad Museums

There are many really excellent museums devoted to trains and railroading around the country, from Sacramento's California State Railroad Museum (an outstanding experience) to a wonderful display of locomotives and railroad equipment at the Smithsonian in Washington, DC. Once again, the Internet provides a comprehensive source of information. Go to www.railsusa.com or type "railroad museums" into a search engine.

INDEX